William Jennings Bryan

MISSIONARY ISOLATIONIST

William Jennings Bryan

MISSIONARY ISOLATIONIST

BY KENDRICK A. CLEMENTS

THE UNIVERSITY OF TENNESSEE PRESS / KNOXVILLE

Copyright © 1982 by The University of Tennessee Press / Knoxville
All rights reserved
Manufactured in the United States of America
First edition

Frontispiece: Secretary of State Bryan on his way to deliver a Chautaucua lecture in 1913. *(Nebraska State Historical Society.)*

Jacket illustration from "The Dove of Peace," by William Henry Walker. Courtesy William H. Walker Collection, Princeton University Library.

Clothbound editions of University of Tennessee Press books are printed on paper designed for an effective life of at least 300 years, and binding materials are chosen for strength and durability.

Library of Congress Cataloging in Publication Data

Clements, Kendrick Alling, 1939-
William Jennings Bryan, missionary isolationist.

Bibliography: p.
Includes index.
1. Bryan, William Jennings, 1860-1925—Views on international relations. 2. United States—Foreign relations—1865-1921. 3. United States—Neutrality.
I. Title.
E664.B87C53 1982   973.91'092'4   82-8342
ISBN 0-87049-364-7   AACR2

TO

Bob Ochs

AND

Anna Spongberg

Contents

Preface   *page xi*
A Note on Citations of the Bryan Papers   *xvii*
1. The Development of a Christian Statesman   *3*
2. Silver, Gold, and Imperialism, 1896–1900   *23*
3. "Friends Are Better Customers than Enemies": Practical Idealism, 1900–1912   *40*
4. Promises, Principles, and Compromises: First Months in Office   *59*
5. "No More Revolutions Will Be Permitted": Latin America, 1913–1915   *77*
6. The Fear of Entanglement, 1914–1915   *96*
7. "Some Nation Must Lift the World": 1915–1918   *113*
8. "Out of the Dark Night of War": 1918–1925   *127*
9. A Life of Christian Service   *143*
Notes   *157*
Bibliographical Essay   *196*
Index   *207*

Illustrations

PHOTOGRAPHS

Secretary of State Bryan, 1913   *Frontispiece*
Colonel William J. Bryan during Spanish-American War   *31*
Campaign portrait of Bryan, 1900   *37*
Bryan at Tierra Blanca, Mexico   *47*
Two Korean stone lions at Bryan's home in Lincoln, Nebraska   *50*
Bryan being welcomed by Nebraskans after his world trip,
    1906   *53*
"No foreign relations these," 1906   *55*
Wilson, Bryan, and Bryan's grandson at "Fairview," 1912   *61*
Cartoon of Bryan as a "lightning rod" for Wilson, 1913   *66*
Souvenir paperweight made from an army sword   *66*
Bryan in California, 1913   *73*
Secretary of State Bryan at his desk   *80*
James Mark Sullivan, Minister to the Dominican Republic under
    Wilson   *86*
Pancho Villa at the head of his troops   *97*
The signing ceremony for four of Bryan's peace treaties,
    1914   *97*
Cartoon published after Bryan's resignation from the State
    Department   *112*
Caricature of Bryan's anti-war activities, 1915   *112*
Bryan with Henry Ford, 1915   *126*
Bryan and his wife at the Washington Naval Conference,
    1922   *126*

TABLES

1. The Votes in the 1896, 1900, and 1908 Elections, by State
    16–17
2. The Votes in the 1896, 1900, and 1908 Elections, by Candidate
    19

Preface

To most people, William Jennings Bryan means the "Cross of Gold," the "Monkey Trial," three campaigns for the presidency, and the "Great Commoner." Most would be surprised to hear that the only public office he held between 1896 and 1925 was two years as secretary of state, from 1913 to 1915, and even the knowledgeable would have to admit that his achievements in that office were far overshadowed by those of Woodrow Wilson. Whether dismissed as a sour old man defending southern bigotry, or celebrated as an architect of twentieth-century American reform, Bryan is seldom thought of as an important influence on modern American foreign policy.

Why, then, study his foreign policy? Although his reputation will always rest mainly on his domestic achievements, his foreign policy record deserves study too. During nearly thirty years of leadership in the Democratic party, he gradually developed ideas about the nation's place in the world that were in contrast to both Republican imperialism and Wilsonian internationalism. Balanced somewhat precariously between traditional isolationism and a deep conviction that Christianity required service to others, Bryan's attitudes mirrored those of millions of Americans who found themselves torn between a fearful desire to escape and an idealistic wish to help, as they faced an increasingly unstable and dangerous world. Indeed, Bryan's foreign policy is of interest to us precisely because it was *not* based upon careful study of the issues or on much practical experience. More articulate and outspoken than most of his followers, Bryan nevertheless revealed their feelings more faithfully than he might have if he had thought more systematically about the issues.

The fact of the matter is that we do not know very much about what ordinary Americans thought of foreign policy in the early years of the twentieth century, when the nation was first experimenting with world power and taking on obligations around the globe. Most studies of the period emphasize leaders like Roosevelt or Wilson who may or may not have expressed general sentiments. Studies of isolationism—a widespread popular sentiment—usually concentrate on either the early nineteenth century or the period after 1918. The reader is thus left with the impression that isolationism somehow disappeared in the early twentieth century when Americans embraced imperialism and internationalism, and that it again mysteriously reappeared after 1918. Although such an interpretation seems implausible and of course is nowhere explicitly stated, it has stood by implication because almost no one has looked closely at isolationist sentiment in the pre–World War I era.

This study does not cover the whole century from Waterloo to the First World War, nor does it explore the whole range of that mysterious entity known as "public opinion" even for the period from the Spanish-American War to World War I. Rather I have tried to trace the evolution of the attitudes of an important leader, outside of the "foreign policy elite," from the 1890s to the 1920s. Through a study of Bryan we can gain insight into the attitudes of millions of Americans confronting a world whose opportunities were enticing but whose perils were frightening in equal measure.

Bryan's career suggests that most Americans did not give up isolationism in 1898 and rediscover it in 1918. Throughout the period they were subject to contradictory emotions. On the one hand, their isolationist fears of the outside world remained strong, while on the other, opportunities for profit and service tempted them to pursue world power. Sometimes one feeling prevailed, sometimes the other, but more commonly Americans felt, in characteristically human fashion, that they might be able to have it both ways at the same time. They could, they hoped, be both influential and safe.

To this somewhat contradictory aspiration John M. Cooper, Jr., in his pioneering study of isolationism during World War I, *The Vanity of Power,* has given the name "idealistic isolationism." In examining Bryan's career I have concluded that the origins of this sentiment can be traced back at least to the Spanish-American War and that Bryan's particular type of idealistic isolationism is perhaps more appropriately termed "missionary isolationism" because Bryan felt, more strongly than most idealistic isolationists, that the United States had a special duty to improve and serve the world while at the same time remaining free of most entanglements.

In seeking to reconcile the contradictory elements of isolationism and idealism, Bryan frequently argued that the United States should exert world leadership mainly by example. "Example," he said, is "the means of propagating truth," and he believed firmly that the United States could influence others by adopting unilaterally such policies as renunciation of the use of force in collecting international debts or disarmament. The idea of America as an example also appealed to Bryan because it gave him an additional argument for domestic reform. The more perfect the nation became, the more it would attract the admiration and emulation of others.

Even before he acquired actual responsibility for administering foreign policy, however, Bryan found difficulty in adhering strictly to the idea of the United States acting in the world only by example. He opposed imperialism as a threat to American ideals and a danger to national security, but he also favored the annexation of Puerto Rico and the holding of naval bases in the Philippines to facilitate trade with Asia. When he entered the State Department in 1913, the temptation to set Latin Americans on the road to democracy and prosperity by means of a paternalistic push or spank overwhelmed him. The superhuman restraint necessary to curb his missionary impulses in the face of so much temptation was beyond him.

On the other side, the outbreak of war in 1914 strongly aroused Bryan's isolationist fears and temporarily paralyzed his idealism. In his panic, no sacrifice of material interests or moral influence seemed too great a price to stay out of the war. Only when the worst finally happened and the nation entered the war in 1917 was his idealism released from the immobilization of fear. Then, like Wilson, he perceived that there were great moral issues in the struggle and a great opportunity for building a better world in the future. From the extreme isolationism of 1914–1917, Bryan swung to near-internationalism in 1919 with his support of an unamended Treaty of Versailles and American membership in the League of Nations.

If Bryan's course in foreign policy was somewhat erratic, it was not without an overall direction that is visible at least in retrospect. When he entered national politics in the 1890s he shared with his followers a parochial suspicion and fear of the outside world. By the 1920s he knew far more about the world, and he had come to believe that both self-interest and duty required a permanent American commitment to its improvement. For Bryan, and to a lesser degree for his followers, the isolationism of the 1920s was a more limited if also more conscious policy than that of the late nineteenth century. In the intervening years opportunity had united with idealism to change the way Americans looked at the world. Try as they might, they could not entirely convince themselves that they had no stake in what happened beyond their own borders.

The question of just how much Bryan spoke for a significant segment of "public opinion" is a very difficult one. Most of his followers did not normally take an active interest in foreign policy questions. Such matters were remote from their daily concerns, and most of them came from groups in American society who have traditionally taken little part in policy formulation. Yet if such people did not usually support particular policies, their suspicion and fear of the outside world tended to have a conservative, restraining effect on policymakers when their concern was aroused. In 1900, for example, the size of Bryan's vote may have helped to cool imperialist ardor in the administration, and certainly the prevalence of antiwar sentiment in the "Bryan sections" of the country in 1915 and 1916 made President Wilson cautious about taking any steps that could be construed as warlike.

Although the main influence of Bryan's followers was probably negative, they also had a large measure of idealism that could be tapped from time to time. The roots of this idealism were in evangelical Protestantism and in a Jeffersonian-Jacksonian belief in democracy as the ideal form of government. When mobilized, this idealism could provide the motive power for an extremely active and aggressive foreign policy. Normally secondary to their isolationism, the idealism of Bryanites could have an important effect on policy, as it did in 1898 or during the campaign to "make the world safe for democracy" of World War I. Perhaps even more important, idealism could neutralize isolationism, so that Bryan, for example, could have a free hand in his efforts to reconstruct governments in the Caribbean.

Bryan believed firmly that it was the principal duty of the politician to reflect and obey the wishes of his constituents. Glorying in his nickname, the Commoner, he spent a large part of his time talking and listening to the people. Both consciously and unconsciously he tried not only to *do* what the people wanted but to *be* one of them. The millions of votes he received in three elections and the thousands of affectionate letters written to him by ordinary people were evidence that to a large extent he succeeded.

Nevertheless, even the Commoner could not be the universal common man. The very fact that Bryan dedicated his life to public service demonstrated that his sense of idealism was somewhat stronger than that of most of his followers, and his greater experience of public life also inevitably broadened his horizons beyond theirs. As a result of these influences, he gradually came to believe that the United States must take a continuing world role that went substantially beyond mere example. By the 1920s it seems likely that he had moved out somewhat in advance of most of his followers in this respect. The gap is hard to measure, however, because Bryan did not run for office in this period and because he spent so much of his time and energy on issues that had little or nothing to do with foreign policy. Above all, the problem did not arise because, with the world again at peace, Americans could once more indulge in the luxury of being both isolationists and idealists with no sense that the two conflicted.

Bryan neither sought nor exerted a vast influence on American foreign policy. Compared with Theodore Roosevelt or Woodrow Wilson, he did relatively little to shape the directions of twentieth-century policy. His significance is rather in what his career and ideas tell us about how Americans reacted to the bold new policies their leaders were proposing. Speaking for a substantial following, Bryan vividly illustrated the contradictory attitudes prevalent in the nation— hope and fear, ambition and timidity, isolationism and idealism. Understanding these internal tensions, we can better understand the vacillations of American policy and comprehend that such convenient terms as "isolationism" and "internationalism" do not adequately express the full complexity of actual events. Almost all Americans wanted their nation to play an honorable, important role in world affairs. Unlike the Roosevelts or the Wilsons, however, they were deeply uncertain of how that could best be done. It is the depth and nature of that uncertainty that Bryan's career helps to illuminate.

In the course of my work on Bryan I have acquired all the debts familiar to scholars. The staffs of the Manuscripts Division of the Library of Congress, of the National Archives, and of the Nebraska State Historical Society in Lincoln were all extremely helpful. I am especially indebted to the many colleagues who have read the manuscript at various stages and who, through helpful advice and suggestions, have at least tried to steer me away from major blunders, even if they have not always succeeded. Armin Rappaport and Lawrence Levine helped at almost every stage from beginning to end, but no less important were the timely and thoughtful suggestions made by Paolo Coletta, Tom Terrill, John M. Cooper, Jr., Lewis Gould, and Charles DeBenedetti. I thank them all and apologize if I have not made as good use of their advice as I should. My cousin and his wife, Mr. and Mrs. Thomas Kendrick, cheerfully put me up during research trips to Washington and turned what might sometimes have been a burdensome chore into fun. My wife, Linda, has read the manuscript more times than I had any right to ask, and her sensible and witty comments have headed me away from many an error. More important, her confidence in me gave me confidence in myself and the determination to persist at difficult moments. No one can give a greater gift. It is the greatest pleasure to say "thank you" to all of the people who have given so generously of their time, skills, and knowledge with so little return.

K.A.C.

Berkeley, California
April 2, 1982

A Note

ON CITATIONS OF THE BRYAN PAPERS

There are three major collections of Bryan Papers: in the Library of Congress, Manuscripts Division; in the National Archives; and at the Nebraska State Historical Society at Lincoln. A fourth, smaller collection is at the library of Occidental College in Pomona, California, but a complete microfilm copy is held by the Nebraska Historical Society and therefore the Occidental papers are here treated as part of the Nebraska collection.

The three main collections of Bryan Papers are cited in this study as follows:

BP   Bryan Papers, Manuscripts Division, Library of Congress

ABP Bryan Papers (or sometimes, Bryan-Wilson Correspondence), National Archives

NBP Bryan Papers, Nebraska State Historical Society, Lincoln (including microfilms of papers held at Occidental College Library)

William Jennings Bryan

MISSIONARY ISOLATIONIST

1

THE DEVELOPMENT OF A CHRISTIAN STATESMAN

When William Jennings Bryan was born, on March 19, 1860, in Salem, Illinois, nearly all Americans were preoccupied by the sectional crisis. Although the Civil War and its aftermath had little direct impact on the Bryan family, the crowding events of those years pushed aside all political issues except those having to do with the internal state of the country. Few Americans, including the Bryans, took much notice of what was happening beyond the borders of the United States. Nevertheless, although foreign policy seems never to have been a topic at the Bryan family dinner table, the bases for Bryan's later foreign policy positions were shaped in his youth.

To an extraordinary degree, Bryan's attitudes, values, and even the course of his career were determined by his father, Silas Bryan. If William ever felt rebellious about his father's firm discipline and strong views, no record of it remains. Silas Bryan was a model Victorian. A fervent Democrat in Abraham Lincoln's home state, he was a professional politician whose religious beliefs molded his political principles. He prayed three times a day wherever he might be and in the evening read aloud from the Bible to his family. As a politician he was never able to rise as high as he wished, but in his later years he achieved considerable success as a judge of the state circuit court. Reserved and thoughtful by temperament, Judge Bryan won wide respect for his upright character and good judgment. In court and at home alike, his stern rectitude was tempered by a sense of humor and by Christian charity. Aunts and grandmothers regularly lived with the family, and the evenings of Bible reading were interspersed with more frivolous occasions when the family gathered around the piano to sing the sentimental popular songs of the period. No rigid doctrinaire, Silas Bryan invited the ministers of all denominations to visit in the spacious home he built in 1866 and even sent a load of hay each year to Salem's Catholic priest as well as to his own Baptist minister and to the other Protestant clergy of the town.[1]

Mariah Jennings Bryan, William's mother, was a lovely woman

whose gentleness softened a character every bit as strong as her much older husband's. When William was young, his father was often away for days at a time on the court circuit, and the boy was much with his mother. The lack of a school nearby reinforced her influence on him. Until he went away to school at the age of ten, she was his sole teacher, drilling him from a speller, a geography, and the McGuffey readers. Each day the boy studied and then declaimed his lessons as he stood on a little table, while his mother worked or listened nearby. From that early association Bryan developed a lasting respect for and pleasure in the company of women. Unlike many politicians of his day, he did not prefer exclusively masculine company and enjoyed discussing political issues with women as well as men. It was not surprising that he became a staunch advocate of woman suffrage.

Life in Salem offered a combination of discipline, hard work, and simple pleasures for young William. There were always chores to be done, and the boy developed from them a robust physique that would stand him in good stead in later years. No one in the family danced, drank, smoked, or gambled, but there were no objections to hunting, and young Bryan became an enthusiastic hunter. On Sundays he avoided the problem of whether to go with his father to Baptist services or with his mother to the Methodist Church by attending both—the Methodist Sunday school in the morning and the Baptist one in the afternoon. Perhaps partly to simplify his life he joined neither church but along with several of his friends became a Presbyterian. If that choice was a rebellion against the limitations of his family life, it was a very mild one. All three of the family churches were evangelical and fundamentalist, and the doctrinal differences among them were minor. Except for his good-natured recollection that the words of the hymns he learned in Sunday school did not always express his feelings as he went about his farm chores on freezing winter mornings, Bryan showed no sign that he ever found the simple, rather limited life of his youth in any way unsatisfactory.[2] Nor was there any particular reason why he should have. His parents were loving if strict, and the values they taught were unchallenged by any outside influences on the boy.

Young Will's earliest remembered ambition was to be a Baptist preacher. One day his father took him to a baptism, of which the central feature was the total immersion of the new church member. After hearing that he too would have to be immersed if he were to achieve his goal, Bryan recalled, he never again said that he wanted to be a Baptist minister. He next decided that he wanted "to be a farmer and raise pumpkins," an idea that probably had something to do with the family's impending move to their new country house. After more intimate experience with farm chores, however, the second ambition gave way to a third, to be a lawyer.[3]

Whether these family tales are apocryphal or not, they forecast with remarkable fidelity the course of Bryan's subsequent career. Although he did become a lawyer like his father and in fact surpassed Silas's career as a public servant, Will never lost his other ambitions. Both as a political leader and in a more direct way as a lay leader in the Presbyterian church, he was always and very consciously a preacher, inculcating faith and advocating the application of biblical morality to daily life. Moreover, like his father he was a gentleman farmer who strongly identified with the interests of the farming West. Silas Bryan rented out most of the five hundred acres he owned in Salem, and Will did little farming on his much loved estate, "Fairview," in Lincoln, Nebraska, but both stayed close to the soil. Like his ideal, Jefferson, Bryan's common man was the small farmer.

Many years later Idaho's colorful Republican senator, William E. Borah, remarked contemptuously that Bryan "never grew an inch after 1896."[4] The remark was both less and more true than Borah could have realized. As a political leader Bryan was much more flexible than Borah gave him credit for, adopting new issues and changing his position on old ones as conditions changed. In foreign policy in particular, a subject to which the Nebraskan had given little thought before 1896, his attitudes and positions changed substantially over the years in response to changing circumstances. Yet at the same time, Borah underestimated the degree to which Bryan's direction had been fixed at an early age. By the Commoner's own account, the basic principles which would govern his response to all issues, public and private, had been determined not in 1896, but nearly thirty years earlier. It was on this bedrock that the changing structures of Bryan's life were always founded. Indeed it was the very solidity of his foundations that gave him his self-confidence, his optimism, his ability to rise from defeat to fight again, his conviction that his cause would triumph ultimately, and his willingness to experiment with various means to his ends. Only near the end of his life, when his fundamental principles themselves were threatened, did he seem to become the rigid, doctrinaire bigot derided by H.L. Mencken.

The source of Bryan's basic convictions was his family, especially his father, despite his close association with his mother. "I have," he said in describing his father's influence on his religious and political positions, ". . . seen no reason to depart from the line he marked out."[5] But both parents had a role in shaping him. It was, after all, his mother who gave him his first exposure to the moralisms of the McGuffey readers, began his training in public speaking, and supervised his physical growth as he did the family chores. Both parents stressed the virtuous personal habits, strong ethics, and active religious commitment that distinguished Bryan's later life. From his father, however, he took the central direction of his life, the decision to become a Christian statesman.

The description "Christian statesman" is particularly appropriate in regard to Bryan because he saw service to others as the fundamental Christian duty and embraced public life because it seemed to offer the greatest opportunity for service. His fundamentalist Protestantism was deep and sincere but was neither tied to any one denomination nor focused exclusively on personal salvation. He accepted the omnipotence of God, the divinity of Christ, and the role of the Holy Spirit as "God's messenger to man, and man's comforter and inspiration." Duty to God came before any earthly goals, and the chief duty expected of man by God was to love and serve one's fellow man. "Example" he regarded as "the means of propagating truth," and "service the measure of greatness." Eternal life after death, he argued, was a "reward" for faith but also a "restraint" upon behavior.[6]

Christianity was a political and social religion for Bryan. What others called the "social gospel," he described as "applied Christianity." He emphasized the importance of forgiveness as a part of Christian life and insisted that a man of faith would demonstrate his faith by his service to others. *"The soul that is warmed by divine fire,"* he declared, *"will be satisfied with nothing less than the complete performance of duty;* it must cry aloud and spare not, to the end that the creed of Christ may be exemplified in the life of the nation."[7] He believed the Christian especially qualified to judge political questions rightly because all political issues could be reduced, at bottom, to matters of right and wrong. Hence the guide for both national and international behavior should be "the moral code which regulates individual life," which he defined as "the theory that we can 'overcome evil with good'—that example is the most potent influence for good."[8]

In keeping with his evangelical background Bryan was a strong supporter of foreign missions. He came of age in a period when the American missionary movement was enjoying an explosive growth— an increase of 50 percent in the number of missionaries overseas between 1870 and 1890, and a rapid expansion into almost all the non-Christian regions of the world, as well as a less successful effort to bring Protestantism to Catholic Latin America. The missionaries generally regarded their function as dual—the saving of souls and the introduction of "backward" peoples to Western culture. For a time, as other cultures first encountered the fascinations of Western technology, they tolerated the Bible along with trade, but after 1890 a backlash of rising nationalism threatened both.[9] When Bryan was young, it was easy to believe that Christianization and Westernization were sweeping the world; by the time of his death that was no longer certain.

For many Americans, missionaries' reports to their churches at home were the first window on strange peoples and alien cultures. Missionaries became the interpreters of other cultures to Americans and thereby exercised an influence on the formation of public attitudes that has never been fully explored. How can we estimate the impact of missionary reports on people who had little other contact with the outside world? In many cases even the highest level policymakers were strongly influenced by missionaries.[10] It is probably not an overstatement to say that at the end of the nineteenth and beginning of the twentieth centuries the missionaries had more influence on American attitudes toward the world, and more exemplified to the world what America stood for, than diplomats, businessmen, or any other group.

Bryan shared the common belief that the function of the missionary was both religious and cultural. His arguments help to clarify the origins of his own foreign policy attitudes and the attitudes of many other Americans of his generation. "The daily life of a missionary," he wrote, "is not only a constant sermon, but to a certain extent, an exposition of western ways. . . . It would be worth while to send Christians to the Orient merely to show the fullness and richness of a Christian life, for, after all, the example of an upright person, living a life of service according to the Christian ideal, is more eloquent than any sermon—it is the unanswerable argument in favor of our religion."[11]

There were, in fact, times when Bryan felt that example could communicate where more direct approaches failed. Although he was seldom at a loss for words, even his eloquence could not bridge all cultural gaps. He faced such a gulf, his wife recalled, one evening when they visited a rescue mission on the New York waterfront. Among the derelicts, he looked, she recorded, "like a creature from another world," and when called upon to speak, he stumbled and found little to say. "It takes a man who has been saved from the depths to reach men like these," he confessed later. "I cannot do it. I lack the necessary past."[12] For the "silver-tongued orator" this was a unique admission, but it sharpened his point that a Christian life could communicate by example even where words would fail.

Secure in the belief that Christian values were superior to all others, Bryan had no trouble in justifying the cost of foreign missions. "If truth must, according to eternal law, triumph . . . , how can it triumph over lower ideals unless it is brought into contact with them? . . . If the Christian ideal is worthy to be followed in America, it is worthy to be presented in every land, and experience has shown that it is an ideal capable of being made universal, for it has commended itself to people of every clime and of every tongue."[13]

To those who argued that Americans should perfect their own society before undertaking the redemption of the world, Bryan drew on his church experience to point out that those who supported home missions were likely to be those who also favored foreign missions, while the critics of the foreign effort were likely to be parsimonious with charity at home as well. Even more important was his argument that the person who withheld service until he perfected himself could never help others. That principle had an application to foreign policy which Bryan did not hesitate to make explicit: "The country which refuses to extend a helping hand to other lands until all its people have passed beyond the need of improvement will do nothing for the world." Countries and individual missionaries would make mistakes and sometimes go astray, he admitted frankly, but that did not relieve them of the obligation to make the effort to serve.[14] In Bryan's mind there was no difference between the American national mission and the Christian religious mission. As the leading Christian nation, America's duty to the world was exactly analogous to that of the Christian individual to support foreign missions.

Bryan did not delude himself that man was perfect or the millennium at hand. Man, he admitted, was weak and prone to error, in need of guidance and control to prevent him from harming himself and others. It was, of course, this view which led him to believe that laws to prohibit the manufacture and sale of alcohol were justified, and which helped him rationalize his approval of various military interventions while secretary of state. Such actions would save men from themselves. But at the same time he also believed that man was basically good and ultimately perfectible: "A man can be born again; the springs of life can be cleansed instantly so that the heart loves the things that it formerly hated and hates the things it once loved. If this is true of *one*, it can be true of any number. . . ."[15]

Almost completely absent from Bryan's religious lectures and writings are references to sin, the devil, and the sources of human evil. In his optimistic world of progress and human perfectibility, evil seems to have been equated with error. He did not regard it as a major independent force in the world, nor did he seem to feel that individuals were ever really bad. They were mistaken, not evil. The atrocities of trench warfare were beyond the comprehension of a man who believed that the human heart instinctively responded to the example of a Christian life.

Because man could be saved by accepting Christ in his heart, Bryan regarded purity of heart as more vital to the future of the world than vast intelligence. Sometimes he verged on anti-intellectualism ("The sin of this generation is mind worship—a worship as destructive as any other form of idolatry"), but provided that cultivation of the mind remained a means rather than a goal in itself, he valued learning as an instrument that could give shape to the urgings of a Christian heart. "The heart," he told a group of educators, "needs a trained mind to assist it if the life is to be largely fruitful. The heart directs but education multiplies the individual's power and capacity for service. . . ." A partnership between mind and heart was the ideal, but the heart must always be the senior partner. "The brain," he pointed out, "will plot a murder or plan a burglary as willingly as it will labor for the welfare of mankind. All, therefore, depends upon the *heart* behind the brain. . . ." "What this country needs," he argued, "is not more brains but more heart—not more intellect but more conscience. . . . The heart must be restored to the throne and made the source of authority."[16]

Exactly what Bryan meant by "the heart" is difficult to specify. At various times he used "conscience," "faith," and "religion" as synonyms for "heart," and what he seems to have believed was that there is in all men a common ethical instinct, divinely implanted, which is the basis for morality. Because he thought that this instinct was shared by *all* men, he believed that appeals based upon it and addressed to it could reach everyone: "Only those who speak from the heart and to the heart employ a universal language. . . ." Regardless of cultural or political differences, therefore, Christianity, which was based upon the common ethical instinct, was appropriate to all peoples everywhere. By extension, if the nation followed "the moral code which regulates individual life," it could hope for universal assent to its policies, although the propensity of man to sin and error did not make such assent automatic. Until everyone reached Christian perfection, there would be disagreement, conflict, and misunderstanding.[17] Nevertheless, a foreign policy based upon Christian principles had an excellent chance of appealing to the hearts of people all around the world.

Evangelical Protestantism was the core of Bryan's foreign policy as it was the center of his daily life. From it he derived many of the basic principles of his policy: the belief that the nation should obey the same moral code as the individual; the conviction that service to others was the first duty to God; the assumption that America, as the leading Christian nation, had a missionary obligation; the belief that although it was necessary to preach to the heathen, the most persuasive argument was the example of a Christian life; and the assumption that because all men were basically alike at heart, all would accept and applaud a truly Christian policy.

Noble though Bryan's aspirations were, his assumptions about the world did not command complete acceptance, even among his countrymen. His critics regarded him as appallingly naive, a victim of "the supreme sentimentality of his countrymen, to whom a lump in the throat makes the whole world kin," and even more serious charges were to be made.[18] One was that by turning all issues into moral questions, Bryan reduced them to struggles of right against wrong, and of course his presumption was that the right was exclusively on his side. That process obliterated subtleties and ambiguities in his understanding of problems, made compromise difficult, and aroused strong emotions in the contending parties. In appealing to the heart, Bryan sought to reach the best in man, but unfortunately it was also possible to tap the worst in the form of unbridled passions. What was more, the world did not, as Bryan assumed, share a common moral sense. On the contrary, although he did not realize it, the very progress in technology that was making the world seem smaller was also causing peoples to become more fiercely protective of their cultural, religious, and national differences. Bryan foresaw an increasingly unified, homogeneous world; the reality has been very nearly the opposite.

Interwined with the religious principles that shaped Bryan's foreign policy attitudes was a series of political convictions. He learned both political and religious principles at his father's knee, and he never saw any real difference between political and religious questions. His religion was oriented to serving men on earth, and his politics aimed at saving their souls as well as solving more mundane problems. "My father was as much at home with ministers as he was with politicians," Bryan recalled. "He saw no necessary conflict—and I have never been able to see any—between the principles of our government and the principles of Christian faith."[19]

The center of Bryan's political principles was faith in the people, and that faith had a religious basis. "The common people," he wrote, "form the industrious, intelligent and patriotic element of our population," and he added that they were "the people to whom the Bible pays the highest compliment it ever pays to any class when it says that the common people heard Christ gladly." "The voice of the people shall be recognized," he declared grandiloquently, "if not as the voice of God, as least as Bancroft defines it, as the best expression of the divine will to be found upon the earth." The success of the United States, he concluded, offered ample evidence that the people could "meet every emergency, rise to every responsibility and prove that their capacity for self-government is as undeniable as their right to self-government."[20]

Despite his tendency to equate *vox populi* with *vox dei*, Bryan's political experience persuaded him that the majority was not infallible. Majorities, he admitted, could be wrong, though he insisted that a minority was more likely to be wrong than a majority. The American people, he thought, were "sound at heart," and if they should "err or be led astray," eventually they would see the truth and correct their mistakes. Perhaps it was that faith that led him to give them three chances to correct one error and elect him president.

Bryan's obedience to the public will could take extreme forms. For example, he thought that representatives of the people ought always to obey their constituents' wills rather than their own judgments, even committing themselves absolutely to keep campaign promises and fulfill party platforms. The Commoner himself went one step further—his identification with his followers extended even to matters of taste in art, music, and literature. He did not regard this submersion of self in the public's desires as a sacrifice or an abasement. So confident was he in the wisdom of the people, so much a part of them was he himself, that to conform to their standards in everything was only natural to him.[21] He admired Jefferson, but in his deference to the public will, Bryan was more a Jacksonian than a Jeffersonian.

Bryan's political ideas also had an important influence on his attitude toward foreign policy. Regarding American democracy as "time's noblest offspring," he was confident that it would, "by the influence of example, excite in other races a desire for self-government and a determination to secure it." "There is not," he declared, "a civilized nation in which the idea of popular government is not growing, and in all the semi-civilized nations there are reformers who are urging an extension of the influence of the people in government. So universal is this growth of democratic ideas that there can be no doubt of their final triumph."[22] Just as he had assumed that the hearts of men were everywhere the same, so he presumed that all men sought democracy. The human race shared both political and religious instincts. "A sense of justice is to be found in every heart," he declared, and that sense of justice was not only "the safest foundation upon which to build a government" but the best guarantee that ultimately "universal peace" would be achieved when men learned, through Christianity and democracy, to trust their hearts.[23]

For all that Bryan usually blurred the distinction between religion and politics, some elements in his foreign policy owed more to political than religious ideas or experiences. In dealing with Latin America his major concern was not religious but political—to demonstrate that democratic procedures could solve existing problems. Likewise his hopes for world peace were only partly founded on his faith in the progress of Christianity in the world. His proposal for national referenda before nations could declare war, and his support of international organization, were political, not religious, ideas. His most famous contribution to the peace movement, his plan for international investigation of disputes, was based on his experience with labor arbitration rather than on religious principles. In fact its basic premise, that investigation of disputes would allow passions to cool and rationality to prevail, seemed directly contradictory to his assertion that the route to international harmony was through appeals to the heart.

A number of Bryan's foreign policy ideas thus derived especially from his political thought. His belief in the universal applicability of democracy and his conviction that the United States ought to promote democracy everywhere were examples. So also was the conviction that reform in the United States would increase America's standing as the leading democratic nation and enlarge its world influence as an example. Somewhat more ominous was the possibility that his faith in the wisdom of the common people might lead him to try to bypass, ignore, or even overthrow nondemocratically selected leaders of other nations in an effort to appeal directly to the people. In combination with his missionary commitment, Bryan's faith in the universal wisdom of the people might lead to a policy of benignly intended but widespread intervention in the affairs of others. The restraints on such a course were his love of peace, his belief in the efficacy of example, and his tolerance. They would not always be enough.

A further restraint, Bryan's isolationism, was widely shared with other Americans and may have been the most important limitation on the national impulse to remake the world in America's image. When Bryan first emerged into national politics in the early 1890s, isolationism was scarcely an active force in American political life. Adopted in the early republic as a defensive policy to prevent the weak, new nation from becoming a pawn in European power struggles and the victim of foreign interference in its internal affairs, isolationism had become an unexamined dogma by the late nineteenth century. Like the Monroe Doctrine it was something to celebrate on appropriate patriotic occasions, as Grover Cleveland did in his first inaugural address in 1885, but it was not usually a conscious policy.[24] Americans of the late nineteenth century did not so much reject the world as ignore it. Henry Cabot Lodge aptly summed up the situation in 1889 with the remark that "our relations with foreign nations . . . fill but a slight place in American politics, and excite generally only a languid interest," and when he proposed a new policy of expansionism his suggestion was unheard beyond a small circle of friends. On the eve of the Spanish-American War, Cleveland's secretary of state, Richard Olney, still lamented that the United States "purposely takes its stand outside the European family circle to which it belongs, and neither accepts the responsibilities of its place nor secures its advantages."[25]

There is some uncertainty about when the words "isolation," "isolationist," and "isolationism" entered the American political vocabulary as descriptions of a particular policy.[26] None of them seems to have been common until after World War I, although the basic concept behind them was explicit from the time of the Revolution and implicit in the decision of the Puritans to build in America a "new Jerusalem," a "city on a hill," in John Winthrop's famous phrase. The essence of isolationism was the rejection of lasting commitments outside the Western Hemisphere, especially where such commitments involved or might involve the use of force. No isolationist objected to the development of economic or cultural links to the outside world, and nearly everyone hoped that the United States would influence at least by example the policy and course of development of other nations. Independence of action was the central goal of most isolationists. George Washington's first draft of his Farewell Address makes the point even more clearly than the familiar final version: "if there be no engagements on our part, we shall be unembarrassed, and at liberty at all times, to act from circumstances, and dictates of Justice—sound policy—and our essential Interests."[27]

Most historians agree that the original policy of isolationism was the result of both circumstances and ideology. Geographical isolation, the weakness of the new nation, and the beckoning wilderness of the West made it natural for Americans to believe that Europe's affairs were no concern of theirs, as well as that Europe should keep hands off the New World. At the same time, the Puritans, the leaders of the Revolutionary generation, and later, expansionists and immigrants, all had positive reasons for rejecting Europe's "decadence," for seeking to create a new, more perfect society in America.

By the late nineteenth century many of these reasons for isolationism were less cogent, but the policy had become so habitual that most Americans never considered any other course. In a period of major social and economic change, they found more than enough to occupy their attention at home.

Ironically, however, the same changes that turned Americans' attention inward were also creating pressures for more active involvement with the outside world. The technology that shrank the oceanic moats and stimulated the growth of industries also produced a flood of goods which led, in turn, to a doubling of American foreign trade between 1870 and 1890. The exodus of businessmen hand in hand with missionaries led to new interests and ties in strange and hitherto unknown regions of the world. Trade and the missionary enterprise required protection, necessitating the building of a new, steel navy beginning in the 1880s, and thereafter the navy itself became a force for greater world involvement. New ideas, the Social Gospel movement and Social Darwinism, were generated in the changes taking place within the United States, but they soon combined with and reinvigorated notions of America's mission as well. The aggressive imperialism of other industrialized nations—particularly England, Germany, and Japan—suggested an inevitable tie between economic development and expansion.[28] By the 1890s the stage was set for a conflict between traditional isolationism and the forces pressing for greater world involvement.

It is notable, however, that not all parts of the United States nor all Americans were affected equally by the forces that eroded isolationism and favored greater world involvement. Such changes most influenced the more urban and cosmopolitan regions of the country. Those people who lived in more isolated, rural sections of the country benefited little from radical social and economic change and clung tenaciously to traditional values.[29] Although farmers of the late nineteenth century sometimes saw foreign markets as a solution to their economic troubles, most of them had no direct contact with any such markets.[30] They dealt with urban middlemen, and it was these middlemen who became the targets of their growing anger. The farm protest movement of the 1880s and 1890s was distinctly antiurban. It widened the gap between city and country, reinforced traditional values among farm dwellers, and made farmers suspicious of anything the "city folks" might want. When William Jennings Bryan spoke in 1896 of the urban East as the "enemy's country," he was expressing a sentiment that farmers of the West and South commonly shared. The forces eroding isolationism had little impact on the rural areas of the country, and in fact the rural-urban split of the period inclined rural people to be less receptive to ideas of change and more assertive of traditional attitudes than they might otherwise have been.

The West was a bastion of the farm protest movement and of isolationism, but both were strong in the South of this period as well. Although the South would be identified with "internationalism" in the twentieth century, that was not true in the nineteenth century.[31] The residue of the Civil War and the quasi-colonial economic status of the region vis-à-vis the North generated an anti-Northeastern sentiment that was never entirely overcome by the leaders of the "New South," with their commitment to industrialization, railroad building, and foreign trade. In the country's most introverted section, isolationism retained its traditional support, which the Populist movement of the 1890s reinforced. The emotionalism of the Spanish-American War swept up southerners along with other Americans, but after it burned away, isolationism sprang up again, like pasture grass after a spring fire.[32]

There was a strong correlation between the regions of the country where isolationism persisted in the late nineteenth and early twentieth centuries and the areas that supported Bryan. Of the fourteen states that he carried in his three presidential races (1896, 1900, 1908), twelve were in the South and two in the mountain West. Four others that he carried in two of the three contests were in the same regions (see Table 1). Even in states he did not win, Bryan always ran better in rural than in urban areas. In short, the areas most disposed to isolationism were also those where Bryan was strongest. Evidently, "Bryanism" and isolationism overlapped considerably. This is not to say that Bryan created isolationism or that his supporters forced an uncongenial position on the Commoner. Bryan was molded by the same forces that shaped most other rural Americans of his day, and it would be surprising if he differed from them in this since he did not on other issues.

Because Bryan lost three elections, it is easy to forget how large his following actually was. In each of his three races Bryan received at least 43 percent of the votes cast, and in 1896 he received 49 percent. Almost 6½ million people voted for him in each election. Since an average of 72.6 percent of the eligible voters took part in all three elections, we can say with considerable certainty that nearly half of the

Table 1. **The Votes in the 1896, 1900, and 1908 Elections, by State**

	Popular Votes						
	1896			*1900*		*1908*	
States	William McKinley, Rep.	William J. Bryan, Dem.	Bryan and Watson, Pop.	McKinley and Roosevelt, Rep.	Bryan and Stevenson, Dem.	Taft and Sherman, Rep.	Bryan and Kern, Dem.
Alabama*	54,737	131,226	24,089	55,512	97,131	26,283	74,374
Arkansas*	37,512	110,103	—	44,800	81,142	56,760	87,015
California	146,688	144,766	21,730	164,755	124,985	214,398	127,492
Colorado*	26,271	161,269	2,389	93,072	122,733	123,700	126,644
Connecticut	110,285	56,740	—	102,572	74,014	112,815	68,255
Delaware	20,452	16,615	—	22,535	18,863	25,014	22,071
Florida*	11,257	31,958	1,977	7,420	28,007	10,654	31,104
Georgia*	60,091	94,672	440	35,056	81,700	41,692	72,413
Idaho†	6,324	23,192	—	27,198	29,414	52,621	36,162
Illinois	607,130	464,523	1,090	597,985	503,061	629,932	450,810
Indiana	323,754	305,573	—	336,063	309,584	348,993	338,262
Iowa	289,293	223,741	—	307,808	209,265	275,210	200,771
Kansas	159,541	171,810	46,194	185,955	162,601	197,216	161,209
Kentucky*	218,171	217,890	—	226,801	234,899	235,711	244,092
Louisiana*	22,037	77,175	—	14,233	53,671	8,958	63,568
Maine	80,461	34,587	2,387	65,412	36,822	66,987	35,403
Maryland	136,978	104,746	—	136,185	122,238	116,513	115,908
Massachusetts	278,976	105,711	15,181	239,147	157,016	265,966	155,543
Michigan	293,582	237,268	—	316,269	211,685	333,313	174,619
Minnesota	193,503	139,735	—	190,461	112,901	195,843	109,401
Mississippi*	5,123	63,793	7,517	5,753	51,706	4,363	60,287
Missouri†	304,940	363,652	—	314,092	351,922	347,203	346,574
Montana†	10,494	42,537	—	25,373	37,145	32,333	29,326
Nebraska†	103,064	115,999	—	121,835	114,013	126,997	131,099
Nevada*	1,938	8,377	575	3,849	6,347	10,775	11,212
New Hampshire	57,444	21,650	379	54,799	35,489	53,149	33,655
New Jersey	221,367	133,675	—	221,754	164,879	265,326	182,567
New York	819,838	551,369	—	822,013	678,462	870,070	667,468
North Carolina*	155,222	174,488	—	132,997	157,733	114,887	136,928
North Dakota	26,335	20,686	—	35,898	20,531	57,680	32,885
Ohio	525,991	477,497	2,615	543,918	474,882	572,312	502,721
Oklahoma	—	—	—	—	—	110,558	122,406
Oregon	48,779	46,662	—	46,526	33,385	62,530	38,049
Pennsylvania	728,300	433,230	11,176	712,665	424,232	745,779	448,785
Rhode Island	37,437	14,459	—	33,784	19,812	43,942	24,706
South Carolina*	9,313	58,801	—	3,579	47,233	3,965	62,290
South Dakota	41,042	41,255	—	54,530	39,544	67,536	40,266
Tennessee*	148,773	166,268	4,525	123,180	145,356	118,324	135,608
Texas*	167,520	370,434	79,572	130,641	267,432	65,666	217,302
Utah	13,491	64,607	—	47,139	45,006	61,165	42,601
Vermont	50,991	10,607	461	42,569	12,849	39,552	11,496
Virginia*	135,388	154,985	—	115,865	146,080	52,573	82,946
Washington	39,153	51,646	—	57,456	44,833	106,062	58,691
West Virginia	104,414	92,927	—	119,829	98,807	137,869	111,418
Wisconsin	268,135	165,523	—	265,760	159,163	247,747	166,662
Wyoming	10,072	10,655	286	14,482	10,164	20,846	14,918
Total	7,111,607	6,509,052	222,583	7,219,525	6,358,737	7,677,788	6,407,982

*Carried by Bryan in all three elections.
†Carried by Bryan in two of the three elections.

	1896				1900		1908	
McKinley (Pres.)	Bryan (Pres.)	Hobart (Vice-Pres.)	Sewall (Vice-Pres.)	Watson (Vice-Pres.)	McKinley and Roosevelt	Bryan and Stevenson	Taft and Sherman	Bryan and Kern
—	11	—	11	—	—	11	—	11
—	8	—	5	3	—	8	—	9
8	1	8	1	—	9	—	10	—
—	4	—	4	—	—	4	—	5
6	—	6	—	—	6	—	7	—
3	—	3	—	—	3	—	3	—
—	4	—	4	—	—	4	—	5
—	13	—	13	—	—	13	—	13
—	3	—	3	—	—	3	3	—
24	—	24	—	—	24	—	27	—
15	—	15	—	—	15	—	15	—
13	—	13	—	—	13	—	13	—
—	10	—	10	—	10	—	10	—
12	1	12	1	—	—	13	—	13
—	8	—	4	4	—	8	—	9
6	—	6	—	—	6	—	6	—
8	—	8	—	—	8	—	2	6
15	—	15	—	—	15	—	16	—
14	—	14	—	—	14	—	14	—
9	—	9	—	—	9	—	11	—
—	9	—	9	—	—	9	—	10
—	17	—	13	4	—	17	18	—
—	3	—	2	1	—	3	3	—
—	8	—	4	4	8	—	—	8
—	3	—	3	—	—	3	—	3
4	—	4	—	—	4	—	4	—
10	—	10	—	—	10	—	12	—
36	—	36	—	—	36	—	39	—
—	11	—	6	5	—	11	—	12
3	—	3	—	—	3	—	4	—
23	—	23	—	—	23	—	23	—
—	—	—	—	—	—	—	—	7
4	—	4	—	—	4	—	4	—
32	—	32	—	—	32	—	34	—
4	—	4	—	—	4	—	4	—
—	9	—	9	—	—	9	—	9
—	4	—	2	2	4	—	4	—
—	12	—	12	—	—	12	—	12
—	15	—	15	—	—	15	—	18
—	3	—	2	1	3	—	3	—
4	—	4	—	—	4	—	4	—
—	12	—	12	—	—	12	—	12
—	4	—	2	2	4	—	5	—
6	—	6	—	—	6	—	7	—
12	—	12	—	—	12	—	13	—
—	3	—	2	1	3	—	3	—
271	176	271	149	27	292	155	321	162

Source: Arthur M. Schlesinger, Jr., Fred L. Israel, and William P. Hansen, eds., *History of American Presidential Elections, 1789–1968* (New York, 1971), II, p. 1874; III, pp. 1962, 2131.

politically active and interested people of the country supported Bryan (see Table 2). If we assume that the women's vote (had women been allowed to vote) would have been divided approximately equally between the candidates, we can estimate that Bryan's following was 12 million to 13 million people. There is no way of determining what percentage of those people were also isolationists, but the correlation between the region where isolationism was strongest and the region where Bryan was strongest suggests that many of them were.

When Bryan entered national politics in the 1890s, isolationism was, even more than in later years, an "impulse" rather than a coherent policy. Insofar as it had any specific focus it implied an aversion to involvement with European affairs. During the silver crusade of the 1890s it acquired a particular tinge of Anglophobia. At this point, however, there was no visible distinction to be made among those groups whom John M. Cooper has identified as "idealistic isolationists," "ultranationlist isolationists," and "internationalists." Those interested in any form of foreign involvement—men like Theodore Roosevelt, Henry Cabot Lodge, or Alfred T. Mahan—were, in Cooper's terms, more properly called "ultranationalists" than "internationalists." They favored world involvement for the United States but cared more for national power, prestige, and security than for international peace, freedom, and justice.[33] Most Americans except for these few were so little concerned with foreign affairs that no distinct positions can be identified. The pressure of events at the end of the 1890s and the first years of the twentieth century, however, would divide the undifferentiated mass into various groups.

Another challenge, too, faced isolationists in the early twentieth century. For the first time many intellectual and political leaders of the nation explicitly questioned isolationism and argued that national interest and patriotism required participation in world affairs.[34] Isolationism had been Americanism. Now people were suggesting that it was really "un-American."

Adding further to the confusion was the fact that after 1898, expansionism, which, in the form of continental Manifest Destiny, had been generally compatible with isolationism, now became a threat to American independence of action in the world. Although most American imperialists strongly asserted that insular imperialism was no danger to isolationism, study of the rhetoric of the anti-imperialists demonstrates that many Americans did not accept their arguments. They feared that possession of distant colonies would entangle the United States in the conflicts and rivalries of Europe and Asia. At the same time, the imperialists themselves found their alternatives limited.

Table 2. **The Votes in the 1896, 1900, and 1908 Elections, by Candidate**

Election Year and Candidates	Popular Votes	Popular Votes Won by Bryan (%)	Eligible Voters Participating (%)
1896			
McKinley	7,102,246*		79.3
McKinley	7,111,607		
Bryan	6,492,559*	46.6*	
Bryan	6,731,635	47.5	
Others	315,398*		
1900			
McKinley	7,218,491*		73.2
McKinley	7,219,525		
Bryan	6,356,734*	45.5*	
Bryan	6,358,737	45.5	
Others	386,840*		
1908			
Taft	7,675,320*		65.4
Taft	7,677,788		
Bryan	6,412,294*	43*	
Bryan	6,407,982	43	
Others	800,626*		

Source: Figures followed by an asterisk are from *Historical Statistics of the United States, Colonial Times to 1970* (Washington, D.C., 1975), II, pp. 1071, 1073. All other figures in the first two columns are from Arthur M. Schlesinger, Jr., Fred L. Israel, and William P. Hansen, eds., *History of American Presidential Elections, 1789–1968* (New York, 1971), II, p. 1874; III, pp. 1962, 2131.

Because of the traditional link between expansion and isolation, they had a far better chance of selling a policy of imperialism to the public than one of internationalism, with its obligations and lack of tangible results.[35] For any number of reasons, the period was one of fluctuating opinions, shifting allegiances, and defensive assertions of old values.

What determined which way various individuals were likely to go? In general, as Cooper points out, internationalists and most isolationists were idealists, an opposed to ultranationalist isolationists, who expressed no interest in the fate of the world, provided the United States was secure. In the generally idealistic rhetoric of American politics, ultranationalist isolationism found few adherents. Most isolationists expressed an idealistic concern for the welfare of the world but insisted that the United States ought to serve the causes of peace, democracy, and justice only by example, avoiding the contamination of involvement. The goals of internationalism and idealistic isolationism were almost the same, and the boundary between them was indistinct. The cases of Bryan and Woodrow Wilson suggest that very small differences might determine which position an idealist took.

Bryan and Wilson got along very well personally because in many ways they were similar in background and outlook. Both were Presbyterians, deeply religious, and committed to applying their religious convictions to public affairs. Both were strong family men. Both were sometimes intuitive rather than analytical in their approach to the world, and both inclined to a somewhat romantic belief in human progress. Both believed strongly in the wisdom of the people and in democracy as the best possible form of government. Both loved their nation deeply and believed that it would help to lead the world toward a new era of peace, justice, and democracy.

Aside from differences of intellect and temperament, about which scholars may still not agree, the most striking differences between the two men were in their educations and early careers. Although Bryan had fine teachers and received a generally good training at Illinois College and the Union College of Law in Chicago, his courses, professors, and classmates lacked the cosmopolitanism that Wilson encountered at Princeton and Johns Hopkins. Wilson did not go to Europe until he was an adult, but as a student, and later as a professor, he moved in a world where trips to Europe for study, business, or pleasure were commonplace and where the doings of foreigners seemed no less important and no more bizarre than the antics of Populist radicals in Kansas or Nebraska. Bryan, on the other hand, studied at a college that offered no courses on the history or institutions of any country other than the United States and no foreign languages beyond one year of German, and his law school program emphasized law as a skill or craft rather than as a philosophical system or as an expression of a culture.[36] After leaving law school he returned to Jacksonville, Illinois, to practice for a time, but restless and ambitious, he eventually settled with his new wife, Mary, in Lincoln, Nebraska. There the young man worked hard to establish himself as a lawyer, a parent, an aspiring Democratic politician in a Republican state, and a voice for struggling farmers. During a period when Wilson's interests were in the wider world, Bryan's attention was fixed firmly on the grassroots.

Not until after his second presidential race, when he was over forty, did Bryan take his first trip beyond the borders of the United States. Wilson first went to Europe at about the same age (in 1896), but the trip was not as much a new experience to him as to Bryan, and even more important, it came before he became a national political leader.[37] However much Wilson and Bryan had in common, Wilson was imbued with Princeton's comfortable familiarity with the world, while Bryan shared Nebraska's suspicion of the metropolitan and foreign. As subsequent experience shaped each man's basic values into a foreign policy, their roads gradually diverged. Each wanted America to serve and lead the world, but they differed in their willingness to trust the fate of the United States to the hands of foreigners. In 1890, Bryan was no more consciously an isolationist than Wilson was an internationalist. In a nation just beginning to define its attitude toward the outside world, such terms had no meaning. For both, however, strong basic values interacted with experience to suggest a direction of development.

In his religion, his education, his rural background, Bryan was a representative man of that heartland of the United States which Paul Glad has called "the middle border."[38] He did not rebel against the values inculcated in home, church, and school, nor did he seek out the books or the teachers or the great cities that might have offered him other values. As he grew older and encountered other ways of doing things and other values, his confidence in what he had learned as a boy did not waver, nor did his faith in the people who held those values. He listened to their problems and sought remedies for their difficulties with a sensitivity to what they wanted only possible in a politician who was truly one of them. They returned his affection and respect with unstinting love, voted for him with enthusiasm in three presidential elections, bought 150,000 subscriptions to his newspaper, *The Commoner,* and flocked to hear him by the thousands as he stumped the country and lectured on the platforms of those late nineteenth and early twentieth century festivals of entertainment and education known as "circuit Chautauquas," after the annual gatherings at Lake Chautauqua, New York.[39] For all practical purposes Bryan never had a private life separate from his public career. Nor is there any evidence that he sought one. His followers were his family—extensions of himself.

Bryan's supporters loved him because they knew he cared about them more than about anything else, and because he perfectly embodied their attitudes and values. He articulated desires they did not even know they had and suggested solutions to problems they recognized but could not solve themselves. As a diagnostician of the ills that beset the middle border, Bryan had no peer.

In terms of foreign policy, the link between Bryan and his followers is more difficult to specify. For the most part, they were not very interested in foreign issues. Except at occasional moments of crisis, the outside world did not affect their daily lives. Provided he did not violate some principle they felt important, they would doubtless have given the Commoner great latitude to follow whatever course he chose in foreign policy. Bryan, however, had no desire to strike out for himself in this area or any other. Sharing the values of his followers in every detail, he was as incapable of knowingly differing from them as he was unwilling to do so. Nevertheless, although he was not intrinsically more interested in foreign policy than they were, Bryan was forced by his leadership position to confront issues sooner and more explicitly. The positions he gradually evolved reflect the reactions of his supporters to a rapidly changing world and to an enlarging American role in that world. Like others, Bryan believed that the United States must seize the opportunity to be a "world power," but the deep convictions that he shared with millions of his followers put special restraints on the way the power would be sought and exercised.[40]

Like others, Bryan's forebears had set out for the West because they felt that a better life could be built there. Yet the gesture of rejection was an ambiguous one. A pioneer's success was a threat and challenge to those he left behind and a temptation to him to bring the message of his success back. When they thought about the world, Bryan and his neighbors felt the same contradictory emotions—the desire to be envied for their success and the fear that envy would arouse hostility, the wish to help others to the happiness they had found but the concern that they might be dragged down rather than others lifted up. The task with which Bryan struggled for thirty years was how to reconcile those conflicting sentiments.

2

SILVER, GOLD, AND IMPERIALISM, 1896–1900

Before 1896, William Jennings Bryan shared the feeling of his neighbors that the world beyond the oceans was of little or no concern to the United States. As he became involved in the monetary controversy, unconcern changed to a belief that at least some interests in the outside world were inimical to America's welfare, and that conclusion reinforced rather than weakened his isolationism. Only after the election, when the Spanish-American War offered the nation new opportunities for world influence, did he begin to move toward the development of a missionary isolationism that promised service to the world without involvement.

In 1896, Bryan was a relatively new but dedicated recruit to the silver cause. "I don't know anything about free silver," he had admitted in 1892. "The people of Nebraska are for free silver and I am for free silver. I will look up the arguments later."[1] Between 1892 and his nomination for the presidency in 1896 he did indeed "look up the arguments," but he did not think them through for himself. He simply accepted an already developed case, with its emphasis on foreign conspiracy against the United States and its assertion that the nation should adopt bimetallism unilaterally. Although silver was a subject of international interest, American silverites took a narrowly isolationist view of the issue.

That was not necessarily the only approach to the matter. Since the 1870s the Republicans had been saying that they, too, favored bimetallism if it could be achieved through agreement among the major commercial nations of the world.[2] The problem was that their course had produced no results, and by 1896, silverites, seeing their economic situation going from bad to worse, doubted the sincerity of the Republican promise and the likelihood of international agreement even if earnestly sought. Hence the Democratic platform of 1896 called for the United States to adopt bimetallism "without waiting for the aid or consent of any other nation."[3] Because of their insistence on unilateral American action, silverites were thus committed to an essentially ultranationalist isolationist foreign policy.

The main reason for the extreme isolationism of most silverites in 1896 was their belief that the nation's troubles were the result of an international conspiracy. A group of American and European financiers, they alleged, had conspired to use their financial power to dominate their governments and compel the adoption of the gold standard in order to enrich themselves further. Since this group controlled the various governments, its political agents were unlikely to agree to international bimetallism. The British, principal competitors of the United States for world trade and dominant in international economic affairs, were regarded as the chief villains in the conspiracy. Those who accepted the conspiracy theory commonly saw the issue of 1896 as a new struggle for independence from England and, like the Founding Fathers, advocated an isolationist foreign policy.

Silverites also insisted that immediate, unilateral adoption of bimetallism would help to break the hold of corrupting elements over the American government and would strengthen the nation's trading position in silver-standard areas of Asia and Latin America. At one stroke, they alleged, unilateral bimetallism would solve domestic economic problems, ensure governmental reform, and improve the nation's foreign trade.

Bryan accepted the conspiracy theory and reflected the Anglophobia endemic among silverites in 1896. In his "Cross of Gold" speech to the Democratic convention, and in his speech accepting the presidential nomination, he argued that unilateral bimetallism would restore American independence, which was imperiled by British financial control. Only when the "fetters of gold" were struck from the hands of Liberty could the United States fulfill its "mission . . . among the nations of the earth" to be "an example in all that is good, and the leading spirit in every movement which has for its object the uplifting of the human race."[4]

A century earlier, George Washington had warned Americans against excessive emotional attachments to foreign nations. Bryan, in 1896, issued a similar warning against foreign economic influence. If foreign investments were allowed to grow freely, he warned in terms now familiar in the Third World, foreign investors would choose the officials and set the policies of the corporations they controlled. In time, he feared, their "influence may be sufficient to decide elections, and ultimately to mould our institutions to conform to European ideals."[5] That the Europeans were eager for an opportunity to remake American institutions to suit "European ideals," Bryan did not for a moment doubt. His immersion in the silver issue had convinced him that little was to be expected from Europe but hostility and selfishness. In such a world, the United States must follow an independent course: "We cannot enforce respect for our foreign policy so long as we confess ourselves unable to frame our own financial policy."[6]

A germ of idealism and world service was apparent in Bryan's 1896 position, but only a germ. The suggestions that unilateral bimetallism would give the United States world influence and economic advantages in certain areas were minor arguments. The real emphasis of silverites in 1896 was on an ultranationalist isolationist policy that would free the United States from foreign influence and permit the solution of domestic problems. Foreign trade and world influence were of little interest to most silverites; their aim was to inflate the currency with silver to relieve the farmers' economic distress. In the cauldron of economic crisis, traditional isolationism combined in some people's minds with equally traditional Anglophobia to produce a new, virulent strain of isolationism that would last well into the twentieth century.

For Bryan and most of his followers, however, Anglophobia did not go very deep. They mouthed it as they mouthed vaguely anti-Semitic slogans—because both were accepted parts of the conspiracy theory, and a conspiracy required villains. Bryan, believing in the universality of conscience, found it impossible to commit himself permanently to the idea of a race or nation as evil. Both by temperament and by religious training, he found the ultranationalist isolationist position uncomfortable. It was incompatible with his optimistic view of human nature. Given an appropriate issue, it would not be hard to move him and those who shared his values from ultranationalist to idealistic isolationism. That issue, the Cuban revolution, was already looming on the horizon in 1896.

The outbreak of the Cuban revolution in February 1895 came at a moment when most American leaders were absorbed by the domestic economic and monetary crises. Despite widespread popular sympathy for the rebels, most politicians were reluctant to see the country embroiled in the Cuban situation. Outgoing president Grover Cleveland made a halfhearted gesture toward mediation, and Congress passed, by lopsided bipartisan majorities, a resolution advocating the recognition of Cuban belligerency, but the administration took no serious steps toward intervention before the election of 1896.[7] During the campaign, despite the efforts of Henry Cabot Lodge to drum up support for a more aggressive foreign policy, the Cuban issue was eclipsed completely by the silver controversy. The Republican,

Democratic, and Populist platforms all contained planks expressing American sympathy for the struggles of the Cuban rebels, but none promised anything definite.[8]

After the election, popular enthusiasm for the rebels was calmed by what amounted to a conspiracy of silence among major political leaders. Former president Cleveland refused comment on all public issues; President William McKinley exerted his influence over Republicans to calm the jingoes; and Bryan, preparing for a renewal of the silver contest in 1900, refused to be distracted from the central issue.

Because Bryan's position on the Cuban issue has been widely misunderstood, it is necessary to examine it here in some detail. In general the Commoner seems to have suffered from a common political malady, guilt by association. Following Richard Hofstadter's suggestion that "after the defeat of Bryan popular frustration in the silver areas, blocked on domestic issues, seemed to find expression in the Cuban question," historians have uncritically lumped Bryan with outspoken silverite jingoes.[9] A recent study of the period argues that he did not try "to stem the popular clamor" but rather "increased it," and even a sympathetic and thorough biographer concludes that he "let himself be swept away with the rest."[10] Such statements are not really accurate.

In the months immediately following the campaign, Bryan was largely occupied with writing his own account of it, *The First Battle*. As the title suggests, his conclusion in this volume was that 1896 was only the first contest of a war that he fully expected would be renewed in 1900 after the Republicans had failed to restore prosperity or to achieve international bimetallism.[11] Confident of ultimate victory, he had no desire to raise extraneous issues or to promote a war which might well redound to the benefit of the incumbent administration. On the contrary, when reporters demanded, in February 1897, that he make a statement on Cuba, he was deliberately vague. "In a matter of duty like this," he said, "there should be but one course, and we should pursue that course without hesitation."[12] What the course should be he did not specify, nor did he renew the pledge of "sympathy to the people of Cuba in their heroic struggle for liberty and independence," which the 1896 platform had extended.

During July 1897 Bryan presided over the sessions of the Trans-Mississippi Commercial Congress at Salt Lake City. Probably his main interest in this meeting of representatives from twenty-one Western states and territories was its endorsement of bimetallism, but he seems to have made no objection when the congress also called for the construction of a Nicaraguan canal, the annexation of Hawaii, and the recognition of Cuban belligerency.[13] Just what these resolutions may have shown about his views is problematical. Since the president had submitted a Hawaiian annexation treaty to the Senate in June, and since the Trans-Mississippi congress included representatives from Hawaii, he probably could not have blocked the annexation resolution if he had wanted to. There is no evidence, however, that he took any particular interest in the question. Certainly he did not become, then or thereafter, an advocate of annexation. On the Cuban issue, the action of the congress merely echoed a resolution which had been passed by large bipartisan majorities in the U.S. Congress in May. Rejected by McKinley as a threat to executive prerogative, the idea of recognizing Cuban belligerency was a meaningless but popular device for expressing sympathy with the rebels. Viewed in this light, the commercial congress's resolution did not go beyond the vague statements in the 1896 platform, and Bryan could hardly have objected to it. Certainly he could have endorsed all of these resolutions without in any way compromising his determination to keep his party's attention focused on the money issue.

By the beginning of 1898, relations between the United States and Spain were rapidly approaching a crisis. President McKinley's efforts to secure a diplomatic settlement were gravely imperiled during February by the publication of the de Lôme letter and the explosion of the American battleship *Maine*. Apprehensively, Republican leaders expected Bryan to proclaim a new crusade for "Free Silver and Free Cuba," but he made no such call. Instead he counseled restraint and urged the nation to support the president's efforts to avoid war.[14] Not until March 9 did he speak out for a bill to increase defense expenditures which had already, with McKinley's support, passed the House of Representatives.[15] Only on April 1, after McKinley had decided that the Spanish were not negotiating in good faith and that war was "inevitable," did Bryan finally endorse intervention. Since the president's views were widely reported in the newspapers, the Nebraskan's position was hardly radical.[16] What was more, he accompanied his call for intervention with the warning that it "may be accompanied by danger and expense," argued that "war is a terrible thing and cannot be defended except as a means to an end . . . when reason and diplomacy are of no avail," and urged the Spanish government to accept compromise.[17] Here, surely, was no irresponsible call to arms; rather this was a sober endorsement of the policy already adopted by the president.

Following his speech on April 1, Bryan remained silent throughout the critical days of early April until the thirteenth, two days after

McKinley had asked Congress for authority to intervene in Cuba. On that day Bryan, speaking at a Jefferson Day dinner in New York, finally gave unequivocal support to American intervention to clean up the Cuban "slaughter house."[18] With Congress virtually certain to declare war, the Jefferson Day speech merely indicated that Bryan, who had lagged well behind much of public opinion on the crisis with Spain, and who had, in fact, tried hard to calm the popular furor, had now caught up with the rest of the nation. Convinced at last that war was inescapable, he was rallying to the flag.

Throughout the year and a half after the election of 1896, Bryan's position on the Cuban issue was much closer to that of the Populist vice-presidental candidate of 1896, Tom Watson, than it was to that of silverite interventionists like Senators William M. Stewart and William V. Allen. Like Watson, Bryan feared that war would sidetrack reform.[19] As Senator James K. Jones of Arkansas, chairman of the Democratic National Committee and a strong Bryanite, pointed out, the hope expressed by some silverites that the expenses of the war would compel the issuing of paper money or the coining of silver was largely ephemeral as long as the Republicans kept their control over the executive and Congress.[20] Whether Bryan accepted the myth, common among silverites in this period, that McKinley resisted war because of the influence on him of American bankers who supposedly held a part of some $400 million worth of bonds issued by the Spanish government to finance the suppression of the Cuban revolution, cannot be determined from the fragmentary Bryan Papers for this period.[21] It is clear, however, that he did not make the "Cuban bond conspiracy" a part of his public argument for going to war. From the outset his concern was exclusively humanitarian. Only that concern led him reluctantly to support the president's decision for war.

Patriotism did not make Bryan trust completely McKinley's assurances that he was entirely altruistic in asking for intervention in Cuba, nor did it make him squeamish about seizing any opportunity to ensure that the administration avoid the temptations of imperialism. In his Jefferson Day speech on April 13 and in a caucus with congressional Democrats earlier in the day he recommended combining a declaration of war with an immediate recognition of the Cuban rebel government.[22] He was not the first to make the suggestion, but his enthusiastic support of it rallied Democrats behind the idea and gave it momentum.[23]

Ultimately, advocates of immediate recognition united in support of an amendment to the war resolution sponsored by Senator David Turpie of Indiana (a Bryan Democrat) but actually drafted by Senator

Joseph B. Foraker (a Republican jingo). As the sponsorship of the resolution indicated, its supporters were a strangely mixed group. Some Democrats merely wanted to embarrass the president and limit his discretionary power. A few senators like Foraker thought that recognition of a weak Cuban government would be a half step toward annexation. A third group, including Bryan, hoped the resolution would prevent just that possibility.[24]

Obviously such a coalition suffered internal strains, but it held together long enough to pass the Turpie Amendment in the Senate on April 16. With the crucial House vote scheduled for Monday, April 18, the administration worked frantically over the weekend to line up the opposition. On Monday morning, however, it appeared they had failed, and the Speaker of the House, Thomas Reed, hastily called a two-hour adjournment to allow one last effort. Their backs to the wall, administration leaders agreed to a compromise. To woo away the members of the coalition whose main fear was the possibility of annexation, they agreed that if the Turpie Amendment were defeated, the House would accept another Senate proposal, the Teller Amendment, which promised that the United States would not annex Cuba after the war. This bargain served its purpose, and early in the morning of April 19 both houses passed the war resolution (without the Turpie Amendment) over the complaints of the remaining dissidents.[25]

The outcome of the struggle over the Turpie Amendment was a modest defeat for Bryan and a foretaste of what would come a year later when Congress considered the disposition of the territories taken from Spain during the war. McKinley had demonstrated not only that he had strong ideas about executive independence but also the skill to make a rebellious Congress accept those ideas. If Bryan's hope was to humiliate and defeat the president in a test of political strength, he certainly failed.

Nevertheless, the compromise finally forced on the administration was a partial victory for Bryan's view of the purpose of the war with Spain. Although he certainly was no pacifist, he was sincere when he said on April 1 that war could be justified only as a last resort, and then only for the highest and most unselfish moral purposes. To some extent the adoption of the Teller Amendment reassured him on that score, but on the very eve of his departure for service as a colonel with the Third Nebraska Volunteers, he warned his fellow citizens, in a major speech at Omaha on June 14, that Dewey's victory over the Spanish at Manila Bay had raised anew the question of war goals. Unless Americans maintained their commitment to the high ideals with which war had begun, he argued, "a contest, undertaken for the sake of humanity" would degenerate "into a war of conquest," and the nation would be open to the charge of having added hypocrisy to greed.[26]

The events of the spring of 1898 were of considerable significance to the development of Bryan's view of foreign policy. In 1896 he had concluded that American policy must be independent; the nation must be free to act in the world without awaiting the permission of others. But he had given little thought to the purposes or standards that would govern such action. Confronted by the Cuban crisis, he concluded that policy must be moral and unselfish, but he realized that altruism would not be automatic. Expansionism had deep roots in American history, and although Bryan, with an isolationist's instinct, felt that overseas imperialism was different and more dangerous than the continental Manifest Destiny of the mid-nineteenth century, both he and his followers were confused about the issue at first. The brevity of the war, which lasted just over four months from declaration to armistice, gave them little chance to reach a reasoned position. In the late summer of 1898, Democratic newspapers were divided over imperialism, and only gradually during the fall, as Bryan and other Democratic leaders spoke out, did the various party factions begin to unite on anti-imperialism.[27] The process was a slow and uncertain one, because in the past expansion and isolation had been compatible. It required a considerable reorientation to see that they might have become contradictory, particularly since the imperialists were proclaiming that nothing had changed.

Like Bryan, President McKinley searched his soul and sounded public opinion, moving toward imperialism in the summer of 1898. While Colonel Bryan, a victim of what he called "military lockjaw," watched helplessly from the swampy Florida training camp to which his regiment had been sent, the president made speeches across the country and gradually embraced expansionism. Bryan, anxious to join the fray, instead found himself expounding "his hellish doctrines to the allygators," as Mr. Dooley irreverently remarked. At the end of September, with an armistice signed, the Commoner obtained a leave and hastened to Washington, where he conferred with Democratic leaders and called on the president to counsel him against imperialism. The warning was in vain, and as Bryan returned to Florida, he was determined to resign his commission as soon as the peace treaty was signed in order to carry his case to the people.[28]

While Bryan still fretted under the constraints of military discipline, others concerned about the dangers of imperialism began to organize.

Colonel William J. Bryan of the Third Nebraska Volunteers with an aide at a Florida training camp during the Spanish-American War. (Nebraska State Historical Society.)

On June 15, the day after Bryan's Omaha speech, a mass meeting was held in Boston's Fanueil Hall to oppose expansionism. Out of the meeting eventually grew, in November, the American Anti-Imperialist League.[29] At first the league produced only generalized anti-imperialist propaganda, but with the signing of the Treaty of Paris on December 10, 1898, it acquired a specific goal. Since the treaty transferred Puerto Rico, Guam, and the Philippines to the United States, members of the league concluded that only one course was practical: to defeat imperialism, defeat the treaty.

Instead of accepting this straightforward approach, Bryan took a position that seemed inexplicable to most anti-imperialists. It would be better, he argued, to ratify the treaty and then liberate the Filipinos. As he told an incredulous Andrew Carnegie, "I do not think that the treaty ought to be rejected, nor do I believe that it ought to be amended. I have confidence in the American people, and prefer to have them settle the question [through legislation to free the islands] rather than leave it to diplomacy or under the direction of the president."[30]

Many anti-imperialists dismissed his idea as crazy or unworkable, but Bryan felt it was a realistic approach to a complex situation. Like Thomas Jefferson, who contributed to American politics the famous warning against "entangling alliances," Bryan had no intrinsic objections to certain kinds of expansionism. If the territory to be annexed were in the Western Hemisphere, did not involve the incorporation of alien races, did not drag the nation into the power struggles of Asia or Europe, and came as a result of the freely expressed wish of the inhabitants, he favored expansion. Although the location of the Philippines raised worrisome issues, he desired the expansion of the influence and commerce of the United States in that part of the world as well as in others. And in the Western Hemisphere he, like Jefferson, found it easy to rationalize the taking of what was available. On that basis he believed that the annexation of Puerto Rico might be acceptable. At the very least, he thought, the United States ought to retain coaling stations in Puerto Rico, Cuba, and the Philippines.[31] Rejection of the entire treaty would eliminate these possibilities.

Practical politics also influenced Bryan's attitude. The anti-imperialist minority might succeed in defeating the treaty in the current session of Congress, but that session would end in March 1899. The new Senate, elected in the autumn of 1898, was controlled by the Republicans and would almost certainly approve the treaty if the president resubmitted it. What was more, even if McKinley took rejection as a directive to renegotiate the treaty, the anti-imperialists would have no control over the provisions of the new treaty, which might, in fact, be even more objectionable than the old one. In the meantime, of course, a technical state of war would continue, and no one could tell whether hostilities might be resumed, more lives lost, and more expenses incurred.[32]

Above all, Bryan's attitude was shaped by his belief that in a democracy the will of the people must prevail. Although, as he freely admitted, the emotionalism prevalent in wartime did not create the best atmosphere for calm and rational decisions, he simply could not accept the idea that a minority in the Senate had the right to thwart the wishes of the people as a whole. Even if the people wrongly (as he thought) chose a policy of imperialism, the decision would not be irrevocable. He was fond of saying, "No question is settled until it is settled right," and he believed that upon sober reflection Americans would realize that imperialism would subvert the foundations of the nation. The best course would be to allow the will of the majority in the Senate to prevail by approving the treaty. This action should then be followed by passing a resolution promising independence to the Philippines. Such a policy would be positive, would allow the United States to protect the islands while the people learned to govern themselves, and would, if successful, clearly demonstrate the will of the majority of Americans.[33]

Unlike many anti-imperialists, Bryan faced reality. He recognized that McKinley was right in arguing that the outcome of the war had thrust a responsibility upon the United States which, however unwanted, could not be evaded. Whether one looked at the matter from the standpoint of American interests in Asia, as most imperialists did, or from the standpoint of the interests of the Filipinos, as Bryan did, some action seemed necessary. The alternative, it appeared, was to abandon the islands to another major power; they seemed too weak to survive alone. Yet Bryan was scarcely enthusiastic about a protectorate. It would give the Filipinos time to establish a stable government, but it would also, like outright annexation, involve the United States in Asian rivalries.[34] The United States would be taking on the burdens and risks of imperialism without tangible rewards, and the process would probably interfere with reform at home.

The fact was that no choice seemed especially attractive, but Bryan, who had taken the easy course of isolationism in 1896, had now matured. Recognizing that responsibility could not be avoided, he urged the ratification of the treaty and the passage of a joint resolution promising independence to the Filipinos after a period of practice in self-government under American guidance and protection.

Whatever the weaknesses of his strategy, Bryan was realistic in understanding that the struggle against imperialism would require sustained commitment. Where other anti-imperialists placed all their hopes on one great Armageddon over the treaty, he, warned by the contest over the Turpie Amendment, realized that McKinley was a formidable antagonist and that the struggle could not be won over-night. Defeat of the treaty in the last hours of one Congress would only throw it into the next, where Republicans dominated. Fur-thermore, he comprehended that the responsibilities thrust upon the nation by war could not be discharged merely by refusing to accept them. Troubled in spirit, he sought among many unpalatable choices a policy that would discharge the nation's obligations without also endangering its security, corrupting its government, and demolishing its chances for reform. In the end he believed that he "never showed more statesmanship" than in following the course he chose.[35]

Statesmanlike though Bryan's program may have been in concep-tion, however, it proved unattainable in practice. Although his sup-port of the treaty may have helped the administration to garner a few of the votes necessary to pass it on February 6, 1899, the united efforts of Bryan and the Anti-Imperialist League were insufficient to pass the supplemental Bacon Resolution, which would have promised the Filipinos independence as soon as a "stable and independent govern-ment" had been created.[36] On February 14, after lengthy debate, the resolution was defeated when a tie of 29 to 29 was broken by the negative vote of Vice-President Hobart.[37] If that decision were to be reversed, it could only be done in the 1900 presidential election.

There was a fair chance of doing just that. The Democrats, split in 1896 between gold and silver factions, began to reunite against imperialism in the autumn of 1898, and there was hope of attracting some anti-imperialist Republicans as well. On this issue, conservative Democrats like Grover Cleveland and Richard Olney found them-selves in agreement with Republicans like Senator George F. Hoar, Andrew Carnegie, and Henry Adams, and even with Populists, Socialists, and Prohibitionists. At least for a moment there seemed a chance of establishing a coalition strong enough to defeat McKinley.[38]

The rock upon which the nascent coalition shattered was the choice of a candidate. No person was acceptable to everyone. Bryan, unpalat-able though he was to many members of the group, dominated the field. He was not only available, he seemed inescapable.

Many anti-imperialists, however, baffled by Bryan's seemingly con-tradictory opposition to expansion but support of the treaty, sus-pected him of the most nefarious motives—a desire to transfer public attention from silver to imperialism as a campaign issue. Nothing could have been less true. Not only was Bryan eager to refight the silver battle of 1896, but he recognized that if he were the candidate, the Republicans, having won once on the issue, would be reluctant to debate any other issue. No matter how hard he pressed the question, it was unlikely that the presidential election would provide any clear referendum on imperialism. Moreover, if he did fight the election partly on imperialism, he would be thrust into alliance with the Anti-Imperialist League, whose most prominent members disagreed totally with him on the silver question. If he spoke out on silver he would antagonize them, and if he failed to do so, he would betray his other followers.[39] From the Commoner's standpoint, no issue could have been less attractive than imperialism for 1900.

Yet despite his objections to the issue, Bryan had no wish to evade it. Believing that the question was of vital importance to the future of the nation, he concluded that the people must have an opportunity to make their wishes known directly. The election offered that chance, and offered it in a particularly clear-cut fashion, since it would be possible in the election simply to ask the people whether they wanted expansion or not. Details of policy could be set aside to be debated later. Thus when the Senate failed to pass the Bacon Resolution, Bryan decided there was no choice about making imperialism an issue in 1900. Whatever the effect on his own fortunes and other issues, duty required action.

If he had any doubts about campaigning on the double issues of silver and imperialism, Bryan did not reveal them in the period before the election. In public and private he stressed both issues, insisting that they were not separate but were aspects of the same fundamental question: whether the government would serve the people as a whole or the interests of a wealthy few. In an echo of a theme of 1896 he suggested that there was a link between "goldbugs" and imperialists: both were supposedly English-influenced. "The Democratic party," he argued, "opposed an English financial policy in 1896; it opposes an English colonial policy now," and he warned that "while the American people are endeavoring to extend an unsolicited sovereignty over remote peoples, foreign financiers will be able to complete the conquest of our own country."[40] The connection between Anglophobia and anti-imperialism was tenuous at best, however, and Bryan never made it a major campaign theme.

Like other anti-imperialists, Bryan's argument against expansion was largely negative. He declared that colonies would enrich the corporations while the people paid ever-increasing taxes to support an enlarged army that would, in itself, be a threat to freedom. He feared that possession of the Philippines would not only involve the United States in quarrels in Asia but would create excuses for other powers to ignore the Monroe Doctrine and meddle in the Western Hemisphere. He suspected that expansion would further complicate the nation's racial problems. And above all, he was convinced that imposition of an unwanted sovereignty on the Filipinos would subvert the basic American principle that governments must derive their powers from the consent of the governed.[41]

If Bryan often stressed what imperialism might do to the United States, he also reminded Americans that world power did not necessarily depend on owning distant colonies. "I want this nation to influence," he said, "not the feeble races only but the strong ones as well; I want it to dominate, not merely inferior races, but also superior ones. I want this nation to conquer the world, not with its armies and navies, but with its ideas. . . . I want this nation to solve the problems of this generation and by doing so not only bless our own people, but give life and hope to those who labor under greater disadvantages than we do." "Example," he proclaimed, "is the means of propagating truth. It is a slow process this winning of converts by example, but it is the sure way."[42]

In his concern with America's world role, Bryan differed from some other anti-imperialists. The same commitment to "applied Christianity" that urged him toward political reform at home led him also to define a missionary obligation for the United States in the world. What was more, Bryan believed that reform at home and world influence were interconnected; the more the nation lived up to its ideals at home, the more other peoples would look to it for leadership. Conservative anti-imperialists like Andrew Carnegie and Grover Cleveland did not share the Commoner's enthusiasm for either domestic reform or America's world mission. Although many members of the Anti-Imperialist League were cool toward Bryan because of his support of silver or because of his tactics in the treaty fight, it is apparent that many of them found another problem as well. At the same time that Americans were wrestling with the question of whether or not imperialism was compatible with their traditional isolationism, they were also being confronted with a choice between ultranationalist and idealistic isolationism. Many conservative anti-imperialists agreed with Bryan about the dangers of imperialism, but his idealistic talk of an American world mission made them almost as nervous as did imperialism itself.

For the most part, Bryan's definition of America's mission was still

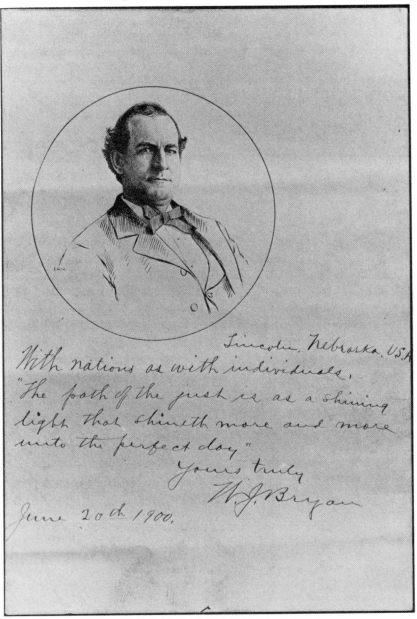

Campaign portrait sent out by Bryan in 1900. (Nebraska State Historical Society.)

vague in 1900. He had turned away from the ultranationalist position
of 1896, but aside from the basic principle that the nation should
adopt reforms in order to make itself a more attractive example for the
rest of the world, his foreign policy stands were somewhat contradictory. He espoused anti-imperialism but endorsed the annexation of
Puerto Rico and the retention of naval bases in Cuba and the Philippines. He warned the nation that taking the Philippines would entangle the United States in international conflicts but suggested a
protectorate over the islands that was likely to have the same effect. He
argued that allowing businessmen to go to the colonies would lead to
problems and conflicts that would involve the government, but he
urged sending teachers and missionaries, whose activities would inevitably produce the same result.[43] As happened throughout his
career, Bryan's idealistic desire to have the nation serve mankind led
him to advocate policies that verged on the very imperialism he
abhorred.

Even without Bryan's ambiguities, the election of 1900 was no
referendum on the imperialism issue. War-born patriotism and
prosperity were more important to the voters than imperialism, and
McKinley played upon these themes almost to the exclusion of any
discussion of expansionism, which Bryan had declared to be the
"paramount" issue. Recognizing the weaknesses of the anti-
imperialist coalition, the president reminded Americans of Bryan's
economic radicalism and won over those for whom the pocketbook
was more important than conscience.[44]

Adding to the difficulty of interpreting the election is the fact that
Bryan and McKinley were not as far apart in their proposals for the
Philippines as they seemed to be on the surface. One called for freeing
the Philippines but keeping them under an American protectorate;
the other advocated annexation but promised eventual independence
after a period of tutelage in self-government. And even more important, there was no difference in tone between the two. From the outset
the anti-imperialists insisted that expansion was morally wrong, while
the administration justified its course as a matter of duty, honor, and
service. The important questions of whether colonies could benefit
the nation economically or diplomatically were seldom discussed. The
overwhelming emphasis on moral issues obscured the fact that both
sides wanted expanding trade and world power and left the public
with the impression that virtue would surely bring its own rewards.
When the rebellion of the Filipinos and the Boer War in 1899 showed
how little native peoples wanted to become "the white man's burden,"
public support for imperialism soon eroded.[45]

One of the great ironies of the election of 1900 was that although Bryan was beaten more soundly than in 1896, he was able to define imperialism in such a way that it was quickly discredited as a policy, and the nation was forced to seek by other methods the world power its leaders were beginning to covet. Although no one realized it at the time, an epoch of world history, the great era of European empires, was on the wane, and a new era of ideological expansionism was beginning. Americans were once again rallying to the banners of idealism in foreign policy as in domestic affairs.

3

"FRIENDS ARE BETTER CUSTOMERS THAN ENEMIES": PRACTICAL IDEALISM, 1900–1912

As he considered the problem of imperialism, Bryan became convinced that both domestic happiness and international influence would result from policies based on Christian principles. When America solved its domestic problems by means of "applied Christianity," it would show other peoples how to better themselves while reaping tangible benefits from leadership in the form of increased political influence and trade. Idealism could be profitable.

Bryan saw no conflict between domestic reform and world leadership, but his program was inconsistent. He was specific and practical in recommending legislative cures for domestic difficulties, but he was apt to be vague and nebulous in explaining how international problems were to be solved. He was far clearer about what his hopes for the world were than about how those hopes were to be realized. Moreover, he assumed a degree of moral progress, rationality, and human goodness in international relations that he did not expect in domestic affairs. He would never have deluded himself that a corporate executive could be made to act morally simply by exposing him to the example of a good person, yet he trusted that an example of moral behavior by the United States could save the world. The aspiration was noble but unrealistic, and it sometimes blinded him to practical problems during these years.

Where his attention was fully engaged, however, Bryan demonstrated that he could make practical suggestions. This was particularly true in regard to American policy in the Philippines. He regarded the rulings of the Supreme Court in 1900–1901 in the "Insular Cases" that the Constitution did not apply to the people of the annexed territories as confirmation of his fear that the imperialists' purpose was to exploit the islanders, not to uplift them, and he argued steadily that the money needed to subdue and protect the new colonies could be used to far better effect at home.[1] In 1904, when his influence in the party was at its lowest ebb, he successfully bartered a promise to support the party's conservative nominee for a renewed promise to put Philippine independence in the Democratic platform.[2] The next year, during a trip around the world, he visited the islands himself. There he conferred extensively with both American officials and Filipino leaders and concluded that "the Filipinos [were] capable of maintaining a stable government without supervision from without."[3] He believed that a protectorate would be desirable for the time being, but he thought that a promise of independence would encourage the Filipinos to take over a large part of their own self-defense. An international agreement to neutralize the islands might be secured among the powers in the area, he believed. Permanent American naval bases in the islands would, however, be desirable to promote and protect trade with the Orient.[4]

The combination of idealistic anti-imperialism and pragmatic interest in trade and political influence that shaped Bryan's attitude toward the Philippines also determined his proposals in regard to Puerto Rico. Outraged that the Supreme Court had held that the Constitution did not apply to Puerto Rico and eager to see self-government granted to the islanders, he nevertheless rationalized continued retention of the island on the grounds that it was "the very base needed for the extension of our trade with, and our influence over, the republics of Venezuela, Brazil and Argentina." It was, he thought, "the key to the East Coast of South America," and as such too valuable to be freed. The benefits of American rule in the form of improved health, education, and agricultural practices, which he had argued did not justify continued retention of the Philippines, seemed to him in this case to sanctify an otherwise unacceptable policy.[5]

Bryan thus allowed national interest to outweigh idealism in regard to Puerto Rico, but elsewhere he was more consistent. He denounced British imperialism in South Africa and India, criticized foreign intervention in the Boxer Rebellion as likely to evolve into imperialism, and applauded the American Open Door policy in China as a constructive alternative to the acquisition of colonies.[6]

He also adhered to principle in opposing the Spooner and Platt amendments to the Army Appropriation Bill of 1901. The Spooner Amendment created a limited civil government for the Philippines and proclaimed the administration's determination to maintain American sovereignty over the islands. It also transferred authority over the colony from Congress to the president and seemed to open the way for large-scale profiteering by American businesses on the islands.[7] The Platt Amendment seemed to threaten the Teller Amendment's promise of independence for Cuba and perhaps to prepare the way for a new imperialist drive in the Caribbean.[8] True to his convictions, Bryan denounced both amendments and tried to rally congressional opposition to them.[9]

His efforts were unavailing. Although there was a good deal of latent opposition to the amendments in both parties, Democratic congressional leaders failed to organize it effectively and refused to take a strong stand against the amendments. The dominance of southerners in the Democratic party in Congress doubtless had something to do with the failure. After the bill and its amendments passed, Washington rumors suggested strongly that the Democrats had cared less about imperialism than about securing the passage of a $50 million rivers and harbors bill that was especially generous to the South and a $5 million federal subsidy for the upcoming St. Louis World's Fair.[10] From the narrowly isolationist viewpoint that characterized most southern Democratic congressmen, what was done to distant colored races was of far less interest than local advantage.

On some issues, in fact, there was more harmony between the narrow sectional perspective of southern Democratic congressmen and the ultranationalism of Theodore Roosevelt than between those congressmen and Bryan's idealistic isolationism. One such issue was the Panama Canal treaty of 1903.

Americans had long been interested in the idea of building a canal through Central America, and that interest had been sharpened by naval problems during the Spanish-American War. In 1900 both parties endorsed the construction of a canal in their platforms. Among Democrats the idea was universally popular, with southerners believing it would bring a bonanza of trade to southern ports and the westerners welcoming any rival means of transportation that might drive down transcontinental rail rates.

Yet despite the wide support for a canal within the party, Democrats could not resist the temptation to play politics with the issue. When Secretary of State John Hay negotiated a treaty with England in 1900 to abrogate the 1850 Clayton-Bulwer pact and thus allow the United States to build a canal alone, Democrats joined with some Republicans in demanding greater concessions from England. A second treaty, laboriously negotiated by Hay in 1901, met most of these objections, but nearly a quarter of the Democrats in the Senate voted against the treaty anyway. Bryan himself, with Anglophobia shaped by the conviction that British bankers were the archvillains in the "gold conspiracy," denounced the new treaty and suggested that the United States defy and insult England by building a canal without asking for British permission. Fortunately for future Anglo-American relations, his irresponsible advice was not heeded, and the treaty was approved by the Senate.[11]

In November of 1903, after Panama's rebellion against Colombia and the hasty signing of the Hay-Bunau-Varilla Treaty, which granted to the United States a canal route through the new nation, the canal issue re-emerged on the political scene. Delighted that the new treaty would allow canal construction to begin at last, Democrats were also keenly alive to the political advantages of exposure of the administration's rumored complicity in the Panamanian revolution.

Senate minority leader Arthur Pue Gorman shared these ambivalent feelings and was, in addition, well aware that if he could devise a strategy that would secure the canal while embarrassing the administration, his own presidential prospects would be considerably brightened.[12] On November 10 and December 15, Gorman proposed a devious strategy to the Democratic caucus. His proposal was that the Democrats use their thirty-three votes (enough to defeat the treaty) to compel a full-scale investigation of the Panama affair, thereafter delivering enough votes to allow the treaty to be approved. To make the threat of defeating the treaty credible, he also succeeded in getting the caucus to adopt a rule that bound all Democrats to vote as two-thirds of the caucus decided. So many loopholes were left in this two-thirds rule, however, that it was obviously intended merely to impress the Republicans with Democratic unity; any Democrat who did not want to be bound by it could easily find excuses to escape.[13]

Gorman's policy was seemingly dictated by personal ambition and sectional interests. Bryan, freed of such considerations by the certainty that he would not be nominated in 1904, was able to react solely on moral grounds. He therefore denounced the administration's intervention in the Panamanian revolt and called for the rejection of the treaty.[14] As it turned out, his position was both better politics and better morality than Gorman's.

The weakness of Gorman's program was that it depended upon almost perfect obedience from all Democrats because the Republicans needed only four Democratic votes to pass the treaty. Maintaining such unity proved to be impossible; Gorman should have realized from the outset that even hoping for it was unrealistic. By the time the treaty came to a vote on February 23, 1904, fourteen Democrats had gone over to the enemy while Republican lines held firm, thus ensuring an easy victory for the administration.[15] To rub salt into the wound, the Republicans also embraced Gorman's resolution calling for an investigation as though they had thought of it themselves. After amending it to remove all references to administration complicity in the revolution, they passed it without a division, rejoicing in the certainty that administration-appointed investigators would be unlikely to find anything discreditable to the president.[16] Thus Gorman's plan to gain both a canal and a political issue for 1904 was destroyed. Having ignored Bryan's advice to fight the treaty on moral grounds, the Democrats' failure left them without either immediate political advantage or the martyrdom of defeated virtue.

Gorman, of course, was the one who bore the brunt of the humiliation inflicted upon the Democrats in the Panama affair, but there were also lessons in the issue that Bryan might profitably have studied. He might, for example, have noted that here was a case where morality suggested one course and national interest another, but he could not imagine such a situation and thus practiced a certain amount of self-deception. Had he been in a position to determine policy, he might well have found the morally impeccable course less easy to follow. It was asking too much to expect congressional Democrats to act from such perfect motives. Indeed, since their isolationism was defined by sectional interests rather than by the idealistic values that were increasingly influencing Bryan's, they did not necessarily even share the Commoner's assessment of the Panama situation. Whether the divergence between Bryan's attitude toward the world and that of southern Democrats in Congress was a sign of a permanent difference or only an indication that his idealism had been awakened before theirs remained to be seen. Up to this point, however, few issues had challenged the idealism or stretched the sectional provincialism of southern Democrats.[17]

Bryan also could be provincial and myopic in his isolationism. His assessment of the problem of European interference in the Caribbean region during this period, for example, was very shortsighted. Traditionally, the United States had accepted the fact that European nations with large economic interests in the unstable Caribbean nations would intervene from time to time to protect their interests. Provided such interventions did not lead to colonization, Americans had generally regarded them with equanimity. With the acquisition of the Panama canal route and the growth of American economic interests in the area in the early twentieth century, however, some Americans began to be concerned about regional security. During the Roosevelt and Taft years, elimination of the threat of European intervention became an important goal of American policy.

Roosevelt and Taft differed somewhat on how to attain their common objective. Roosevelt concluded that the United States should act as policeman and debt collector for the Europeans, taking on the burden of intervention to maintain stability and fiscal responsibility and thus eliminating any excuse for others to do it. This approach was embodied in his Roosevelt Corollary to the Monroe Doctrine, first proclaimed in 1904. Taft's policy, dollar diplomacy, was based on the theory that private American investments should be used to stabilize the Caribbean nations economically, and that economic development would assure political stability. American capital, Taft thought, would not only promote growth and order, but it would diminish European excuses for intervention by transferring a part of the foreign debts of the Caribbean nations to American hands. Although both programs were regarded by Latin Americans as imperialistic, and neither secured the stability in the area for which its supporters hoped, these failings were secondary matters to American policymakers. The fact that after the winter of 1902 there were no new European interventions in the Caribbean was ample justification for the policy in their eyes.

Bryan rejected both Republican approaches to the problem. The Monroe Doctrine, he believed, gave the United States all the authority it needed to deal with European threats to the hemisphere. Corollaries and extensions were not necessary.[18] His position was thus entirely traditional. He visualized external danger as coming only in the form of conquest. The more subtle problems of economic domination did not concern him. In his view the Monroe Doctrine did not exist to "shield" the Latin American nations from "the performance of international duties and obligations," and he therefore accepted the nineteenth-century American view that European intervention to collect debts was acceptable provided it did not result in the annexation of territory.[19] Oblivious to changing conditions in the Caribbean, he assumed that the arrangements of the past would continue to work in the future.

In essence, Bryan's position was based on the unexamined assumption that intervention could be dealt with after it had taken place. Republican leaders believed that it would be wiser to avoid the problem in the first place. Their approach would protect American interests at the cost of Latin American goodwill lost in preemptive interventions. Bryan's policy, on the other hand, fitted well with traditional isolationism and would not jeopardize relations with the Southern Hemisphere, but it offered doubtful protection for growing American interests in the region. Neither position was entirely satisfactory.

The problem became acute in 1904 when the international court at

The Hague ruled in a 1902 debt dispute between several European nations and Venezuela that the nations that had sent warships should be paid first.[20] The decision put a premium on the use of force in such disputes and created a risk that debt collection could turn into permanent occupation. Bryan, who had applauded the original submission of the dispute to the court, did not comment on the ruling, and when the president announced the Roosevelt Corollary in response to the decision, Bryan criticized him for exaggerating the danger of "imaginary" European threats. Instead, he suggested, the United States should set an example for the Europeans by unilaterally renouncing the use of force to collect international debts.[21] Idealistic in tone, the suggestion was, in fact, perfectly compatible with the sort of provincial isolationism that had characterized southern Democrats' policy in the Panama struggle.

Nevertheless, for all the naivete of his suggestion, Bryan was groping toward a more positive policy. He became intensely interested in Latin America during the early 1900s and made several trips in an effort to see the area for himself. In 1902 he visited Cuba for the inauguration of the island's first independent government, and during the next decade he went back twice more. He also traveled several times to Jamaica and Puerto Rico, and three times to Mexico. His most extensive Latin American trip lasted from January to April 1910 and included visits to Cuba, Jamaica, Peru, Bolivia, Argentina, Brazil, Chile, and Puerto Rico.[22] From this firsthand experience he gradually developed proposals that he believed were both idealistic and practical.

The central goal, as Bryan saw it, was to increase American political and economic influence in Latin America without imperialism. If that could be achieved, it would reduce any risk of foreign intervention while at the same time enlarging American trade opportunities. Obviously, however, unless the Latin Americans themselves wanted American trade, admired and emulated the United States, and actively supported common goals, the policy could not work. Agreeing essentially with Roosevelt on the objectives of American policy, Bryan hoped to achieve them not by coercion but by winning the hearts and minds of the people.

The first vital step was to renounce the use of force in hemispheric relations. It was partly for that reason that he opposed the Platt Amendment, the Panama Canal treaty, and the Roosevelt Corollary. By giving up intervention, he argued, the United States would set an example for European nations, and even more important, it would create a new atmosphere of trust in Latin America. In the past, he

Bryan at Tierra Blanca on one of his trips to Mexico before he became secretary of state. (Nebraska State Historical Society.)

pointed out, foreign investors had exploited the area's weakness by demanding excessive interest rates on loans because of the risks—but then had used their nations' navies to collect the debts and remove the risks. That practice, said Bryan, was both exploitative and shortsighted; giving it up would win friends and probably new customers as well. "While our plans should be unselfish," he argued, "they would probably prove profitable in the end, for friends are better customers than enemies, and our trade is apt to develop in proportion as we teach the natives to live as we do."[23]

The suggestion that Americans should "teach the natives to live as we do" revealed the missionary strain in Bryan's isolationism. Although he argued for governmental restraint, he strongly supported the efforts of legitimate businessmen, missionaries, and teachers to export American culture, economic values, and political systems to Latin America. The missionary or teacher overseas, he believed, served as a perpetual example to the natives of the superiority of American culture and religion and as a clear proof of the nation's commitment to the ideal of service to the rest of the world. In addition, he also strongly supported the idea of bringing foreign students to the United States. With the hyperbole of the true believer, he argued that "a hundred students educated in the United States and returned to their nations . . . , would do more towards extending our trade and our civilization than an army of a hundred thousand men. The federal government could well afford to establish a school and educate all the students that would be sent here from South America and Asia."[24]

To round out his proposals, Bryan recommended retention of Puerto Rico and the establishment of minimal tolls for the Panama Canal. Keeping Puerto Rico, he argued, would make the Caribbean and the east coast of Latin America readily accessible to American commerce, while moderate canal tolls would help to open up the rest of the continent. Limiting tolls to levels that would just cover operating expenses would stimulate hemispheric trade, discourage other nations from building a competing canal, and—of course—benefit Bryan's own constituents by promoting rate competition with the transcontinental railroads.[25] As elsewhere in Bryan's ideas, the values of his followers intertwined with idealism to create a particular form of missionary isolationism that was far more committed to involvement and service in other areas of the world than some isolationists would have liked, but more resistant to formal, governmental obligations than internationalists would choose.

Similar principles also governed Bryan's evolving attitude toward Asia. Convinced that there as elsewhere in the world democracy was making steady progress, he argued strongly that Americans, both through private and governmental actions, should do as much as possible, short of political involvement, to encourage it. He applauded the efforts of American teachers and missionaries in Asia as in Latin America and deplored what he regarded as Theodore Roosevelt's alarmist militarism. Visiting Japan in the midst of public celebrations of the victories of the Russo-Japanese War, he was nevertheless sure that the Japanese preferred peace to war and would not follow an aggressive policy.[26] Optimistically blind to what he did not wish to see, Bryan held resolutely to his belief that the world welcomed the United States as friend, teacher, and above all, as example. Even when he contributed to an erosion of that image himself, as when he supported the exclusion of Oriental immigrants, he nevertheless remained serenely confident of American superiority and of the eagerness of Orientals to imitate the American example.[27]

Like many missionaries, Bryan was a sort of cultural imperialist. He was so sure that democracy and Christianity offered the routes to earthly perfection and eternal salvation that he could not imagine that other peoples would not embrace them eagerly if only they could be given the good news. Conversely, he regarded all other forms of government and religions as inferior and inevitably destined to pass away. His confidence in the ultimate success of his doctrines allowed him to rely upon the force of example rather than on coercion to spread the gospel, but at the same time it also made him blind to the virtues and values of other cultures.[28] Thus his foreign policy embodied a curious paradox—a resistance to imperialism and intervention coupled with an eagerness to guide, instruct, preach, and otherwise meddle in the internal affairs of other nations. Although such assistance was offered with only the most benevolent motives, its recipients sometimes found it difficult to distinguish from more overt and vigorous forms of intervention.

Nevertheless, subtle though the distinction may be, there was an important difference between the policy which Bryan advocated and the one which his Republican opponents followed. While both sought to influence the course of development and policies of other nations, Roosevelt and Taft believed that such influence could only be founded upon force or the threat of force; Bryan, on the contrary, strongly criticized reliance upon force and held that coercion could not bring about the changes he sought. Even if both attitudes implied

These two Korean stone lions, brought back from his trip around the world in 1905–6, flanked the entrance to Fairview, Bryan's home in Lincoln. (Nebraska State Historical Society.)

a certain amount of interference in other people's affairs, Bryan's policy was far less likely than his opponents' to lead to wars and international conflict.

Bryan realized, however, that conflict had always been a part of international life and that unless he could advance a program for reducing or eliminating it, his hopes for the peaceful evolution of a democratic world were likely to be frustrated. It was precisely for this reason that his program for an international network of investigation treaties became the keystone for his whole structure of American foreign policy.

Not surprisingly, Bryan's peace plan grew out of his concern with a domestic problem, the settlement of labor disputes. Arbitration of such disputes by an "impartial tribunal," he had argued in 1896, would solve most of them.[29] In the autumn of 1904 the signing of a series of bilateral arbitration treaties between the United States and other nations led him to broaden his perspective to include international as well as domestic disputes. The problem with such arbitration proposals, as Bryan saw it, was that no nation, including the United States, was willing to promise in advance to settle all issues through arbitration. Especially in crucial matters of national interest and honor, the nations insisted upon reserving freedom of action. Nevertheless, Bryan still thought that the principle of an "impartial tribunal" might offer a way out of the dilemma, provided the tribunal's functions were confined solely to investigation of disputes, not to recommending settlements. If they knew that they would not be bound by the outcome, he argued, nations would have no objection to submitting all disputes to investigation, even sensitive questions of national honor. What was more, the time necessarily involved in investigation would allow popular excitement to cool, while the results of the investigation would be likely to indicate the way to a peaceful solution of the original problems.[30]

Like much of the rest of his foreign policy, Bryan's peace plan was a mixture of the pragmatic and the idealistic. By relying solely upon investigation rather than upon compulsory arbitration, he hoped to surmount the obstacles to the peaceful settlement of disputes that were erected by nationalism. That much, at least, of his program was realistic, but his belief that investigation of disputes alone would guarantee their peaceful settlement represented a leap of faith.

He and many other American and Western European peace advocates thought, however, that such faith was justified by the apparent spread throughout the world of education, Christianity, and democracy. Not only would educated men recognize that might and right were not necessarily synonymous, but religion would help to harness their brutish, belligerent instincts while bringing to the fore loving and charitable emotions. The connection between education and religion was, in Bryan's view, essential: "Head and heart should be developed together." Education would enable an individual or nation to perform tasks skillfully, but only religious faith could ensure that the tasks chosen would be beneficial to the world rather than selfish or destructive.[31] Such an enlightened people, he reasoned, would inevitably demand a greater share in running their own government, and the progress of democracy would, in turn, further stimulate the peace movement. Not only would a religious, educated people have moral and intellectual objections to war, but they would realize that because the masses bear the burdens of war, a government of the people had powerful reasons of self-interest for avoiding it.[32]

The decade before 1914 was the heyday of the peace movement in the Western world. Although in retrospect the optimism prevalent among the world's leaders seems ludicrous, Bryan was no more naive than many other statesmen and politicians. On the contrary, he was more realistic than many. During his travels around the world he predicted overoptimistically that democracy would make rapid strides in such unlikely places as Japan, China, and Russia, but he nevertheless understood that perfection had not yet been achieved either in human nature or in breaking down the barriers of nationalism. His peace program was designed to take account of the practical problems while moving toward a day when war could be eliminated totally. Unlike Tolstoi, whom he admired greatly, he did not believe that all individuals must be perfected before steps could be taken toward world peace. A gradualist and reformer by temperament and conviction, Bryan believed that the world could pull itself up by its own bootstraps, using existing organizations and techniques to move toward perfection. In such a process the United States would, of course, continue to pursue its mission as example, guide, and teacher. This meant, in his view, following a fourfold policy of domestic reform, reduction of armaments to the lowest levels consistent with self-defense, encouragement of Americans to go abroad as teachers and missionaries, and support of international agreements for the settlement of conflicts.[33] "To take the lead in such a movement would establish our position as a world power in the best sense of the term;" to do any less would be to shirk a clear Christian duty.[34]

Characteristically, Bryan began a tireless campaign to popularize and achieve the adoption of his peace plan as soon as he had developed it. During his 1905–1906 trip around the world, he advanced it in an

Exuberant Nebraskans welcoming Bryan in New York in 1906 after his world trip. (Nebraska State Historical Society.)

address to a Bankers' Club banquet in Tokyo, and in London he urged it upon the delegates to the Interparliamentary Union, who unanimously endorsed it. Returning from this triumph, he reiterated it during a much-publicized speech at a welcome-home ceremony in New York, and thereafter pressed it enthusiastically upon any group willing to give him a hearing.[35] His first tangible success with the proposal, however, did not come until the administration of President William Howard Taft, who was himself an ardent peace advocate.

When an international peace conference at Edinburgh endorsed his peace plan in June of 1910, Bryan seized the opportunity to bring the meeting's resolutions to Taft's notice. He was convinced after conversations with some members of the British cabinet, he told the president, that Great Britain would be willing to sign a treaty with the United States based upon the principles of his investigation plan. Such an agreement, he believed, would set an "example" which "would be followed until war would become almost impossible."[36] In Taft, Bryan found a sympathetic listener. The president had long believed in the efficacy of international courts and arbitration for the settlement of disputes, and in the autumn of 1910 he instructed Secretary of State Philander C. Knox to negotiate a series of treaties that would provide for the arbitration of all issues, including the delicate questions of national honor, which were normally excluded from such treaties.[37]

Making the arbitration proposal broad was essential if the treaties were to be really effective in settling serious international disputes, but it also raised the question of whether nations, including the United States, would agree to limit their freedom of action so drastically. Hence, Taft sought some formula that would allow nations to save face and yet would make arbitration probable in critical cases. The solution to his problem was suggested by Bryan's proposal of international investigation to establish the facts in a dispute. Presumably, if the parties could agree on the facts, they could also agree to a peaceful settlement.[38] The first two treaties with England and France were submitted to the Senate in the summer of 1911 and included a provision for a Joint High Commission of Inquiry, which would determine the facts and could recommend arbitration. Since even a recommendation for arbitration had to have nearly unanimous support from the members of the commission, and since each government had to approve a specific arbitration agreement after the investigation, national interests seemed to be in little danger from the treaties. Nevertheless, many senators, apparently annoyed at Secretary Knox's failure to consult with them before the treaties were signed,

This cartoon, "No foreign relations these," welcomed Bryan on his return to Nebraska from his world tour in 1906. (Nebraska State Historical Society.)

expressed fears that acceptance would endanger American security. The fears born of ultranationalist isolationism were very near the surface.

The main isolationist objection to the treaties was that the United States might be binding itself, legally or morally, to arbitrate any dispute as recommended by the investigators. On that point even supporters of the treaty differed. President Taft and others held that the nation had at least a moral obligation to arbitrate if it were recommended by the investigators, but other equally enthusiastic proponents argued that the Senate's freedom to reject arbitration was unimpaired.[39] Adding further to the confusion was the fact that Theodore Roosevelt, who had supported arbitration treaties of his own while president, now reversed himself and thunderously denounced the new treaties.[40] With the supporters of the treaties thus divided, their opponents attached a series of reservations so crippling, in Taft's opinion, that he gave up the whole project.

Bryan was a great supporter of the Taft treaties, as well he might have been. "The world's peace is no longer a dream; it is very nearly a glorious fact," he proclaimed. Above all, he was delighted with the president's adoption of his investigation scheme, which he described as "plainly the most important provision of the treaty."[41] Whether it was that or not, the investigation clause was certainly the most popular part of the treaties.[42] For the first time, Bryan had hit upon a policy proposal that evoked Americans' idealism without threatening their desire to remain unentangled in the world's problems, and he basked in the public approval.

Bryan's appeal to missionary isolationism was not enough, however, to save the treaties, nor were his best political efforts. In editorials in *The Commoner* and in letters and conversations with members of the Senate he urged support of the treaties but to no avail. And when he tried to find a ground for compromise between Roosevelt and Taft, he was no more successful than others who tried to patch up that famous quarrel.[43]

Despite his disappointment over the outcome, Bryan learned valuable lessons from the battle over the Taft treaties. When, as secretary of state, he drafted his own peace treaties, he eliminated the controversial arbitration clauses and proposed only investigation. Furthermore, recognizing that Secretary Knox's tactless treatment of the Senate had multiplied obstacles to the passage of Taft's treaties, he bent over backward to make himself agreeable and accessible to the Senate. Above all, he formulated his own proposals to satisfy the widespread American desire to serve the world without being involved with it.

His reward was the virtually unanimous votes by which his treaties were passed.

Between 1900 and 1912, Bryan began to come to grips with the daily problems of foreign policy and to articulate a general philosophy for dealing with them. In some cases his suggestions were practical and entirely feasible. He knew exactly what he wanted in Cuba and the Philippines, and he had programs for achieving it; he thought that the Panama intervention was wrong, and he was willing to risk delaying the construction of a canal to correct the injustice; he understood why Taft's arbitration treaties had run into opposition, and he knew how to avoid the problem in the future. In all of these cases familiarity bred practicality.

Sometimes, however, what masqueraded as practicality was something else. From Taft's tribulations Bryan learned how to deal with the Senate, but his willingness to abandon arbitration and depend solely on investigation to solve international conflicts was less a result of practical politics than of his idealistic isolationism. Regardless of the Senate's attitude, he would have believed that "benevolence, unarmed, is mightier than selfishness equipped with sword and mail."[44] It was precisely that faith that led him to advocate unilateral reduction of armaments and the abandonment of debt collection by the navy in Latin America.

Bryan often sounded naive or foolish when he advocated meeting the threat of European intervention in Latin America simply by adopting an exemplary American policy of restraint, or when he suggested that world peace could be achieved merely through the investigation of disputes. But such naivete struck a deep chord of idealism in American breasts. A generation deeply imbued with faith in human perfectibility and inevitable progress easily believed that the efforts of individual Americans working overseas—teachers, missionaries, and honest businessmen—could really change and improve the world. So important did Bryan think these efforts that he believed that the government should support them, at least to the extent of maintaining overseas bases, building an Isthmian canal, and perhaps subsidizing the education of foreign students both in their countries and in the United States.

In sum, Bryan evolved between 1900 and 1912 a missionary isolationism in which traditional reluctance to become involved with the world's problems coexisted in an uneasy balance with an idealistic desire to begin the creation of a better, more peaceful world. Groping to stake out a position distinct on the one hand from Rooseveltian imperialism and on the other from ultranationalist isolationism, he insisted that it was possible to serve without involvement. Unless a man were willing to struggle toward perfection, he argued, he would remain an animal, "content to eat and drink and die." Progress would come only through continuous effort and the willingness to take risks. The individual or nation that followed only traditional paths might be safe but stagnant.[45] Deeply convinced that "example [is] the means of propagating truth" and "service the measure of greatness," his faith in ultimate success, despite the evident obstacles, was secure.[46] Whether the public would respond to the challenge he posed, and whether the balance between the two elements in his policy could be maintained, remained to be seen. Only time and experience would show whether the faith would be justified and the challenge met.

4

PROMISES, PRINCIPLES, AND COMPROMISES: FIRST MONTHS IN OFFICE

On December 21, 1912, Bryan went from Miami, where he was building a new house, to Trenton, New Jersey, to confer with president-elect Woodrow Wilson. Each had previously doubted his ability to work with the other, but the meeting went very smoothly. For nearly four hours the two Democrats discussed cabinet appointments and the legislation to be introduced by the new administration. Later, over lunch, Wilson offered Bryan the appointment as secretary of state, and the Commoner accepted.[1]

Neither Wilson's decision to offer the post to Bryan nor Bryan's to accept it had been arrived at easily. Wilson had moved steadily toward Bryan's position on domestic reform and respected his party strength, but the new president was skeptical about Bryan's abilities and perhaps a little afraid that he would be a rival rather than a supporter.[2] For his part, Bryan was doubtful of his own administrative talents and reluctant to force himself upon Wilson, although he was eager to have a part in passing the reforms for which he had fought so long.[3] In the end, it was this common goal and the belief that Bryan could advance it that brought the Commoner into the cabinet. Neither man thought that the administration would be seriously concerned with foreign policy.

Despite Wilson's doubts, Bryan soon proved useful. Not only was he a much more conscientious secretary of state than his Republican predecessor, but his view of foreign policy coincided almost exactly with that of the president. He also provided valuable assistance in getting Wilson's program through Congress, and because of his personal idiosyncrasies, he drew to himself some political criticism that might otherwise have fallen on Wilson. As one journalist put it, "Everybody speaks a kind word for our honored President and then gives the Secretary of State both barrels with nails in the charge."[4]

One of Bryan's peculiarities which drew more ridicule than criticism was his refusal to serve alcohol at State Department functions. Although he had secured the president's approval for this policy before accepting his appointment, and though he warned the diplomats before the first state dinner, his attitude was widely regarded as rural barbarism among European and metropolitan American newspapers.[5] Indeed, the reaction was out of all proportion to the importance of the issue. "People who had never tasted the stuff [grape juice]," said one reporter, "rushed out and drank it in order to loathe it with more vigor." One might think, he added, "that in times past people went to state dinners for the purpose of being hauled out by the legs in a condition of alcoholic coma."[6]

The issue of "grape juice diplomacy," a minor matter at most, was soon eclipsed by a more serious criticism of Bryan's behavior. This was the result of the fact that, while secretary, he continued, though less frequently than before, his Chautauqua lectures. These lectures were of great importance to Bryan. They enabled him "to keep in touch with the people" and to "present a message worth while to those to whom it is worth presenting"; they renewed his faith in the people, kept him attuned to the interests and concerns of the masses, and satisfied his compulsion to preach as nothing else could do.[7] They allowed him to escape briefly from the isolation and restraints of a position which is, after all, the most rigidly formal and apolitical of cabinet posts, characteristics that steadily grated on Bryan's nerves. Nevertheless, perhaps feeling that his behavior was somewhat suspect, Bryan unfortunately yielded to the temptation to overexplain. Instead of saying merely that he found the lecture platform a refreshing change, he went further and argued that he needed the fees of $250 to $500 per lecture to supplement his annual salary of $12,000.[8]

Strange though this claim of insufficient salary sounded on the lips of an exponent of Jeffersonian simplicity in government, it was actually reasonable. Bryan's expenses, including the costs of the entertaining required by his position, were very high, and unlike many others in government, he had no outside income except what came from his writing and lecturing. Even so, his announcement caused an outburst of public and congressional criticism which was only reduced, not stilled, when the president assured the nation that the secretary of state was not neglecting his duties.[9] For the critics of the administration, Bryan's continuing appearances on the Chautauqua platform with Swiss bell ringers and magicians offered too tempting an opportunity to give up.

If the attacks on Bryan for his views on alcohol and lecturing were essentially trivial, the charge that he debauched the Foreign Service by flooding it with incompetent political cronies deserves more attention. There can be no doubt that he believed in a spoils system. When

On October 7, 1912, Wilson called on Bryan at Fairview. With them here is Bryan's grandson. (Nebraska State Historical Society.)

he was attacked for having written a letter seeking jobs for "deserving Democrats," he replied frankly and without embarrassment, "I am glad to have the public know that I appreciate the services of those who work in politics and feel an interest in seeing them rewarded." However, definite limits were imposed on the secretary. "My debts were larger," he said later, "and in an appointive way, my assets smaller than those of any other cabinet member."[10] One of the richest sources of patronage, the consular service, was closed off from the outset. In spite of Bryan's pleas, Wilson barred this field by retaining the service's longtime chief, Wilbur J. Carr, and issuing an executive order modeled on those of Roosevelt and Taft which kept the consuls under civil service.[11] Elsewhere Bryan met similar frustrations. The chief diplomatic posts in Europe went largely to Wilson's major campaign contributors, and even within the State Department itself the Commoner had little freedom to choose his assistants. Since most of the clerks and minor officials of the department were under civil service, Bryan could only shuffle assignments and bring in a few new people.[12]

At the policymaking level of the department the secretary's power to appoint was also circumscribed. He was allowed to select his old friend, former governor John E. Osborne of Wyoming, as first assistant, but Second Assistant Alvey A. Adee remained in office, and Wilson and his friend Edward M. House selected two successive third assistants, Dudley Field Malone and William Phillips.[13] The post of counselor, which in the Wilson period was the second-ranking departmental position, was filled first by John Bassett Moore and later by Robert Lansing, both of whom owed their appointment more to the president than to Bryan.[14] The same was true of the four chiefs of the department's geographical divisions, of whom Bryan chose only the least important, the head of the Near Eastern Division, Dean Albert H. Putney of the Illinois College of Law. Of the others, House's friend William Phillips served as both third assistant secretary and chief of the Western European Division, Edward Thomas Williams secured the Far Eastern desk primarily because of strong support from American missionaries in China, and Boaz Long was appointed to the Latin American desk largely on the recommendation of Vice-President Thomas Marshall.[15] Although Bryan concurred in all of these appointments, with the exception of some reservations about Phillips, they were certainly not his personal choices.

Bryan found his greatest opportunity for making appointments in the Foreign Service, where the new administration replaced twenty-two of thirty-five ministers within the first year. Even here, however, the secretary's freedom was not as great as he wished. The most important posts in Europe and Asia were monopolized by the president, leaving Bryan to fill only the minor positions. Frustrated, the secretary suggested a novel plan of rotating appointments among "deserving Democrats" on a yearly basis so that the party could build up its ranks of ex-ministers, but Wilson rejected the idea. In the end, Bryan had to be content with the relatively few positions he could control himself or secure as favors from other cabinet members.[16]

Had Bryan really had a free hand, there can be little doubt that he would have cleaned house from top to bottom in the State Department. As it was, contemporary critics who accused him of debauching the Foreign Service with legions of political hacks were less than just. Although their argument that skilled careerists had been replaced by unskilled politicians was true in some cases, they failed to note that many of the experts who were fired owed not only their original appointments but also subsequent advancement as much to political influence as to the expertise they had acquired along the way. What was more, many of the Republican diplomats were totally out of sympathy with the aims of the new administration. For all their lack of experience, the new men, unlike such holdovers as Henry Lane Wilson in Mexico, at least did not try to sabotage new policies. As the Democratic appointees acquired experience and knowledge, they proved to be, on the whole, adequate representatives of the United States abroad, neither much better nor much worse than their Republican predecessors.[17]

Despite the criticism leveled against Bryan's appointments, only one Democratic diplomat was involved in a real scandal. This was James Mark Sullivan, minister to the Dominican Republic, whom Bryan had appointed at the urging of Wilson's private secretary, Joseph Tumulty, Senator James A. O'Gorman of New York, and Congressman James Hamill of New Jersey. As revelations in the *New York World* and an official investigation later showed, Sullivan, a lawyer and prize fight promoter of dubious reputation, had been supported for the post by New York backers of the Banco Nacional of Santo Domingo, who hoped to profit from the minister's influence with the Dominican government. Those hopes, the investigation demonstrated, had not been disappointed, and what was worse, the minister had deliberately lied to the State Department about conditions in the Dominican Republic in order to secure American backing for a corrupt and illegal regime that was friendly to the Banco Nacional interests. There was not enough evidence to prove graft on Sullivan's part, but his behavior was flagrantly improper, and Bryan, who had been lax in investigating the candidate's background and qualifications, was held responsible by the public.[18] Adding to the general impression of misdeeds were the publication of Bryan's "deserving Democrats" letter during the investigation and the obvious reluctance of the administration to undertake any investigation at all.[19] Although Sullivan was scarcely typical of Bryan's diplomatic appointments, his case helped to create an unfortunate impression that time will probably never erase.

Morale was always something of a problem for Bryan in the State Department. He was able to win a somewhat grudging liking from members of the department, but many of them also thought both the secretary and the president impractical dreamers and some of the secretary's departmental appointees incompetent hacks. A series of leaks to the press for which each group tended to blame the other exacerbated the situation, despite the fact that Bryan himself correctly identified the main cause of the problem as sloppy security procedures within the department which allowed reporters to snoop unimpeded. Perhaps most demoralizing of all, however, was the fact that Wilson seemed frequently to ignore the department altogether. Not only did he take decisions into his own hands in cases that interested him, but sometimes he implemented policies without consulting the department and even without using its diplomats, choosing instead to work through a series of special agents who might entirely bypass the State Department. For two years he dealt with Mexico in this manner, and during the war almost all of his most delicate negotiations were handled by special agents.[20] Under such circumstances maintaining departmental morale was almost impossible.

The appearance of sloppy amateurism in the State Department was increased by Bryan's own methods. As he admitted cheerfully, he was no administrator. He stuffed telegrams into his pockets, scrawled official messages on the backs of old envelopes, and heaped documents in untidy piles on his desk. Yet his memory for facts, dates, and quotations was remarkable, and out of the apparent chaos that surrounded him he seemed able to pluck what he wanted. His wife, Mary, also imposed a semblance of order on him and helped enormously with the research he was too impatient or too busy to do himself.[21] Bryan simply refused to let himself be bogged down in details. He was concerned about basic issues of policy, and he let others worry about the mechanics of administering it. In that attitude, which was shared to a great extent by Wilson, was both strength and weakness. The two knew where they wanted to go and refused to let trivia distract them, but sometimes their eyes were so fixed on the horizon that they tripped over pebbles in their way.

Yet despite difficulties and criticism, Bryan at first regarded the secretaryship as an opportunity to put his ideals into practice rather than as a burden. Above all, it meant a chance to place America in the forefront of the world peace movement through promotion of his novel peace plan. He had made the freedom to pursue this plan a condition of his acceptance of the appointment, and he lost no time after the inauguration in drafting a treaty proposal, which he submitted to the president and cabinet in April 1913.[22] Essentially unchanged from the original proposal of 1905, the draft treaty provided that "all questions of whatever character and nature" in dispute between the signatories should be "submitted for investigation and report to an international commission" and that "the contracting parties agree not to declare war or begin hostilities until such investigation is made and report submitted." The methods and times of selecting the investigating commission, a proposal of a year's time limit for the investigation, and a proposal that during the investigation each party promise not to increase its armaments unless menaced by a third party were removed from the draft for separate negotiation with other powers when members of the cabinet expressed fears that they might impede agreement.[23]

Having secured cabinet acceptance of his proposal, Bryan next approached members of the Senate Foreign Relations Committee and within a week won their approval as well. With these hurdles crossed, he then called together the diplomatic corps to explain his program and by the beginning of July had won support in principle from twenty nations. On August 1, 1913, the first treaty was signed with El Salvador, and during the following year nineteen more were completed. This group of twenty treaties was then submitted to the Foreign Relations Committee in July 1914. Recognizing that previous secretaries had sometimes lost treaties for want of sufficient wooing of the Senate, Bryan sent a letter to each senator explaining the treaties and asking for ratification, wrote himself and got the president to write to the chairman of the Foreign Relations Committee, and spent two days in the office of the clerk of the senate informally answering questions and talking to senators. The result of these strenuous efforts was an overwhelming vote of approval for all of the treaties on August 13, 1914.[24] Inasmuch as the ratification of the treaties coincided with the beginning of World War I, it is evident that they were hardly a panacea for the world's conflicts, although some

Bryan often served as a "lightning rod" for President Wilson, taking the brunt of attacks really aimed at the White House. This cartoon, by William Henry Walker, appeared in *Life,* November 20, 1913. (William H. Walker Collection, Princeton University.)

Below: In the summer of 1914, Bryan had some old army swords melted down to make paperweights as souvenirs for the diplomats who signed his peace treaties. On the back was inscribed "Diplomacy is the art of keeping cool." (Library of Congress.)

peace advocates and groups hailed them in such terms, and had the times been different, Bryan might well have won the Nobel Peace Prize for them.[25] Their fundamental principle, the use of investigation to delay war, thus allowing time for passions to subside and public opinion to be mobilized for peaceful settlement of issues, was sound. Though the treaties were never used, the principle subsequently found its way into many international agreements, including the charters of both the League of Nations and the United Nations.[26]

From the standpoint of the immediate interests of the United States, the worst thing about the Bryan treaties was that the major nations—Britain, Italy, Germany, and Japan—all either refused to sign treaties or else used Bryan's eagerness for them to wrest concessions on other matters from the secretary. Thus Germany, with whom a serious dispute would soon erupt, supported the principle of the treaties but refused to limit its own freedom of action by signing an agreement; Japan used Bryan's eagerness for a treaty to bargain on the touchy issue of Japanese landownership in California; and Britain used the opportunity to put pressure on Bryan to reverse himself on the matter of exempting American ships from paying tolls in the Panama Canal.[27]

The toll exemption had been passed during the Taft administration, but it had originated in the Democratic Congress and had strong support in most Democratic circles. In 1912, Bryan, always eager to strike a blow against the railroads, put an endorsement of it into the party platform, and Wilson obediently applauded the idea. Only after the election did the new president discover that the British regarded the exemption as a violation of the Hay-Pauncefote Treaty and had already protested it strongly. Realizing his mistake, Wilson quickly reversed himself and at an early cabinet meeting in March suggested repeal of the exemption law. Caught by surprise, Bryan asked for time to consider the matter, pointing out to both the president and the British ambassador that since the canal would not open for another year, the problem was scarcely urgent.[28]

Knowing that a request for repeal would surely be regarded by some of their Anglophobic followers as a sell-out to London, neither Wilson nor Bryan was eager to endanger the president's domestic program by arousing their anger. Although he was committed to the idea of repeal and repeatedly assured the British of that fact, Wilson did not ask Congress to act until March 1914. As he had anticipated, many members strongly opposed the idea, and repeal did not actually pass until mid-June.[29]

Bryan took almost no role in the repeal effort, not even announcing publicly that he favored it until April 1914. Perhaps knowing how hard the secretary found it to reverse a position he had once adopted, Wilson took the matter into his own hands, conducting negotiations with the British through his friend Edward M. House and Sir William Tyrrell, private secretary to Foreign Secretary Sir Edward Grey, and using Treasury Secretary William G. McAdoo and Postmaster General Albert S. Burleson to manage the fight in Congress. Bryan, in announcing that a private poll showed that a majority of delegates to the 1912 Democratic convention now favored repeal and in endorsing the idea himself, may have helped to swing a few wavering Democrats' votes, but it was obvious that he was never very happy with repeal. In this case the desire to set an example of moral behavior for other nations was weakened by an even stronger urge to serve the needs and wishes of his rural supporters.[30]

It was ironic that Bryan felt so severe a strain over this issue. The president insisted that repeal was "a point of honor," a matter of strict regard for international morality in living up to a treaty. This argument, added to the secretary's loyalty to the president and the subtle hints from the British ambassador that Sir Edward Grey would find it much easier to submit Bryan's peace plan to Parliament if the tolls exemption matter were out of the way, should have made it easy for Bryan to embrace repeal. As with the silver issue after 1896, however, he found altering any of his public positions almost impossible.[31] This loyalty to past promises was a rare virtue in a politician, but it could, as in this case, create an unnecessary inflexibility.

Yet such determination to honor commitments could accomplish a great deal against considerable odds. For twelve years, with hardly more than the most halfhearted support from his own party, Bryan had been promising independence to the Filipinos. Now, as Emilio Aguinaldo, the leader of the Philippine independence movement, reminded him, the time had come to begin to fulfill those promises.[32]

Realism, however, dictated caution. Wilson had never been an ardent anti-imperialist and even in 1912 had modified the platform's promise of independence to include a period of tutelage in self-government. This view was shared also by most members of the cabinet, and Bryan's reply to Aguinaldo, urging patience upon the Filipinos, was thus so cautious that the Philippine leader strongly suspected a betrayal.[33] For the moment the secretary could only await an opportunity to move in the direction he desired.

That opportunity was offered by the submission to the president of two new reports on the Philippines, one from an old friend, Professor Henry Jones Ford of Princeton, whom Wilson had sent on a fact-finding tour of the islands just before inauguration, and the other from within the War Department, which was charged with administering the islands. Surprisingly, both reports agreed that the Filipinos were capable of controlling many of their own affairs and urged substantial self-government for them. Impressed by these reports, the president agreed to a suggestion made by Secretary of War Lindley M. Garrison and the chairmen of the House and Senate committees dealing with the islands that a new governor general of the Philippines be appointed and entrusted with the delicate task of transferring some power to the Filipinos.[34]

No sooner had the president agreed to the appointment than Bryan had just the man for the job—for once, patronage and principle could be allies. His candidate for the post, chosen at the suggestion of Manuel Quezon, Philippine commissioner in Washington, was Francis Burton Harrison. Scion of a wealthy New York family, Harrison was young, vigorous, able, committed to Philippine independence, and best of all, a former congressman acceptable even to Democrats doubtful about independence. Within a week of Bryan's original suggestion, Wilson submitted Harrison's name to the Senate, and two weeks later the new governor was on his way to Manila with dramatic instructions to inform the Filipinos that everything he did would be directed toward "the ultimate independence of the Islands."[35] Here at last was the promise of independence that Bryan had so long sought.

Having embarked upon the new policy with some misgivings, Wilson was, to Bryan's delight, quickly confirmed in his program as a result of the violent opposition to it from American businessmen in Manila and their Republican supporters in Congress and the press at home. Convinced by the protests that retention of the islands as colonies benefited only the special interests, Wilson reaffirmed his promise of independence in his 1913 Annual Message and supported a bill introduced by Chairman Jones of the House Insular Affairs Committee, which specifically promised independence in its preamble. Although Republican opposition to any such promise and southern Democratic demands for immediate independence delayed passage of the Jones Bill until August 1916, after Bryan's resignation, its eventual passage was nevertheless a profound personal triumph for him.[36] Not only had he been instrumental in overcoming the resistance of the president and Congress to independence, but in a much broader sense his appeals to the American conscience over the years had recalled Americans to their historic commitment to freedom. Having been among the first to recognize the threat to American ideals embodied in imperialism, he had also the persistence to fight on through the long years of disappointment and defeat when many others gave up. His ultimate victory was a tribute to the best in his commitment to American idealism.

If the Philippines represented a triumph for Bryan's sense of the American mission, long-standing problems with Japan offered an equal and ultimately, it turned out, insuperable challenge to it. The heart of the issue was the old problem of Oriental immigration to the United States, now appearing in the specific guise of state laws intended to restrict or eliminate Oriental landownership. Although this particular issue was thrust upon Bryan by the Japanese ambassador the day after inauguration, it had deep roots in West Coast history. As early as 1855, California passed the first of a series of laws designed to restrict the rights of Orientals, and repeated invalidation of such laws by the courts only increased Californians' determination. Recognizing the importance of the issue to westerners, national administrations had tried with little success to solve the problem. The most recent attempt to restrict immigration, Theodore Roosevelt's "Gentlemen's Agreement" of 1906, was still in effect but had, like earlier efforts, failed to satisfy the West. Between 1906 and 1912 anti-Oriental legislation was introduced in every session of the California legislature, and only the most vigorous persuasion by Republican presidents kept Republican majorities from passing it. By 1910, passage of some sort of law in California to forbid landownership by Oriental aliens seemed only a matter of time. Republican Governor Hiram Johnson favored it but blocked legislation out of courtesy to a Republican administration in Washington and in hopes of securing a $1.5 million subsidy from Japan for a proposed California exposition to celebrate the opening of the Panama Canal. With the growth of support for restriction in California and the change of administration in Washington, however, the governor's opposition to a land law disappeared. Accepting the inevitability of a law, Johnson now became a supporter to make political capital for himself while embarrassing the Democrats in Washington.[37]

Although California's proposed law seemed to offer a clear threat to the new administration's desire to place the United States before the world as a nation of superior virtue worthy of emulation, neither Wilson nor Bryan was especially concerned at first about the California situation. On the contrary, both were on record as favoring restriction of Oriental immigration to the United States, and provided the California law did not specifically violate the 1911 Japanese-American Treaty of Commerce and Navigation, they did not see any objection to it. Moreover, their traditional Democratic states' rights theories made intervention in the internal affairs of a state distasteful to them.[38]

Their reluctance faded as it became clear that Japan was seriously disturbed about the impending legislation. Wilson thereupon decided to make a direct appeal to Governor Johnson, though Bryan doubted that Johnson would be willing to cooperate. Through Congressman William Kent, a California Progressive, Wilson asked Johnson to consider a law like that of the District of Columbia, which would simply limit landownership to aliens who had applied for American citizenship. Since Orientals could not apply for naturalization, California's object could be achieved in a way that would not offend sensitive Japanese racial pride.[39]

Choosing to see Wilson's indirect approach as an insult to his office, Johnson rejected all efforts at compromise and supported a bill providing, in the most offensive possible terms, that aliens "ineligible to citizenship" could not own land in California. The issue was now inescapable. When Johnson rejected direct overtures from Wilson and Bryan as well as indirect appeals from Samuel Gompers, Theodore Roosevelt, and William Howard Taft and indicated that he intended to sign the bill into law, Wilson decided that although the situation was hopeless, a dramatic gesture must be made to pacify Japan. Accordingly, on April 22 he proposed to the cabinet that Bryan go to California to plead the administration's case. The secretary, recognizing the futility of his task, consented only when his colleagues agreed that the trip might soothe Japan.[40]

This assumption that Bryan's trip could do no harm and might do some good seems questionable in retrospect. When Bryan left Washington, the California Senate had not yet acted on the bill, and enough legislators were opposed to various aspects of it to make its passage open to question. Furthermore, such influential newspapers as the *Sacramento Bee* had advocated moderation on the issue. As soon as Bryan's trip was announced, however, opposition to the bill was associated in the minds of many Californians with subservience to Washington, and the law acquired new and powerful supporters. Although the Japanese were pleased with the trip, its actual effect may have been harmful to their cause.[41]

Nevertheless, Bryan was an effective advocate of the administration's position, pleading vigorously and cogently for the passage of a law that would avoid offense to the Japanese. Alarmed by the secretary's success, especially in the Senate, and feeling his own leadership slipping, Governor Johnson struck back with an emotional harangue to the legislators and by leaking the supposedly secret transcripts of the sessions with Bryan to the press to stir up public opinion. When a so-called "compromise," the Webb Bill, replaced the objectionable phrase, "ineligible to citizenship," with the equally obnoxious declaration that only those "eligible to citizenship" could own land. Bryan recognized defeat. After the Webb Bill passed the legislature on May 3, the secretary returned to Washington to try to pacify the Japanese.[42]

Given the situation in California, the administration could not reasonably have expected to accomplish much except to placate the Japanese. Bryan discovered when he got back to Washington that Tokyo was pleased at his effort but was not prepared to drop the issue. On the contrary, with public opinion in Japan at a fighting pitch, the government sent so belligerent a note to Washington that Bryan was compelled to ask Ambassador Chinda to tone it down for fear it would worsen the crisis. Chinda agreed, but the Japanese were not mollified.[43]

With war fever apparently sweeping Japan, the American cabinet met in an atmosphere of crisis to debate what steps to take. Several members, backed by the military, urged sending a small force to the Philippines as a warning and first line of defense. Secretary of the Navy Josephus Daniels, strongly seconded by Bryan, disagreed with this advice. Such a gesture, Daniels and Bryan argued, would be both impotent and provocative. Although seriously concerned about Japanese belligerence, the president agreed with Bryan that for the time being diplomacy rather than military preparation must be the method for dealing with the situation.[44]

Wilson and Bryan recognized the gravity of the situation, but they had little to offer the Japanese. Deadly serious Japanese protests were answered belatedly and with little more than soothing phrases that reiterated the palpable falsehood that the issue was economic rather than racial. On this basis Bryan suggested that the federal government might buy the land of any Japanese who wanted to leave California, but the Japanese rejected that proposal as inadequate. As the steamy Washington summer approached, only Bryan's unsuspected diplomatic talents of endless patience and boundless goodwill kept strained relations from shattering. At one point, when Ambassador Chinda asked in discouragement if the American position were final, Bryan assured him that "nothing is final between friends;" it was a phrase that summed up the secretary's attitude.[45]

The first glimmer of a breakthrough in the crisis came not from the Americans but from the Japanese. In midsummer a special three-man Japanese mission arrived in Washington to work with the Americans on a draft of a new bilateral treaty that would accept the status quo in

Bryan, Governor Hiram Johnson, and Robert F. Rae (not identified) during Bryan's unsuccessful trip to California in April 1913 to dissuade the California legislature from passing a law restricting land ownership by Orientals. (Library of Congress.)

California but prevent the passage of similar laws elsewhere. On August 19, after preliminary discussions, the treaty draft was officially forwarded to Washington by the American ambassador in Tokyo.[46]

On the whole, the draft treaty seemed to offer the basis for a reasonable compromise between the two nations, and the Japanese were enthusiastic about it. On the American side, Wilson, absorbed by a major struggle with Congress over tariff reform, authorized Bryan to proceed with discussions of the treaty. The secretary, feeling that no single state should have the power to endanger the safety of the whole nation, was eager for the proposal to be accepted. By mid-January 1914, agreement had been reached on all but final details, and at that point Wilson, angered by a tactless attempt by California representatives to push through Congress a bill barring all Oriental immigration, authorized the secretary to present a treaty draft to the Senate Foreign Relations Committee. A few days later the Japanese gave way on their last objection to the treaty and agreement seemed at hand.[47]

The treaty was never signed. While Wilson felt that assuring the Japanese that their citizens would receive the same treatment as the people of other nations in the United States was only simple justice, he also warned Ambassador Chinda that for the federal government to appear to dictate racial policies to a state was extremely dangerous. Nevertheless, by early 1914 he might have been willing to run even this risk had he not feared that anger aroused on this issue would damage his pending domestic program. Accordingly he asked the Japanese for permission to delay submitting the treaty to the Senate, and the Japanese government unwisely agreed. On March 24, partly as a result of its failure to reach agreement with the Americans, the Japanese ministry was replaced by a far more militant one. Regarding the proposed treaty as insufficient balm for Japan's wounded pride, the new ministry junked it and returned to old demands for nullification of the Webb law. Since the Americans had nothing to offer on this subject, the stalemate was renewed.

In January 1915, Ambassador Chinda tried to return once again to the draft treaty, but by that time Wilson was alarmed about Japan's intentions in China and was unwilling even to talk about the matter until reassured about "her willingness or unwillingness to live up to the open door in the East."[48]

In dealing with Japan, Bryan and Wilson found that domestic political realities severely limited their ability to follow an idealistically pure policy. On the land issue the United States set no moral example for anyone to follow. Yet one cannot escape the suspicion that had the president and secretary cared more about the issue, had they perhaps not agreed deep in their hearts with the attitude of the Californians, had they been a little bolder and more willing to take a political risk, more might have been accomplished. Although nothing they could have done in this case would have averted the rivalry between the two nations over China, undoubtedly racial tensions between Japan and the United States exacerbated and complicated other issues as well. Without an atmosphere of mutual trust and respect, no real diplomatic progress was possible on any issue.

Within the limitations imposed by the president's reluctance to take domestic risks to pacify Japan, Bryan did the best he could. His tact and diplomacy in California were matched only in his dealings with the Japanese themselves. Whatever small success there was in averting a crisis and maintaining at least superficially friendly relations was largely to his credit. At the same time, he seems also consistently to have underestimated both Japanese sensitivity on the issue and the importance to Americans of settling it satisfactorily. His argument against sending ships to the Philippines at the outset of the crisis was only partly a result of his aversion to the use of force; it was also based on a belief that the Japanese would not fight, that they could be talked out of their anger. Although he freely admitted the imperfections of the nation in many areas, its racial attitudes were for Bryan—like most of his contemporaries—not subject to discussion. At bottom it was this lack of real commitment to justice for the Japanese that made the administration's policy a failure.

Throughout the events described here runs a pattern of commitment to idealism tempered by concern for extremely practical matters. While setting a high example by refusing to serve wine, Bryan also took the precaution of warning the diplomats ahead of time so that they could fortify themselves against the ordeal. In seeking to replace the corrupt advocates of dollar diplomacy with new representatives of a moral diplomacy, Bryan never forgot that the apostles of virtue could also be political friends. In the Philippines the secretary was perfectly willing (as he had always been) to settle for a promise of ultimate independence in place of immediate liberation; like Wilson he had deep doubts of the ability of the Filipinos to govern themselves without instruction from the United States. And in the case of the dispute with Japan over California's land law, he was no more willing than Wilson to endanger domestic legislation in order to establish a principle of racial equality in which he did not really believe.

Bryan was discovering, in short, that translating ideals into policies was more difficult that he had thought. Unfortunately, not all issues were clear-cut matters of right against wrong; often, one good, desirable aim had to be traded for another equally good, as in the Panama tolls controversy with Britain. Having had nearly all his previous political experience in opposition, where all issues appear black and white, Bryan had been able to escape this knowledge. Now it was borne in upon him every day. It was one thing to denounce imperialism, another to end it; it was easy to criticize Republicans' handling of East Asian relations, appallingly difficult to devise workable alternatives. Robbed of his innocence, Bryan increasingly longed for his old role of critic rather than actor. The fault lay not so much in his commitment to noble ideals as in his inability to understand that the ideal was never attainable and in his inexperience in judging which compromises were necessary and how to make them.

5

"NO MORE REVOLUTIONS WILL BE
PERMITTED":
LATIN AMERICA, 1913–1915

Secretary of State Bryan hoped fervently to use American power creatively in Latin America. Nowhere did he have a freer hand; nowhere did the United States traditionally have more influence. It seemed easy, at first glance, to replace the mistaken policy of dollar diplomacy, which Bryan defined as the use of "diplomatic influence to advance the interests of American investors without a scrupulous regard to the merits of the claim," with a policy in which the United States would set an example of moral behavior, constitutionalism, and political excellence that others would be eager to imitate.[1] With the exception of a few limited successes, however, Bryan actually spent his time in office merely laying the groundwork for the new policy, or intervening to set recalcitrant imitators on the right track. Idealism proved to have unexpected results.

When great missionary instincts are backed by great power, the temptation to force the heathen onto the road to salvation frequently becomes overpowering. So it was with Bryan in Latin America. Having set goals that were too grand in their aspiration to reconstruct the political and social structures of whole nations and that were too vague in their relation to the actual conditions and needs of the people involved, he ended up on the old treadmill of intervening in order to create conditions that would make future intervention unnecessary. It was the "responsibility" of the United States, as "the dominant influence in the western hemisphere," to use its strength in "the service of Latin America."[2]

To enlarge America's moral influence, Bryan was determined to alter past policy so that exploitative businessmen would be deprived of government support and so that the weight of American disapproval would be thrown against revolutions and other disorders. More positively, he intended to encourage the development and strengthening of constitutional and democratic processes that would permit gradual reform.

The first phases of Bryan's program were put into effect almost immediately upon his taking office. He declared that the American businessman would be encouraged to work and invest abroad, but only if he behaved responsibly, giving "a dollar's worth of service for every dollar that he asks as recompense," and if he refrained from attempting to subvert or control governments for private profit. "The malefactors of great wealth," as Theodore Roosevelt had dubbed them, were to be tamed both at home and abroad. In addition, Bryan and Wilson stated in a press release on March 11, 1913, that the American government would henceforth promote stability by refusing to recognize any regime that came to power by "disorder, personal intrigues, and defiance of constitutional rights." By these means, Bryan believed, instability and disorder could be expunged from the hemisphere, stability and constitutionalism encouraged, and the way opened for example to exert its beneficent influence.[3]

It was not the traditional security interests of the United States that led the new administration into intervention. It intended to protect the Panama Canal, as the Taft and Roosevelt administrations had, but World War I soon relegated such security problems to a back seat in favor of nobler and vaguer aims. The administration did attempt to enlarge the American naval base at Guantanamo, Cuba, and it hoped to acquire a new base at the Môle Saint Nicolas in Haiti; it tried to buy an option on a possible canal route in Nicaragua, and it produced low-key promotional programs for American business and investment projects overseas.[4] But none of these were central focuses of administration interest or major causes of intervention.

On the contrary, Bryan tried very hard in the early days of the administration to show that material concerns were not central and that he could offer new solutions to the hemisphere's problems and conflicts. Believing that one source of Latin America's troubles was the area's dependence upon private bankers for capital, a situation that produced astronomical interest rates and occasional intervention, he recommended that the U.S. government move into investment banking. The government, he suggested, could issue bonds at 3 percent interest, reloan the money to the Latin nations at 4½ percent, and use the profit to help retire the loan. It was a novel idea, many years ahead of its time and offering substantial advantages, but it had one serious problem in that it made no provision for defaults. Under such circumstances either loans would become outright grants or the United

States would be drawn into intervention itself—neither particularly attractive possibilities. Perhaps aware of these risks, Wilson gently rejected the proposal as too "novel" and "radical" for the country to accept without long thought and discussion. Bryan did not give up easily and continued to press the idea at all opportunities, but the rejection was final.[5]

A second project of the secretary's, a Pan-American nonaggression treaty, fared no better. Originally conceived by Representative James L. Slayden of Texas, the treaty project was pursued by both Bryan and Colonel House, and it was partly this division of authority that doomed it. Although he was enthusiastic about the idea of a treaty when he heard of it in the autumn of 1913, Bryan was too distracted by the Mexican Revolution to do much about it and left it to House, who made some progress during the spring of 1914 but abandoned it after the European war broke out.[6] Even before that, despite all the talk of hemispheric harmony, no one, including some of the larger Latin American nations, was really committed to such a treaty. Given the disparities of size and strength among hemispheric neighbors, promises to settle all disputes peacefully were unrealistic, and by 1915 the administration itself was so frequently intervening in the Caribbean that the treaty could only have been an embarrassment.

A third proposal of Bryan's, of great symbolic importance in demonstrating the administration's difference from its predecessors and determination to follow a new course, was for a treaty of apology with Colombia. Having long believed that Colombia had been grossly wronged by Roosevelt's highhanded behavior in Panama, Bryan was delighted to find that negotiations between the two nations had already begun under Taft, although, of course, a Republican administration had found it impossible to make any apology. Upon entering office the new secretary reopened negotiations, and after long haggling with Bogotá over the exact wording of the apology clause and the amount of money to be paid to Colombia, a treaty was signed on April 6, 1914. Unfortunately, however, although Bryan was assiduous in his support of the treaty in the Senate, he was unable to overcome Republican opposition to any apology, and the treaty, even without the apology clause, was not approved by the Senate until 1921, after Bryan left office, Theodore Roosevelt died, and oil was discovered in Colombia.[7] Although the willingness of the administration to consider an apology raised the prestige of the United States in Latin America, its inability to get the treaty approved partially nullified the achievement. Probably it had never occurred to Bryan that his

Secretary of State Bryan at his characteristically messy desk. (Library of Congress.)

fellow countrymen might be less eager than he to purify all aspects of America's behavior if that process was costly or embarrassing.

The resistance of Americans to purification, however, was in the long run less troublesome to the secretary's hopes than the intransigence of the external world, as problems in dealing with Nicaragua demonstrated. In that country, vital to the United States because of its potential canal route, uprisings in 1910 and 1911 had worsened a serious economic situation and had led President Taft to prop up a friendly government with American marines. Democrats in the Senate were angry over the president's failure to ask Congress's permission before sending troops and refused to approve treaties he negotiated. When Bryan entered office, the crisis remained unresolved, and it seemed likely that if money were not forthcoming from the United States, the Nicaraguans would mortgage their canal route to European bankers.[8]

Secretary of State Knox had tried to deal with the Nicaraguan dilemma by negotiating treaties which offered either an American customs receivership like that in the Dominican Republic or the purchase of an option on the canal route. Bryan, unwilling to associate himself with his predecessor's mistakes, sought a different means of achieving the same end. For its part, the Nicaraguan government, desperate for money and aware that only American support kept it in office, was willing to do whatever was necessary for its survival. Hence the Nicaraguans suggested, and Bryan accepted, a plan to establish an American protectorate like that created by the Platt Amendment for Cuba. When the secretary proposed such a scheme to the Foreign Relations Committee, however, Democrats were almost unanimously opposed, and Bryan had to retreat to the canal option scheme instead.[9] He had made a serious blunder. In seeking to make his policy different from Knox's he had embraced a proposal that was in fact substantially more imperialistic sounding than anything the Republicans had offered.

With the protectorate proposal dead by August 1913, Bryan sought alternative ways to assist Nicaragua while awaiting Senate approval of the canal option. When the president rejected his suggestion of a direct governmental loan, he, like Knox, turned to the bankers. In October, having brought the full weight of the State Department to bear on behalf of the Nicaraguans, he was able to secure a loan for them at much lower rates than usual. The Nicaraguan government was grateful but recognized the loan as merely a stay of execution, not a pardon. Without the continued backing of the United States it could not long survive. Hence the Nicaraguans insisted upon including the provisions of the Platt Amendment in the new canal option treaty, and Bryan, making sure to have their request in writing, accepted their wishes despite the previous opposition of the Foreign Relations Committee.[10]

The specific Nicaraguan request for a protectorate helped to moderate Senate opposition to the idea, but new difficulties quickly appeared in the form of the opposition of other Central American states to any protectorate in the area. Bryan dismissed such objections as not serious, but when the Foreign Relations Committee, after six months of delay, finally took up the treaty in June 1914, the protests, along with the allegations of imperialism and accusations of favoritism to the bankers, provided valuable ammunition for treaty opponents. On July 12, 1914, Chairman William J. Stone of the Foreign Relations Committee informed the secretary that there was no hope for the protectorate. Bryan thereupon dropped the protectorate scheme once and for all, but Stone could not get a favorable vote from the committee on any canal option treaty until mid-December, and thereafter a filibuster threat from Senators Borah and Root postponed the treaty indefinitely. Not until eight months after Bryan's resignation, as the result of a rumored German attempt to grab the canal route, did the Senate finally approve the treaty.[11]

Relations with Nicaragua offered a unique test of Bryan's ability to solve old problems in new ways. Policy toward that country was almost exclusively the secretary's. Wilson took an interest in what was done, and Bryan kept him informed, but the president let the secretary run things completely, even when he disagreed with what was being done.[12] The result was disaster. An undemocratic regime was sustained in office by methods which, when they had been pursued by Republicans, Bryan had righteously denounced. A military intervention begun by Taft and never approved by the U.S. Congress was prolonged, and most of the other states of Central America were deeply antagonized. When those states, frustrated and alarmed by the American policy, took their protests to the Central American Court of International Justice, the United States and Nicaragua refused to abide by the court's decision, thus undermining one of the few cooperative organizations in the area.[13] Not even a successful policy could be held up as justification of these disasters. Since Nicaragua survived throughout the period without any of the treaties, one can only wonder whether they could possibly have been as essential as Bryan thought.

Bryan was concerned about American interests in the canal route, and he genuinely hoped to help the Nicaraguans. Without seeing that the two objects were incompatible, he concluded that keeping the current, pro-American government of Nicaragua in power was desirable, because allowing further revolution would worsen the economic situation, reduce American influence, and reduce the chances of ultimate stabilization. Such reasoning was of course extremely shortsighted and narrow, but Bryan was neither the first nor the last leader to indulge in it.

Elsewhere in the Caribbean, Bryan's policy followed a distressingly similar pattern. In the Dominican Republic he again inherited complex problems and handled them in the same unfortunate fashion. Gradually, and without intent, he moved by a series of small steps toward a military intervention that eliminated the possibility of the very constitutional democracy he sought. Under a 1907 treaty turning over the Dominican customs service to the control of American collectors, the island republic had enjoyed four years of unwonted prosperity and political stability until, in 1911, the assassination of the nation's president destroyed all the painfully made gains. Taft used American troops to restore order and to impose a provisional president, but the provisional government collapsed just after Wilson came to office. In April 1913, José Bordas Valdés assumed the provisional presidency on the understanding that he would serve no more than a year, pending revision of the election laws by a constitutional convention.[14]

By the summer of 1913, Bordas was feeling the lure of permanent office despite the arrangement under which he had taken office. Other Dominican factions promptly organized a revolution against him, and Bryan, outraged, informed the rebels that the United States felt "profound displeasure" at such "pernicious revolutionary activity" and might withhold customs revenues from a revolutionary regime.[15] This was to prove the first of a long series of blunders. While it was true that Bordas had not yet actually *done* anything illegal and hence remained the "constitutional" president, his intention to perpetuate his regime was so blatant as to make the rebels' actions fully understandable if not legal. In choosing to put himself unequivocally on the side of Bordas, Bryan was encouraging that slippery gentleman and evincing a foolish regard for form over content. From that mistake followed others.

The new American minister to the Dominican Republic, James Mark Sullivan, arrived in Santo Domingo in the midst of this first crisis. Plunging immediately into his duties, Sullivan arranged a cease-fire at the cost of a promise to the rebels that the United States would supervise congressional elections to guarantee their honesty. Bryan, delighted by the end of the revolution, conveniently ignored this promise until it was almost too late. Reminded of it at the last moment, he tried to wriggle out of it but eventually capitulated to the extent of sending a group of Americans and Puerto Ricans "as individuals" to observe the elections. What he would have done had the observers reported the elections rigged remains unclear, but fortunately they thought they were reasonably honest, a conclusion which the victory of Bordas's opponents made plausible.[16]

The outcome of the December 1913 elections put the United States in a most awkward position. Having endorsed Bordas as the constitutional president, and in a sense, having accepted the legality of the congressional elections as well, the Americans were committed to both congress and president. This raised the interesting problem of which the State Department would back if the two clashed, which with presidential elections scheduled for April 1914 seemed increasingly likely.

No sooner did the Dominican congress meet in early 1914 than conflict began. Bordas asked for money to suppress revolutionary activity, and the congress refused. In fact some members of the congress began themselves to prepare their factional forces for a revolutionary struggle against Bordas. Alarmed by the growing split, Bryan arranged a meeting between Bordas and his chief factional opponent aboard the U.S.S. *Petrel*. These surroundings proved conducive to agreement, but Bordas had no sooner returned to the presidential palace than he began removing his opponents from office. The secretary of state, beginning to suspect that he had been victimized, indignantly refused Sullivan's suggestion that customs revenues to Bordas be increased to allow the president to suppress his enemies. The United States, Bryan informed Sullivan, had no interest in subsidizing Bordas's illegal reelection.[17]

The Secretary's partial recognition of the problem came too late. By the end of March 1914, a revolution against Bordas was under way and Bryan reluctantly authorized an increase in the funds granted to the Dominican government. The United States, he told Sullivan in a telegram specifically endorsed by Wilson, would uphold constitutional government, although he did not attempt to explain why Bordas, rather than the congress, was the only exemplar of constitutionalism.[18]

American aid did not save Bordas. Sullivan reported the success of Bordas's forces, but the opposite was actually true, and by the beginning of July the rebels were at the gates of Santo Domingo. In the meantime their continually repeated assurances that all they wanted was free elections had exerted a powerful appeal on Bryan. When Bordas spurned the secretary's request for a cease-fire to be followed by elections and instead conducted a rigged election of his own, Bryan at last cut his ties to the provisional president. Early in July he recommended to Wilson that the Dominicans be compelled to accept a new provisional president (deposing Bordas), that American-supervised elections be held, and that it be made clear that no future revolutions would be tolerated. "No opportunity for argument should be given to any person or faction," he advised, and enough American force should be sent to "present the plan and see that it is complied with."[19] The power of example was to be augmented with bayonets.

After getting Wilson's approval of this drastic plan, Bryan dispatched the navy with instructions to bombard the island unless all factions agreed to a truce. American commissioners, sent to the island on his orders, then used the truce to force the resignation of Bordas and to select Dr. Ramon Báez as provisional president pending elections in October 1914. Báez was guaranteed full American support, including the use of troops if necessary to maintain order. In October the elections were held under American supervision and the winner, Juan Isidro Jiménez, received Bryan's assurances of full support at his inauguration in December. At the end of 1914 the secretary was confident that the election had at last "cleared up" the Dominican situation and had "vindicated" his policy. Jiménez, Bryan was convinced, would surely agree to adopt a series of reforms recommended by the Americans.[20]

Having by this time totally abandoned any pretense of leading by example, Bryan made it clear that he would tolerate no deviation from his conception of how events ought to proceed in Santo Domingo. Jiménez's failing health was ignored. A bitter split between Jiménez and the Dominican congress was entirely disregarded, and when the congress moved to impeach the president, a perfectly constitutional action, Bryan made it clear that he would back the president "to the fullest extent." "The election having been held and a Government chosen by the people having been established," he informed malcontents, "no more revolutions will be permitted."[21]

Bryan's success in avoiding full-scale military intervention in the Dominican Republic (it would come a year after he left office) was the result of luck, not of a wise policy. His confidence that he knew better than the Dominicans what they needed led gradually and almost imperceptibly to outright control of the island by the United States. The desire to serve and lead had changed into the drive to command

James Mark Sullivan, Minister to the Dominican Republic under Wilson. Sullivan's flagrantly improper behavior led to a major investigation. (Library of Congress.)

and dominate. His aims, to be sure, remained benevolent throughout, and he sought no gain for himself or his nation, but the result of his policy was just about the same as though he had been the most dedicated imperialist.

In the midst of Bryan's difficulties in the Dominican Republic, he faced similar problems at the other end of the island of Hispaniola, in Haiti. To some extent the problems were connected in that a revolution in one nation affected the other as arms and revolutionaries traveled back and forth across the border; more fundamentally the problems in each country were separate but parallel cases of political and financial instability.

By 1913, Haiti owed to its various creditors, internal and external, about $36 million (with an annual income of about $5 million) and had pledged about 80 percent of its customs revenues to the repayment of these debts. If political conditions had been stable, the government might have been able to manage with the remainder, but between 1885 and 1911 ten of the eleven presidents were either killed or overthrown, and in the Haitian back country the *cacos,* a group of professional revolutionaries, offered a ready-made revolution to the highest bidder.

American interest in Haiti had for some years centered upon the Môle Saint Nicolas, a fine harbor on the northern tip of the island just across the Windward Passage from Guantanamo. By 1911, President Taft feared that French or German interests, which dominated Haiti's economy and foreign debt, might use their economic position to gain control of this port, and hence the Taft administration urged American firms, including W.R. Grace and Company, the National City Bank of New York, and Speyer and Company, to invest in Haiti to maintain an American influence. Nevertheless, by 1913, American investment in Haiti was still negligible.[22]

Bryan's first concern in Haiti was the protection of the Môle Saint Nicolas, and he sent the first assistant secretary of state, John Osborne, to Port-au-Prince in June of 1913 to see about buying it. Osborne failed in the purchase attempt, but he got a promise that the harbor would not be turned over to another power. When a revolution that winter overthrew the Haitian government, Bryan made renewal of the promise a condition for the recognition of its successor.[23]

Others had more ambitious plans. Roger Farnham, vice-president of the National City Bank of New York and president of the American-owned Banque Nationale d'Haiti, had for several years believed that Haiti, like the Dominican Republic, ought to have an American collectorship. He had not succeeded in convincing either the Haitian government or the Taft administration of this, but he now undertook to win over Bryan. How Farnham, the New York banker, contrived to meet and gain the trust of the apostle of the common man remains a mystery, but it was soon clear that the secretary of state regarded the banker as his chief expert on Haitian affairs. Farnham's influence was greatly increased by the fact that the supposedly impartial experts of the Latin American division of the State Department were also under his spell.[24]

Bryan was perfectly willing to accept a receivership in Haiti, but only if the Haitians wanted it, and it was precisely this condition that was the sticking point, since no Haitian showed the slightest interest in such a proposal. Farnham's task, therefore, was to overcome this objection, which he proceeded to do by withholding Haitian governmental funds in the Banque Nationale in order to put pressure on the government to ask for a receivership and by feeding to the State Department incessant rumors of impending German or French intervention. The Germans and French, for their part, hearing rumors of possible American intervention, added fuel to the fire by asking to be included in any receivership arrangement.[25]

Although the outbreak of World War I in the summer of 1914 removed any real danger of European intervention in Haiti, Farnham continued to regale the State Department with rumors that some such scheme was imminent. Bryan seems to have taken these tales with a grain of salt, but it is difficult to tell exactly what he believed. He continued to urge the receivership plan on the Haitians as yet another revolution began and progressed during the autumn of 1914. President Oreste Zamor, in the hope of saving himself, agreed to the idea in October but was too late; a new president, Davilmar Théodore, was soon installed in Port-au-Prince.[26]

The latest shake of the Haitian kaleidoscope had come while Bryan was campaigning in the West for Democratic candidates in the congressional elections, and he returned to Washington determined to clean up the Haitian mess once and for all. The United States, he informed President Théodore, would not recognize the new government until a customs agreement was signed, an American financial adviser approved, and a nonalienation pledge made for the Môle Saint Nicolas. Théodore at first seemed amenable to these demands, but a riot in the National Assembly quickly made him back down. Instead he offered preferential economic concessions in the hopes of buying American recognition, an obvious bribe which Bryan virtuously and indignantly spurned.[27]

Early in 1915, Farnham again increased the pressure, asking the

American government for a ship with which to transfer the Banque Nationale's gold reserves to New York. The ostensible reason for this extraordinary move was the fear that President Théodore was about to seize the gold. Bryan, considerably embarrassed, nevertheless complied with the request, and the Haitians, whatever their previous intentions, obligingly confirmed Farnham's predictions by seizing the remainder of the bank's gold and issuing a flood of worthless paper money. As the secretary of state pondered whether or not this latest disaster justified intervention, the outbreak of a new revolution fortuitously relieved his difficulty.[28]

By the spring of 1915, Bryan's hopes for a peaceful, orderly, moral world were dissolving in chaos as disaster after disaster threatened American policy throughout the world. Relations with Germany and Japan deteriorated rapidly, while in Mexico, the Dominican Republic, and Haiti, reverse followed reverse. Desperate at this destruction of his dreams, Bryan seems throughout this period to have been hopeful only of finding some way to cut the Gordian knot of his troubles; finally, when the last hope was gone, he had no recourse but to resign. In the meantime, in his despair and desperation, he endorsed and even recommended uncharacteristically violent solutions to the nation's problems.

It was against this general background, as well as the more immediate background of a growing Haitian revolution, that Bryan at last came to recommend "forcible interference" to impose a political and economic solution on Haitian problems. Admitting that such an arrangement would please the Banque Nationale and that he disliked intervention "on purely business grounds," he was convinced in this case that the welfare of Haiti as well as the interests of the bank dictated action. A permanent solution, he recommended, should include American supervision of Haitian elections (earlier recommended by Robert Lansing during Bryan's absence), American customs control, and a definitive non-alienation pledge for the Môle Saint Nicolas.[29]

Events now moved rapidly toward their tragic climax. On February 20, Bryan, having secured the approval of Wilson but without consulting the Haitians, sent an American commission to Haiti to supervise a general election—apparently totally unaware that in Haiti the president was elected by the Assembly, not by the people. On the same day the French again requested inclusion in any customs control arrangement. Hearing of this overture, Farnham immediately asserted that the French and Germans, although at war in Europe, planned some sort of joint action in Haiti, a fantastic story that achieved temporary credibility in the State Department only because the latest president of Haiti, Vilbrun Guillaume Sam, flatly refused even to talk to the American commission. To Bryan, such incredible intransigence could only be the result of Sam's belief that he would receive foreign aid. On the verge of recommending immediate military intervention, Bryan drew back only when the French announced that they accepted the American right to unilateral intervention. In May, in a last attempt to avoid the necessity of using force, the son of an old friend of Wilson's, Paul Fuller, Jr., was sent to Haiti to try to achieve agreement on a receivership plan. By the time Fuller's mission failed in June, Bryan had already left office, but his policy remained. On July 28, taking advantage of another revolution as excuse, American troops were landed in Haiti, and the country began nearly twenty years of complete American control.[30]

It is tempting to argue that Bryan's policy in Haiti was the result of sinister manipulation by Roger Farnham, but the essential directions of policy and the crucial decisions were Bryan's own. Although Farnham fed the State Department deliberately biased information, and the department's supposed experts made incredible blunders (such as their ignorance of how the president was selected) and were overly business-oriented, the secretary of state's decisions were ultimately based upon his own conclusions and desires. As with the Dominican Republic, Bryan's wish to be of service to a "less fortunate" people, reinforced in this case by Farnham's advice and Bryan's own fears about the Môle Saint Nicolas, led him gradually from assisting to controlling.

Bryan never understood that American-style democracy had no meaning in either country. In place of traditional parties each country had factions loyal only to individual leaders and concerned far more with the spoils of office than with adopting any sort of program. A free election was pointless because no group offered anything for the country at large. What was more, as soon as one was in office, the others, having no principles except the pursuit of power, immediately united to pull it down. Until some group was able to secure a broader popular basis of support, therefore, neither American election observers nor troops could be expected to break the cycle of revolutions.

In Mexico, on the other hand, revolution meant something quite different. There, despite factional differences, what might be called a revolutionary consensus emerged on broad social, political, and economic reforms. As they did elsewhere in the Caribbean, Wilson and Bryan at first frowned on revolution in Mexico and insisted that what the country needed was a free election with all parties participating under proper constitutional forms. Gradually, however, it became apparent to the president in particular, that a revolution in this case might actually be more beneficial to the country than an election. Although he did not abandon his hope of ultimately seeing constitutionalism restored in Mexico, Wilson's discovery led him to modify his policy. As he came to accept the necessity of revolution and even the possibility of revolutionary dictatorship to make reforms, he thought of American intervention as a tool with which to assure the success of the revolution rather than as a means for suppressing it. Only after even limited intervention had failed, indicating that the revolutionaries did not welcome it, did he move finally to the most difficult position of all—passive nonintervention. In his willingness to accept real self-determination in Mexico, and in his recognition that revolution might be a democratizing process, Wilson returned to an older concept of the American mission, to an idea of the eighteenth and nineteenth centuries—that of the United States as an example of successful democratic revolution.

When Bryan and Wilson came to office, Mexico was just beginning thirty years of revolutionary upheaval. From 1876 to 1911 the nation had been ruled by Porfirio Díaz, whose military dictatorship had offered stability beneficial to landowners, the military, the church, and foreign investors, but which oppressed the peasants, crushed workers, and almost eliminated any middle class. In 1911 an enfeebled Díaz was overthrown by Francisco Madero, who dreamed of restoring democracy to Mexico, a goal which was too novel for the upper class and too conservative for some peasant radicals. Deposed and executed in a military coup in February 1913, Madero became a rallying symbol for revolutionaries who had despised him while he was alive, and a revolutionary movement calling itself "Constitutionalist" and proclaiming its desire to restore Maderista democracy quickly grew. The Taft administration, on its way out, preferred to leave this particular problem to Wilson and hence withheld recognition of the government of Victoriano Huerta, the new dictator.[31]

Wilson and Bryan were morally appalled by the murder of Madero and, regarding recognition as implying approval, withheld it. Their hope was that if Huerta could be isolated from outside help, he would be forced to resign, thus clearing the way for the restoration of democracy. This policy immediately aroused substantial opposition from American businessmen with interests in Mexico and from their Republican allies in the United States, but neither Bryan nor Wilson had much sympathy with such complaints. More serious, from their point of view, was that Britain, the only other nation whose interests in Mexico came near to equalling those of the United States, insisted upon recognizing Huerta—a lead most other nations were eager to follow. Wilson and Bryan suspected strongly that British policy was dictated by oil interests, but it gradually became apparent that there was less difference between the two nations than appeared on the surface; once the British understood that the Americans were really serious in following a policy they regarded as mistaken, they were quite willing to follow the American lead insofar as doing so was compatible with minimum protection of their own interests.[32]

Throughout the summer and early autumn of 1913, Wilson and Bryan sought a simple, clean solution to the Mexican problem. Taking the Constitutionalists at face value, Bryan believed that the only issue was the restoration of political democracy, and hence he recommended the sending of an American commission to supervise nationwide elections (the same idea he would later press in the Dominican Republic and Haiti). Wilson ultimately agreed and appropriately chose a friend of Bryan's, John Lind of Minnesota, to carry out the mission of getting the Mexican factions to lay down their arms and submit their differences to an election. Lind's total failure in this naively conceived project was followed, in October, by Huerta's dissolution of the Chamber of Deputies, arrest of 110 opposition deputies, and assumption of dictatorial powers.[33]

The events of October 1913 jolted Wilson's and Bryan's complacent assumption that an election would solve all of Mexico's problems. A further shock came later in the month when another of Wilson's agents, William Bayard Hale, for the first time asked the Constitutionalists directly what they wanted. He discovered that they did not want an immediate election. Their first priority was a complete military victory that would crush the old ruling class, and they deeply resented any American interference beyond allowing them to buy weapons in the United States. The impression of Constitutionalist insistence upon a real revolution, not just a change in rulers, was confirmed when, late in December, the Constitutionalist agent Luis Cabrera had several meetings with a State Department representative in Washington.[34]

By the beginning of 1914, Wilson had changed his attitude and concluded that "a radical revolution was the only cure."[35] He continued, however, to assume mistakenly that the rebels would welcome American assistance. Although they were pleased when he announced that he would lift a long-standing ban on the sale of arms to them, they wanted no other help. Wilson, failing to understand this, sought what he called "a psychological moment" to strike a final, crushing blow at

Huerta. That moment came in April when the Tampico Incident (the temporary arrest by Huertista forces of some American sailors who came ashore in Tampico to buy supplies) offered a justification for the landing of troops at nearby Veracruz.[36]

Bryan was alarmed by Wilson's rush to intervene and was inclined to settle the Tampico Incident without resorting to force, but when the president overruled him, he went along loyally. Nearly universal Mexican outrage at the American invasion of Veracruz, however, soon suggested that the secretary had been wiser than the president. As the situation became increasingly critical, Bryan advised Wilson to give up plans for enlarging the intervention and to accept a mediation offer from Argentina, Brazil, and Chile. To Bryan's delight, the president agreed.[37]

Wilson, however, had merely shifted methods rather than objectives. During the mediation he tried to get Huerta to resign in favor of a provisional government which would institute some of the Constitutionalist reforms before calling an election, and his insistence on these hopeless demands doomed the conference. Nevertheless, Huerta, recognizing the handwriting on the wall, resigned at last in mid-July. Predictably, there then followed a scramble for power among the various factional leaders of the rebels. In this struggle the Americans could do little except to try, through the various special agents still in Mexico, to ameliorate the treatment of foreigners by the rebel chieftains. In the fierce struggles for power, their efforts had little effect.[38]

By the autumn of 1914, Wilson at last recognized the virtues of nonintervention. The temptation to meddle still existed, but the president was now more skeptical about what intervention could accomplish in Mexico and more confident that the revolution would ultimately benefit the people. He was satisfied, in short, that Mexico was gradually moving toward a democracy similar to that of the United States, and that confidence made him willing, despite continuing provocations and temptations, to let nature take its course.

Still, between January and March of 1915, as the continuing factional struggles isolated and endangered the large foreign population of Mexico City and cut off shipments from Yucatan of sisal, the raw material for the manufacture of binder twine, Wilson again stepped to the brink of intervention. On March 6 he informed Constitutionalist leaders that the United States would hold them "personally responsible" for harm to foreigners in Mexico City, and a week later he authorized an ultimatum demanding the immediate reopening of Yucatan ports for the shipment of sisal. An actual conflict over these issues was averted when the Constitutionalists made minor concessions, but there was no doubting the president's determination. Evidently his commitment to nonintervention was limited by an even stronger commitment to protect American interests.[39]

Bryan's attitude during the crisis of early 1915 was ambivalent. His humanitarianism was outraged by the conditions inflicted upon foreigners in Mexico City, and his western constituency put a good deal of pressure on him to protect the sisal supply; yet at the same time he disliked the idea of using military force. The suggestion, made by Robert Lansing, of holding the Constitutionalist leaders "personally responsible" for conditions in Mexico City appealed to him because it seemed to avoid the implication of war. Similarly, he reluctantly accepted Wilson's decision to threaten the use of the navy to reopen the ports of Yucatan only because he convinced himself that this could be a limited, minimal intervention unlikely to lead to large-scale hostilities.[40] As it turned out, the crisis passed without conflict, more by good luck than good planning.

Like falling drops of water, each successive problem eroded Bryan's restraint a little more, bringing closer to the surface the missionary urge to set things right in the world. In March, Bryan was still uneasy about the idea of intervention in Mexico, but by June, when he resigned, he seemed to have overcome his last doubts. The cause of this shift was apparently the defeat of Pancho Villa by Venustiano Carranza, a disaster from Bryan's point of view because it removed the one Mexican leader who had seemed amenable to American guidance. Agreeing with the president at a cabinet meeting on June 1 that the civil war in Mexico showed no signs of abating, the secretary of state endorsed Wilson's proposal that the United States might have to recognize one of the factional leaders in order to bring the conflict to an end. Significantly, however, Bryan went beyond the president's recommendation of purely diplomatic pressure to suggest the possibility of military intervention also.[41]

By June 1915, Bryan and Wilson had virtually exchanged attitudes about Mexico. At first, Bryan had advocated restraint and nonintervention. Even as late as April 1914 the secretary counseled against the Veracruz landing as the president sought a pretext to use force against the Mexican dictator. Then, as the prospects for democracy seemed to dim in Haiti and the Dominican Republic as well as in Mexico, Bryan gradually lost faith in natural processes of development and moved toward intervention in all three cases, while Wilson concluded that at least in Mexico, intervention could achieve very little and was likely to be destructive in many ways. Although he never said so explicitly, it is possible that the president came to understand a crucial distinction between the Caribbean and Mexican revolutions that Bryan never grasped—that the Mexican Revolution, although divided in leadership, had widely supported goals and a broad base of popular support, whereas the incessant coups of Haiti and the Dominican Republic were merely factional squabbles with no broad goals or movements behind them. Conceivably stability could be imposed by intervention in the Caribbean states, but in Mexico interference only stimulated nationalist hostility. The tragic irony of Bryan's attitude toward Mexico was that after years of predicting the evolution of democracy all over the world, he failed to recognize the most promising example of the process on his own doorstep.

When he resigned in June of 1915, Bryan was deeply discouraged and depressed about his ability to reshape the world as he thought it ought to be. His experience with Latin America suggests that a large part of the reason for his frustration was an all-too-human impatience at the slow pace of "inevitable" progress. He really believed that the world was developing toward universal Christian democracy, but once in office, he felt that there must be some way the enormous power of the United States could be used to speed up the process. Unable to admit even to himself that his actions were contradicting and subverting his own goals, he assured his successor that the administration's increasingly dictatorial policy in the Dominican Republic was embodying at last "our altruistic values."[42]

In the Western Hemisphere, Bryan created a policy to fit a world that never existed. Unable or unwilling to absorb the details of actual conditions and problems, he imposed on the complex reality an artificial structure and order, assumed the existence of popular goals that were absent, and counted upon values and habits of behavior that had never developed. Had the world been as he wished it, his policies might have worked, but had it been as he wished it, they would not have been necessary. In the real world they were neither appropriate nor effective.

6

THE FEAR OF ENTANGLEMENT, 1914–1915

In dealing with the Western Hemisphere, Bryan's isolationism was not aroused, and his missionary impulses were restrained only by the ability of Latin Americans to resist his smothering embraces. When World War I began in 1914, however, almost the opposite was true. The war stirred isolationist fears that temporarily suppressed the secretary's idealism. His innovative policy of neutrality as well as his insistent urging of mediation on the president were the result of his apprehension that the United States would not escape entanglement in the war unless it could somehow end the conflict.

Bryan thought of and phrased his isolationist positions in idealistic terms. Rarely mentioning the dangers the war presented to the United States, he argued that the nation had a duty to stay out. By so doing it could demonstrate that at least one nation was able to solve conflicts peacefully, and it could make its mediation services available to the belligerents. He advocated even the sacrifice of some profits and the postponement of some conflicts over neutral rights—not, he said, because such issues might drag the nation into war, but because America must demonstrate its moral superiority in order to set an example for others. Ending the war was in the true national interest and the path to international service. Not fear but duty dictated a policy of nonintervention, Bryan insisted, although an outside observer might have had difficulty seeing the difference.[1]

President Wilson agreed generally with Bryan about the desirability of neutrality and the importance of setting an example for the world, but he did not share the secretary's deep and chilling fear of world involvement. Believing that some moral and legal issues were more important than neutrality, Wilson concluded that America would lose its ability to lead the world if it did not defend its principles. As Bryan moved more and more toward idealistic isolationism, Wilson moved toward internationalism. Under the pressure of crises with Germany, subtle differences became basic disagreement over policy.[2]

At first no differences were apparent. The president and secretary

For a time, Wilson and Bryan regarded the flamboyant Mexican revolutionary Pancho Villa, shown here at the head of his troops, as a savior of Mexico. (Library of Congress.)

Below: Signing the Bryan peace treaties with France, Great Britain, Spain, and China, September 15, 1914. (Nebraska State Historical Society.)

agreed that neutrality was the only reasonable course, and Wilson, grief-stricken by the illness and death of his wife, was grateful to leave the details of the policy to the State Department.[3] Eager to fulfill the president's injunction to the nation to be "impartial in thought as well as in action," Bryan had the department's lawyers prepare a lengthy neutrality proclamation setting forth neutral duties, and he made every effort to see that citizens of the warring powers residing in the United States respected that neutrality.[4]

The first sign of difference between Wilson and Bryan was not evident to either man. It grew out of Bryan's suggestion that if Americans were discouraged from lending money to the belligerent governments, they would be less likely to form emotional attachments to one side or the other. Wilson at first supported the secretary's loan ban, agreeing that loans would be "inconsistent with the true spirit of neutrality." There was, however, an important difference in the way the two men saw the issue. Robert Lansing sarcastically described the secretary's position as "only . . . idealistic," but in fact that description was truer of Wilson than of Bryan, whose attitude was shaped by isolationism as well as idealism. When Lansing, who was neither an idealist nor an isolationist, pointed out to the president in Bryan's absence that the loan ban was damaging American trade and recommended circumventing it by authorizing the extension of "credits" but not loans, Wilson accepted the modification.[5] Wilson now realized that what he had initially viewed as an idealistic effort to starve the war economically was in conflict with the equally idealistic and perhaps even more important aims of maintaining freedom of the seas and open trade. Bryan, busy on the campaign trail and sure that the president shared his own belief in the primacy of noninvolvement in the war, apparently never realized that the loan ban had been subverted.[6] Neither man seemed to see that the issue had revealed an important difference in emphasis between them.

Perhaps one reason they did not see what was happening was because on another, similar issue they found themselves in complete agreement. This was the question of arms sales to the belligerents. Before the war both had endorsed the principle of a ban on arms sales, but after August 1914, they both rejected it. The reason was simply that although an arms sale ban would be *idealistic,* it would not be *neutral.* It would benefit the well-armed Central Powers and injure the poorly armed Allies, a conclusion reinforced by support for the idea among German-American groups. Even though many of Bryan's followers in the Midwest endorsed the idea of an arms embargo, he could not accept it while he was secretary of state. Uncomfortable though it must have been to him to run against the will of the public and to give up an idealistic proposal to maintain the legal requirements of neutrality, as long as he held office Bryan had to accept such compromises with perfection. For a crusader of his temperament, the position was not easy, although in this case he managed to persuade himself that the greater goal of idealistic service would be promoted in the end because a threat to cut off arms sales would be seen by the Allies as blackmail and would diminish America's standing as a potential mediator. The president, reflecting on the damage that Jefferson's embargo had done to the American economy before the War of 1812, agreed with Bryan, but for reasons that suggested trouble ahead. The administration's united opposition doomed arms embargo proposals in Congress, but the agreement of president and secretary of state was more tenuous than either realized.[7]   216448

On matters of trade with the belligerents, Bryan and Wilson also agreed initially on policy, but again a serious difference lurked beneath the surface harmony. To Wilson, freedom of trade and the rights of neutrals were idealistic aims of the first importance, worth defending even at the risk of war. Bryan would have sacrificed trade to stay out of war on the grounds that only by so doing could the country maintain its moral purity and lead the nations to better ways of settling disputes. These two positions were not necessarily in conflict if definite, binding rules governing trade could be agreed upon between belligerents and neutrals. Provided that trade did not threaten American isolation, Bryan favored it as enthusiastically as anyone in the administration. For that reason he made strenuous efforts during the autumn of 1914 to win endorsement by the belligerents of the statements of neutral rights contained in the Declaration of London of 1909. The small-navy Central Powers quickly agreed, but the British, relying largely upon blockading the Continent to win the war, would not accept the declaration.[8]

Angered by British intransigence, Bryan directed one of his assistants in the State Department to draft a strong protest note, but in the secretary's absence during October it was Lansing who delivered the draft to the White House. There Colonel Edward M. House, fearing that the note might cause a break with England, persuaded Wilson to let him shorten and moderate it. Even this brought complaints from the Anglophile American ambassador in London, Walter Hines Page, and subsequently Lansing cabled to Page a proposal that the British announce their adherence to the declaration while at the same time adopting policies that would effectively circumvent it. Lansing's concern was a possible loss of British trade over an issue that seemed to him unimportant, and his attitude convinced the British that they had nothing to fear from the United States. Consequently they rejected the Declaration of London and tightened their restrictions on neutral commerce. On his return from his campaign trip Bryan discovered that Lansing had abandoned the Declaration of London altogether and informed the belligerents that the United States would defend its neutral rights on the basis of traditional international law—a weak reed at best.[9]

It is not difficult to understand why Bryan failed to protest the abandonment of the Declaration of London. Assuming that Wilson shared his commitment to isolationism, he could not imagine that the president would consider the abstract issue of neutral rights an adequate reason for going to war. Nor, of course, could he have imagined the problems that would be created by the German use of submarines after early 1915. Although not as advantageous as the Declaration of London, traditional international law seemed in the autumn of 1914 an acceptable protection for American interests because it provided a basis for postwar negotiated settlements of claims arising from British seizures of American ships. Confident that he and the president saw eye to eye on the basic direction of American policy, and unable to foresee the future, Bryan simply did not feel that the issue was of sufficient importance to justify a major confrontation with Lansing, House, Wilson, and Page.

The way was thus cleared for further concessions to the British to promote "practical" interests. In December, Lansing worked out informal arrangements between American exporters and the British government under which the Americans agreed to withhold food shipments from Germany in return for freedom from petty harassment by the Royal Navy. The lost trade with Germany, though insignificant economically, represented a substantial concession of principle.[10]

A less obvious but more important concession came late in December 1914. On December 26 a formal protest was sent to the British about their treatment of American merchant ships. Depicted by the press as a strong statement of the American position, in fact the note was quite the opposite. By admitting that "imperative necessity to protect . . . national safety" might justify actions otherwise illegal, the State Department left a loophole in its argument through which the British could squeeze a defense of everything they had done. Bryan, who had been the instigator of the American protest (though not of its crippling concession), was eager to debate with London every line of the British reply. Wilson, however, soon made it clear that in his eyes a modus vivendi had been reached. "The two governments," he told the secretary of state flatly, were "in substantial agreement about the principles involved;" there was no reason for further protests.[11]

Even to Bryan, who had been scarcely aware of the erosion of his neutrality policies, it was now becoming evident that the Allies were to receive special treatment in order to safeguard increasing American trade. But even as that fact was thrust upon him, he found it difficult to grasp its full implications. Weighed down by the pressure of daily crises, he plodded on through the first six months of 1915. Finally it took the explosion of German torpedoes to arouse him.

One of the many problems that distracted Bryan's attention from what was happening to his neutrality policy was a conflict with Japan over China. Like Roosevelt and Taft, the Democrats had made preservation of the Open Door in China a key part of their East Asian policy, but they did not simply continue what their predecessors had begun. Believing that a policy that had been intended originally to lead China toward democracy had been perverted into a program designed to enrich American businessmen, they sought to free it from the influence of such people and to restore it as an example of American superiority to European imperialism. Symbolic of their intent was Bryan's insistence that the United States send to China only "men of pronounced Christian character," a view which led him to veto a Unitarian as minister to China and to install a former missionary as chief of the State Department's Far Eastern Division.[12]

Another indication of the new policy was the hasty and ill-considered decision, made by Bryan and Wilson against all expert advice, to withdraw from participation in an international loan to China. The Taft administration had labored long and hard to win American participation in this project on the theory that it was the only way to exert influence on the behavior of other nations in China. Bryan and Wilson ignored such arguments and concluded that the loan was merely intended to enrich favored bankers. Hence they announced that the government would not press American bankers to participate in the loan. The bankers, who thought the whole project excessively risky anyway, were delighted to have an excuse to make their escape.[13]

The decision to recognize the new Chinese government was made equally blindly. When the republic was proclaimed in February 1912, both Bryan and Wilson urged Taft to recognize it, but the president, guided by the advice of experts who considered the new government neither democratic nor stable, and who wanted to preserve hard-won cooperation with other powers in China, refused. None of these considerations influenced the new administration a year later. In China they saw what they wanted to see, and for cooperation with other nations they sought to substitute American leadership by example. On April 1 the administration announced that as soon as the new Chinese government was formally organized, the United States would recognize it unilaterally; other nations were invited to follow the American lead.[14]

Again the experts were appalled, but of course the president and secretary of state were less concerned with the realities in China than with demonstrating American moral leadership. They did not realize that the practical result of their idealism would be to reduce American influence on the behavior of other nations in China. The Japanese in particular, already nursing a grudge against the United States as a result of the land law controversy, were delighted that the Americans seemed to be withdrawing from Chinese affairs. They were only too willing to take advantage of the opportunity.[15]

When the war began in 1914 the Japanese lost no time in acting. On August 23, refusing to accept restraints proposed by their British allies, they declared war on Germany. Their object was to seize German holdings in China while the other powers were too busy to stop them. They assumed the Americans would do nothing and soon found they were right. Bryan favored a proposal to declare all of Asia a neutral zone in order to protect China from just such a situation, but in the confusion at the beginning of the war the proposal was delayed until too late, if indeed it had ever had any hope of acceptance.[16]

Bryan was, with good reason, deeply suspicious of Japanese intentions in China. Nevertheless, recognizing American weakness and committed to isolationism, he advised the president that the Japanese occupation of Kiaochow and seizure of the Shantung Railroad (which implied domination of the whole province of Shantung) must be accepted. The best the Americans and Chinese could hope for, he thought, was that the Japanese would honor their promise that "the occupation is temporary and that the final action in regard to the railroad will be determined after the war is over." Despite persistent rumors that the Japanese had no intention whatsoever of returning any of the seized territory to China after the war, a hands-off policy remained the official American position throughout the autumn of 1914.[17] Impotence put any practical alternative to moral leadership out of reach.

In January 1915 it began to be apparent that rumor actually had underestimated Japanese intentions. On January 18, amid injunctions to the Chinese of total secrecy, the Japanese delivered the infamous

Twenty-one Demands. The fruit of several months' careful planning, these demands were designed to make China virtually a Japanese colony, and so great was the Chinese terror that it was not until more than three weeks later that the American minister, Paul Reinsch, was informed of their extent.[18]

After Reinsch's initial report, it took three weeks to get full details of the demands. Another three weeks were lost in fruitless debate about what to do, and more than two weeks were required to draft an American protest. All told, almost two months passed between the submission of the demands and the sending of the American protest note on March 13.[19] By the time the Americans acted, the Chinese had already made substantial concessions.

Reflecting the indecision which lay behind it and the great reluctance of the administration to take on another crisis to add to those already pressing upon it, the March 13 note was scarcely a ringing reaffirmation of the Open Door. It began with the assertion that a strong protest would be justified, but it undermined its own argument with the admission that "territorial contiguity creates special relations between Japan and these districts." This unfortunate phrase, like the "imperative necessity" clause in the protest to the British, vitiated the American case. When they replied, the Japanese seized upon it to justify their position.[20]

Noting that the Japanese professed concern about American desires to acquire a naval base in Fukien Province, and that they offered not to force China to accept Japanese advisers (one of the most obnoxious of the original demands), Bryan discerned in the Japanese reply a hope of compromise. Ignoring Reinsch's warning that any compromise would constitute appeasement of Japan at China's expense, the secretary informed Tokyo on March 26 that the United States wanted no base and proposed that the Chinese put the Japanese on an equal footing with other foreigners in choosing foreign advisers. Neither side took the slightest notice of this proposal.[21]

In the next three weeks Wilson, who had been cool to Bryan's compromise proposal from the start, gradually became convinced that the demands, no matter how modified, were "clearly incompatible with the administrative independence and autonomy of the Chinese Empire and with the maintenance of an open door to the world." Rather than urging the Chinese to give in to some Japanese demands, as Bryan had suggested, Wilson felt that "we shall have to try in every practicable way to defend China," and he warned that "we shall have to be very careful hereafter about seeming to concede the reasonableness of any of Japan's demands or requests."[22] As in their policy on

Germany, the president and secretary were increasingly at odds, with Wilson adopting a tough line while Bryan retreated from involvement and conflict.

The secretary was not happy about giving up the search for accommodation, but he loyally supported the president. On April 29 he handed to the Japanese ambassador a memorandum which in effect withdrew his compromise proposal and threatened a public protest if the Japanese did not back down. The ambassador professed great alarm at this prospect, and his government obligingly withdrew the most objectionable of the demands, but in fact these were delaying tactics. The demands were quickly reinstated in new guises, and a long memorandum from the Japanese arguing that the demands had been so softened as to be unobjectionable did not deceive anyone. On May 3, Bryan submitted to the president the draft of a note protesting most of the demands as infringements on China's sovereignty and America's treaty rights and a press release condemning a rumored Japanese ultimatum to China as well. Two days later, following receipt of reports from Reinsch of major Chinese concessions, both were handed to the Japanese ambassador.[23]

As had been the case all along, American policy had no visible effect on events in China. The day after receiving the American protest, the Japanese government decided to send an ultimatum to China. Dispatched on May 7, it demanded full acceptance of the latest demands before 6:00 p.m. on May 9. The Chinese, who had already on May 1 offered to accept almost all of what was now demanded, immediately gave in to the rest and by the end of the month had signed treaties embodying the agreements. Bryan, who had feared that a Sino-Japanese war was imminent, was profoundly relieved, particularly since the sinking of the *Lusitania* on May 7 had thrust the United States into the midst of a far more serious crisis.[24]

Never an advocate of a vigorous American defense of China against the Japanese, Bryan by this time was more than willing to drop the matter entirely, but Wilson wanted to go at least one step further. During the first moments of concern over the ultimatum of May 7, Lansing had suggested an application of Wilson's nonrecognition doctrine to the Chinese situation. By refusing to recognize the validity of any agreement that violated American treaty rights, he argued, the United States would protect its rights for future negotiations. The president liked this idea and instructed Lansing to draft a note embodying it. On May 11, the United States informed Japan that it would not "recognize any agreement or undertaking" which impaired "the treaty rights of the United States and its citizens in China, the political or territorial integrity of the Republic of China, or the international policy relative to China commonly known as the open door policy."[25]

Just what the American note meant was open to considerable doubt. Wilson and Lansing seem to have regarded it as a protest, although it was not explicitly such. The Japanese were angry about it, but Bryan assured them that it was meant not as a protest but as a clarification of the American position and a precautionary statement to make clear that *future* infringements on American rights would not be acceptable. With this the Japanese had to content themselves for the time being.[26]

The note of May 11 was, in retrospect, in many ways typical of American policy in China during Bryan's tenure as secretary of state. Throughout, that policy had been dictated by the desire to keep American hands clean, to protect American moral purity; practical, concrete actions to help China were rejected. Cloaked in the language of service, in fact the policy was selfish and narrow. Indeed, it did not even protect American interests in China adequately; all were left to fend for themselves. Unwilling to take any action in China that entailed a risk of conflict with other powers, Wilson and Bryan convinced themselves that an independent policy would be virtuous and effective. The result of their self-delusion was that the United States lost whatever small influence it had on events in China, while at the same time its moral preachings antagonized and confused the Japanese. Bryan, who would have acquiesced in what he could not prevent in China, was perhaps slightly less unrealistic than Wilson, and the president, in protesting Japanese actions, may have been somewhat bolder, but the differences between them were minor. For both of them the invocation of the Open Door policy in China offered an easy excuse for doing nothing while at the same time it protected their self-satisfied sense of righteousness.

At the heart of the failure in China was not only the refusal of Japan to follow the American lead but the Japanese determination to exploit the American withdrawal rather than to imitate it. In Europe at the same time similar problems faced American policy as the belligerents rejected American leadership and exploited what they saw as American weaknesses.

From the beginning of the war Bryan believed that both self-interest and duty required continuous American efforts to promote peace. Mediation would minimize the risk of being sucked into the war by violations of American rights, and it would also guarantee America's moral leadership in the world. The president shared the secretary's eagerness to lead the world to peace but was less fearful of the consequences of involvement. He realized, moreover, that as long as either side thought it could win, mediation would fail. He was sympathetic to Bryan's various peace proposals during the first months of the war, but he did not feel the same sense of urgency and hence gave them little attention.[27]

In any case, Bryan was not Wilson's chosen agent for the pursuit of peace. That task fell to Colonel House, whose subtlety and closeness to the president made him the perfect spokesman. Wilson liked Bryan, but he doubted his capacity for a mission of such extreme delicacy, and he may have somewhat feared the Commoner as a potential rival for the title of world peacemaker. When the time seemed ripe in early 1915 to send an American agent to Europe in search of peace, it was House, not Bryan, who went. This was a deeply felt blow to Bryan, who believed himself uniquely qualified for the mission, but he accepted his disappointment gracefully and did his best to assist House.[28]

Arriving in London in February 1915, House followed up promising leads but soon discovered they led nowhere. Neither side was prepared to make real concessions, and without such concessions no compromise was possible. It was clear long before House finally left in June that no breakthrough would be made. His reports, combined with a drastic turn for the worse in German-American relations, created an atmosphere of deep gloom in Washington.[29]

The principal cause of this depression was the announcement made by the Germans on February 4, while House was still on his way to London, that, effective February 18, German submarines would sink Allied merchant ships without warning in a war zone around the British Isles. Neutral ships were not to be attacked deliberately, but the Germans warned that the British practice of using neutral flags to disguise their ships made it difficult for submarine commanders to avoid mistakes.[30]

It was immediately apparent to everyone in Washington that there must be some protest against the German policy, which in effect established a blockade of the British Isles while at the same time rejecting all of a blockade's traditional safeguards for neutral lives and property. Counselor Lansing, commissioned to draft a protest, produced a sharp note warning the Germans that the United States would hold them to "strict accountability" for harm to American ships or citizens. On February 10, approved by the president and secretary of state and accompanied for balance by a protest to the British about the misuse of neutral flags, the note was sent.[31] No one had stopped to wonder what "strict accountability" meant, whether it would be invoked no matter how an injury befell an American or his goods, or how it would be enforced.

These practical problems soon presented themselves. The German government, somewhat taken aback by the American reaction, temporarily delayed and subsequently slightly modified the new policy but eventually decided that the American warning was meaningless and authorized the navy to begin using submarines as planned. On March 28 came the first test of the American threat when the British ship *Falaba* was sunk by a submarine and an American engineer, Leon C. Thrasher, killed. The American press was outraged, but caution prevailed in the State Department. Lansing pointed out that even under traditional rules, the sinking was justifiable if the ship had tried to escape, and Bryan, who had already suggested that the submarine might have made old rules of naval warfare obsolete, now argued that an American who traveled in the war zone, knowing the risks, might be guilty of "contributory negligence."[32]

Wilson agreed with Bryan and Lansing that the case required caution and deliberation, but a growing split between him and the secretary on basic policy soon became apparent. Once satisfied that the facts of the case merited a protest under existing international law, Wilson believed national interest required him to make one. As Lansing pointed out, however, any specific protest would in effect be a protest against submarine warfare; since the submarine could only attack without warning, it followed that if such an attack was wrong in one case it was wrong in all.[33]

Bryan, on the other hand, doubted that the United States could, without risking being drawn into the war itself, compel the belligerents to change their methods of warfare. He therefore concluded that, at least for the duration of the war, the only practical course for the United States was to refrain from exercising certain rights—especially the right of travel in the war zone. Following the war, such issues could be settled by negotiation and perhaps damages claimed. Between Wilson's and Bryan's positions, it became increasingly obvious, there was no ground for compromise.[34]

For a time it appeared that Bryan had carried the day. Although on April 22, Wilson, stung by German demands that he place an embargo on the sale of arms to the Allies, directed Bryan to prepare a protest in the *Falaba* case, he agreed to withhold any demand for reparation until after the war. Bryan, believing that the death of one man was not worth a war, was delighted. Now doubly convinced that he was right, he also argued successfully against retaliation for the bombing of the American ship *Cushing* and the torpedoing of the American tanker *Gulflight,* even though three men were lost in the latter sinking. He even urged the president to consider a new protest to London about British violations of American neutral rights to balance the protest to Berlin in the *Falaba, Cushing,* and *Gulflight* cases.[35]

Then, on May 7, before the draft of the protest to Germany was completed, came the shattering news of the sinking of the *Lusitania* and the loss of 128 American lives. Extraordinary though it seems in retrospect, apparently no one in the administration had imagined such a catastrophe. Now, instantly, the whole nation was swept up in debate over the issue which would also come to divide Bryan and Wilson. Some felt, like the president, that honor was more important than peace; others joined Bryan in thinking that some sacrifice of neutral rights was reasonable if the country could thereby stay out of war. Thus what had been a private issue between the two men that could, given the great liking and goodwill between them, be compromised to some extent, now became a national political question upon which compromise was increasingly difficult. Wilson asked the nation for calm deliberation, but it was obvious that such calm was unlikely to prevail.[36]

On May 11, angered by a German memorandum that apologized for the loss of American lives but offered no concession on submarine warfare, Wilson read to the cabinet the draft of a strong protest note. Avoiding any discussion of the facts of the case that might have offered the Germans a means of finding a face-saving formula for apologizing, and labeling in advance any offer of reparations as inadequate, the note left the Germans a simple choice between stopping and continuing submarine warfare. Nothing less than complete cessation, said the president, would satisfy the United States.[37]

Bryan, listening to the president, was staggered. If the note were sent, he thought, it meant that his advice had been rejected and that all possibility of compromise had been abandoned. Unless the note were modified by an offer to postpone settlement of the issue until after the war, or ameliorated by a simultaneous protest to the British, he told the president after the meeting, he would sign it only with the greatest reluctance. Wilson thought any offer to postpone settlement weakened the American case too much, but he suggested that the State Department issue an informal "tip" to the press saying the same thing. Bryan was relieved, but before the tip could be released, other cabinet members convinced Wilson that it would undermine the effect of the protest, and he withdrew his permission. Two days later, unsoftened, the note was sent.[38]

Defeated, Bryan might well have resigned at this point, but he continued to hope that somehow he might persuade the president to change direction. Wilson, however, seemed adamant, rejecting Bryan's suggestions for a ban on American travel in the war zone or a new protest to the British. When House in London suggested the vague possibility that a reciprocal lifting of blockades might be arranged, Bryan grasped eagerly at this straw, but nothing came of it.[39]

By mid-May, the secretary was deeply discouraged, and his depression may have led him to be slightly indiscreet. In a conversation with Constantin Dumba, the Austro-Hungarian ambassador, he emphasized that although the United States insisted upon the terms of its note to Germany, it was eager to settle the issue peacefully. Dumba, already convinced that the United States would never fight, interpreted this statement to mean that the Americans would give in. This was patently ridiculous, but it cost Bryan a good deal of time and trouble to secure a correction from the erring diplomat and contributed to the secretary's strain.[40]

In fact the outlook was less black than it seemed to Bryan. German leaders, though scornful of the United States, were reluctant to antagonize the neutrals just at this moment because they feared that neutral Italy, wavering on the brink of belligerency, might be pushed into the laps of the Allies. Accordingly, secret orders were sent to submarine commanders to refrain from attacking large passenger liners, and on May 30 a note inviting a lengthy discussion of the facts of the case was sent to Washington.[41]

This appeal to the principle of Bryan's peace treaties was most welcome to the secretary of state, but Lansing, Wilson, and a majority of the cabinet feared that a lengthy investigation would give the impression that the United States did not take the matter seriously. When the American ambassador in Berlin reported that the German purpose was to "keep the *Lusitania* matter 'jollied along' until the American people get excited about baseball or a new scandal and forget," Wilson decided that no compromises were possible. On June 5 he gently but finally rejected Bryan's renewed suggestions for a ban on war zone travel or a protest to London.[42]

On June 4, while still reflecting on Bryan's suggestions, Wilson completed and read to the cabinet the draft of a new note to Germany that reiterated the simple point that the use of submarines to attack ships without warning was a violation of the "principles of humanity." When a discussion indicated that most members of the cabinet supported the president's position, Bryan realized that the end was at hand. Calling Wilson aside at the end of the meeting, Bryan told him that if the note were sent, he would have to resign.[43]

The following Monday, after a weekend of rest and reflection, Bryan confirmed his decision to resign. Finishing up some last chores that morning, he had a long talk with Wilson in the afternoon that convinced both men that their positions were irreconcilable but removed some bitterness. When the cabinet met on June 8, Wilson read the final draft of the note and then announced Bryan's resignation. The next day, as the note was sent to Germany, the resignation became effective.[44]

To most people, Bryan's resignation was explicable only as cowardice—quitting under fire—and few could understand how he could have signed the first note and balked at the second. Even within the government, where he had won many friends during the past two years, there was personal regret at his departure but mystification as to its cause. Only a relatively small number of old-time supporters, German sympathizers, and pacifists supported his decision, and then often for the wrong reasons. An even smaller group understood that the resignation stemmed from fundamental differences with Wilson, not from a flash of temperament.[45]

Bryan himself confused the issue by giving two inconsistent explanations of his decision. In one he asserted that a new section which opened the possibility of negotiations was added to the note without his knowledge and implied that had he been aware of the change, he might not have resigned. In the other, he said, contradictorily, that it was the president's refusal to apply the investigation principle of the peace treaties that led to the resignation.[46] Neither version was entirely accurate. Wilson's rejection of the investigation principle was an immediate cause of the conflict between the two men, but that was only part of the problem.[47]

The most essential difference between Wilson and Bryan over neutrality policy was that Bryan's attitude was shaped primarily by isolationism, whereas Wilson's was determined by idealism. It was that emphasis on isolationism which led Bryan to insist on neutrality policies that went beyond normal custom and the requirements of international law; it was isolationism that made him willing to postpone settlement of even the *Lusitania* controversy until after the war; and it was the fear of involvement that made him propose mediation so insistently. Wilson, on the other hand, was increasingly disturbed by the war's shattering of international standards of decency, morality, and law. Although he declared that the nation was "too proud to fight" over the *Lusitania* controversy, that was hardly a reassurance to Bryan. Pride is a volatile emotion, particularly when it is based upon a sense of moral superiority. Anger at Germany's refusal to recognize American superiority as well as the temptation to impose the nation's standards on the chaotic world tended to undermine Wilson's restraint, with the result that pride might just as well lead the president to war as keep him out. Unchecked by Bryan's isolationist fears, Wilson's idealism, pride, and anger all eroded his commitment to neutrality. As the secretary of state had foreseen from the outset, the pressures on the United States, both from within and without, were so great that virtually the only way to maintain neutrality was somehow to bring the war to an end before it was too late. Wilson was beginning to feel that only by sharing the burdens of war could the United States win a share in shaping the peace; Bryan still believed that only by standing above the conflict could the nation lead the world into the paths of righteousness.[48] Both were idealists, but the difference in policy determined by their attitudes toward isolationism was fundamental.

Beyond the differences with Wilson over neutrality policy, Bryan had another, more personal reason for resigning. The Commoner was not at peace with himself. Throughout his period in office he had been unable to strike a workable balance between idealism and isolationism. He had performed the duties of office competently enough, but it never seemed possible to bring everything together in a policy that was effective, idealistic, and yet protected American independence of action. Compromises were constantly forced on him, and his well-meant actions had unexpected and unwanted results, as in his dealing with the Caribbean states, and his great hopes evaporated in controversy and frustration, as in Asia. Unable to admit that perhaps missionary goals were incompatible with isolationism, Bryan took refuge in the belief that the fault lay not in the policy but in his ability to implement it. Remembering the days when, as a critic of American policy, the world had seemed simple and choices clear, he longed to be free of the burdens of office. His resignation was an act of protest and a sacrifice, but it was also a liberation.

In 1906, in a rare moment of self-analysis, Bryan had written: "I don't know that the Presidency will ever be my proper place. I do know that advocacy of what I consider right is always my proper place."[49] Almost ten years later that insight returned to him again, and lifting up his eyes from the papers on his desk, he strode forward onto the stage, renewed, refreshed, and himself once more.

When Bryan resigned from the State Department in June 1915, Wilson's supporters dismissed him as a crank who had run out when the going got tough. William Henry Walker's cartoon, "Don't make me laugh, Mr. President, I have a crack in my lip," in *Life,* July 1, 1915, was kinder than many. (William H. Walker Collection, Princeton University.)

Below: Bryan's antiwar activities were caricatured by William Henry Walker in *Life* on Nov. 11, 1915. The title was that of a popular sentimental song, "I didn't raise my boy to be a soldier." (William H. Walker Collection, Princeton University.)

7

"SOME NATION MUST LIFT THE WORLD":
1915–1918

Once Bryan had thrown off the terrible responsibility of keeping the nation out of war, his idealism re-emerged to limit his isolationism. Continuing to believe that the issues behind the war were none of America's concern and that involvement would be a mistake, he nevertheless began to look forward to the end of the conflict and to wonder how America ought to share in the peacemaking. At first he thought mediation might be the way, but as the nation was drawn into the battle, he, like Wilson, concluded that only belligerents would set the peace terms. He did not welcome war, but when it came he reasoned that even out of such a catastrophe might come opportunity. "Some nation," he declared, "must lift the world out of the black night of war into the light of that day when peace can be made enduring by being built on love and brotherhood." Such leadership, he felt sure, was the "task that God in his Providence has reserved for the American people."[1]

Believing that "for 1900 years the gospel of the Prince of Peace has been making its majestic march around the world" and has been becoming "more and more the rule of daily life," Bryan regarded the war as the death throes of the old philosophy that "might makes right." It presented to the United States, as the exemplar of Christian democracy, a unique opportunity to lead the exhausted belligerents to a permanent peace based on Christian principles. Thus, paradoxically, where others saw in the war the end of progress, Bryan thought it a challenge to take a major step forward.[2]

Between 1915 and 1917, Bryan tried, as he had while secretary of state, to arrest the drift toward involvement and to encourage mediation. Since to a large extent his efforts paralleled those of pacifists and German-Americans, much of the urban press pigeonholed him in one category or the other. He quickly learned to avoid this trap. When German-Americans tried to use him, he refused to speak under their auspices, and at other times he emphasized that he was more concerned with avoiding the particular perils of this war than with maintaining an abstract pacifist principle. The essence of his message was that American national interest, not loyalty to the fatherland or ideological pacifism, should be the basis for national policy.[3]

Convincing the American people that their interests would be well served by continued isolation was not easy in the summer of 1915. On the contrary, deteriorating relations with Germany and increasing dependence on trade with the Allies made involvement in the war ever more likely. On August 19 a German submarine sank the *Arabic*, killing two Americans and compounding the still unresolved *Lusitania* case. When the British exploited this new German-American crisis by placing cotton on the contraband list and thus making cotton sales to the Central Powers almost impossible, Bryan was convinced that the increased dependence of southern planters on Allied markets would make settling problems with Germany even more difficult. Any protest to Germany should, he urged, be accompanied by another to Britain, and the government should free the planters of exclusive dependence on Allied markets by buying or loaning money on the cotton crop.[4]

Bryan's advice went unheeded. Although the German ambassador, Count Johann von Bernstorff, somewhat relieved the crisis on September 2 by promising that large liners would no longer be sunk without warning, the administration did not take the opportunity to protest British behavior. Instead the State Department lifted the remnants of Bryan's loan ban and permitted the Allies to float a half-billion dollar loan in the United States, which tied Americans even more closely to the Allied cause. Bryan protested what seemed to him a sadly mistaken course, but to no avail.[5] Other more serious changes in American policy were in the offing.

During the early months of the war Wilson had agreed with Bryan that increased American armaments were more likely to push the nation into war than keep it out. In the spring of 1915, however, as public pressures for preparedness grew, and as relations with Germany, Japan, and several Caribbean nations worsened, the president began to change his mind. That summer he planned a program for the expansion of the army and navy, and early in the fall he began a discreet campaign to win congressional support for his plans. On November 4 he announced his conversion to preparedness and urged the immediate passage of his program. His proposals, although far more limited than those advocated by such bellicose citizens as Theodore Roosevelt, seemed a fire bell in the night to Bryan, who regarded any preparedness program as dangerous and provocative.[6]

As in the struggle against imperialism, Bryan found himself forced by the preparedness controversy to refine his isolationism. In both cases he was compelled to recognize that the nation could not fulfill what he regarded as its duty if it simply rejected all world responsibility. And just as his anti-imperialism had combined a fear that expansion would contaminate the United States and a faith that Americans could find better ways to exert world leadership, his opposition to preparedness was both a selfish desire to escape the burdens of war and a generous urge to help the belligerents.

In opposing preparedness Bryan was once again reflecting commonly held opinions among his supporters. The South and West, the Bryan sections of the country, opposed preparedness, and Bryan shared their conviction that "No nation has any intention of attacking us, and if any nation had such a design, the ocean is a barrier which makes a successful attack impossible." Moreover, even if American isolation were not a sufficient protection by itself, at the rate the European belligerents were "killing off soldiers and burning money," American strength was "increasing RELATIVELY as other nations exhaust themselves." Since the issues of the war were of no interest to the United States, there could be no possible need for a costly preparedness program, especially since the nation was already spending for defense "ten times as much as we are spending on the department of agriculture."[7]

Those who advocated preparedness, Bryan suspected, usually cared more about their own profit than about the national interest. Because Congress, which reflected the views of all the people, was not in session while Wilson developed his preparedness program during the summer of 1915, Bryan feared that the president had been misled by misrepresentations in the eastern press and by such leaders as Theodore Roosevelt, whom Bryan characterized as "a human arsenal, a dreadnought wrought in flesh and blood." "The common people," who "heard Christ gladly when he was preaching his gospel of 'peace on earth, good will toward men,' " could not possibly want any such program as Wilson suggested. Its supporters must therefore be the shadowy powers behind the press and behind such politicians as Roosevelt—the bankers, the armaments manufacturers, and their allies like the Navy League (a private organization founded in 1902 to build public support for the navy), who stood to profit from war. He urged a congressional investigation of what he described as a well-organized conspiracy "supported by unlimited means," and although forced to back away from wild charges leveled at the Navy League, he continued to make the conspiracy argument central to his antipreparedness campaign.[8]

In many ways Bryan's antipreparedness fight was a return to the themes of 1896—the people threatened by a conspiracy of the special interests. It was almost as if, having been released from the constrictions of office, the Commoner was reverting to an earlier, more conspiratorial view of the world, a vision more in keeping with the provincialism of his youth than with the greater sophistication of his middle years. Alarmed by the growing popularity of preparedness and believing that the nation was moving toward war, he tried to persuade himself that American interests were not endangered except by the selfish machinations of the powerful, and that the public—his public—wanted peace at almost any price.

Yet even as he campaigned against preparedness, Bryan admitted that head-in-the-sand isolationism was neither desirable nor practical. "I cannot agree . . . ," he wrote, "that either national necessity or national welfare requires non-intercourse between nations." Commerce brought practical benefits, and even more important, the exchange of ideas was a route to progress. "Wisdom," he said, "has no pent-up habitation. . . . As individuals grow in breadth of mind, depth of thought and clearness of vision by a comparison of views, so nations are enlarged, strengthened and developed by intercourse. . . ." The nation might wish to limit its commitments to other countries, but it had an obligation to truth and progress to make its ideals available to the world. The war, Bryan suggested, was the real test of America's conviction that better methods could be found to solve international conflicts. To abandon the ideal when it was most threatened was to acknowledge its unworkability or to shirk the responsibility of leadership. The real basis for the Commoner's opposition to preparedness, a correspondent suggested to Wilson, was "his Christian conviction that this great Nation should stand forth as an example to all Nations and peoples of the earth in refusing to even prepare for war."[9] In that attitude the isolationist was reunited again with the missionary.

In preference to preparedness, Bryan urged Americans to avoid all threats, treating both belligerents as friends rather than enemies, to apply the principle of impartial investigation to the disputes with Germany, to set aside insoluble disputes to be dealt with after the war when tempers had cooled, and continuously to seek opportunities for offering mediation. This was precisely the same program he had urged on Wilson prior to his resignation, and the president was no more receptive now than he had been then. Nevertheless, Bryan believed that his suggestions were both practical and reflective of the real wishes of the American people.[10]

Convinced that he knew better than Wilson what Americans wanted, Bryan urged the president to seek a direct expression of public opinion before committing the nation to war. Except in the event of a direct attack, he argued, a declaration of war ought to be preceded by a national referendum. He first suggested this idea in July 1915 and thereafter pressed it steadily, fully confident that given the opportunity the people would almost always choose peace over war and that whichever they chose, they ought to have a direct voice in so crucial a decision. The proposal had a double appeal to him, satisfying both his conviction that the people wanted peace and his commitment to democracy, but others did not see it as a panacea. Neither the public at large nor Congress evinced much interest in the idea.[11]

Bryan's most formidable challenge to Wilson's control of foreign policy came not on the question of a referendum on war but on the adoption of voluntary restrictions on American neutral rights. During the spring of 1915, Bryan had become convinced that Americans must be kept off belligerent vessels in the war zone in order to eliminate dangerous incidents. Those who needlessly exposed themselves, he had argued, were guilty of "contributory negligence." Wilson's rejection of his suggestion was one of the reasons for the secretary's resignation after the sinking of the *Lusitania,* and when the *Arabic* was sunk in August, Bryan revived the idea publicly, adding to it a proposal that American ships be forbidden to carry passengers and munitions at the same time.[12]

Early in January 1916, following the sinking of the liner *Persia* and the loss of two more American lives, resolutions embodying Bryan's suggestions were introduced into Congress by Democratic congressmen Claude Kitchin, Dan V. Stephens, Jefferson McLemore, and Senator Thomas P. Gore. Bryan endorsed the Gore-McLemore Resolutions, as they came to be known, enthusiastically, and there was such general support for them, particularly among Democrats, that they seemed sure to pass. Wilson, who objected strongly to any such curtailment of American rights, now found that he could not command a majority in Congress. Only by shifting the ground of the debate to the question of the president's right to control foreign policy free from congressional interference was he able, with great difficulty, to defeat the resolutions.[13]

Although disappointed at the loss of the resolutions, Bryan felt that he had won most of what he wanted. A congressional majority, he pointed out in a front-page editorial in *The Commoner,* had not supported the resolutions, but most congressmen had made clear their desire to keep Americans out of the danger zone and the nation out of war. The president would have to heed the warning. For the first time in months involvement in the war did not seem quite so inevitable.[14]

On March 24, 1916, when the French channel steamer *Sussex* was torpedoed and four Americans were injured, Bryan's slender gains were obliterated. House and Lansing called for an immediate break in diplomatic relations with Germany, and Wilson sent a note on April 18 that warned the Germans that unless submarine warfare against "passenger and freight-carrying vessels" was terminated at once, the United States would have to sever relations. Bryan, on his way to New Orleans when the note was announced, got off the train at St. Louis and hurried to Washington. There he urged members of Congress to insist on a peaceful settlement of the crisis, but in fact there was nothing anyone in Washington could do about it. Wilson's note had put the initiative into German hands, leaving Berlin the choice of whether or not to force a break with the United States. As it happened, they chose to announce that they would give up submarine warfare, but they coupled this concession with an ominous threat that unless the United States compelled the Allies to live up to the "laws of humanity," Germany might have to go back to the submarine. The president rejected the condition, but matters were now largely out of his control.[15]

Like most Americans, Bryan regarded the *"Sussex* pledge" as a solution to the submarine problem and a triumph for Wilson. On this basis he was able to overcome previous reservations about Wilson's handling of foreign policy and to announce his support of the president's renomination. At the Democratic convention in St. Louis, though not a delegate he was called upon to speak, and he responded with a speech lauding Wilson and the platform. Following the convention, he campaigned enthusiastically for the president through twenty western states, evading his own doubts by arguing that Wilson's domestic record and success in keeping the nation out of war entitled him to a second term. When the election was over it became apparent that the Commoner's evocative combination of peace and domestic reform still carried a powerful magic in many areas of the country. Fifteen of the twenty states in which Bryan campaigned went for Wilson and provided the margin of his narrow victory.[16]

Encouraged by the support for his position implicit in the election outcome, Bryan decided it might now be time to shift the focus of his efforts from keeping the nation out of war to promoting mediation. From the beginning of the war he had felt that ending the war through American mediation would be the ideal way of rendering disinterested service to the belligerents and the only sure method of keeping the nation from being sucked into the conflict. As secretary of state, he had constantly urged mediation on the president and was never satisfied that enough was being done to press it upon the belligerents. One of his reasons for resigning was to free himself to urge mediation publicly.

Immediately after his resignation, however, Bryan had found that the growing crisis with Germany made it imperative for him to concentrate all his efforts upon arousing public opposition to the drift toward war. During the summer of 1915, friends urged him to consider traveling to Europe himself to promote mediation, but for the time being he believed it was more important to carry his antipreparedness case to the people. Although he had suggested such a trip to the president in the autumn of 1914 and still found it appealing, he was temporarily willing to let leadership of the private mediation effort be taken over by others.[17]

With Bryan out of the running, others took up the mediation project. The result was Henry Ford's ill-fated peace ship expedition which departed for Europe in December 1915. Ford was eager to have Bryan join the group, but the Commoner, perhaps warned off by the sideshow atmosphere attending the project, did not sail on the ship. Wishing the effort well, he promised to join it later in Europe, but when the mediators squabbled among themselves and even Ford gave up and came home, Bryan found pressing reasons to stay in America. An official government mediation offer, he concluded, would have more chance of success than any private effort.[18]

In the winter of 1916, with the election over and the *"Sussex* pledge" reducing tension with Germany, Bryan revived the idea of a trip to Europe. On December 6 he called at the White House to acquaint Wilson with his plans. The president had already been thinking about making a peace proposal when the moment was ripe, and now, forewarned of Bryan's idea by Ambassador Gerard in Berlin, he decided to act at once. Very soon, he told the Commoner, he intended to send a note to the belligerents asking them to state their war aims. As this was a step Bryan had been urging since the beginning of the war, and one that he felt certain would reveal a basis for compromise, he immediately gave up his plans for a private trip. Leaving Wilson with a request that he be included on any peace commission, he returned home, filled with high hopes.[19]

On December 12 the Germans formally asked American assistance in arranging a peace conference. Delighted, Bryan immediately cabled British Prime Minister Lloyd George to urge the Allies to seize the moment, and in telegrams to the belligerent ambassadors in Washington, he implored their assistance to the same end. When, on December 18, Wilson sent his message asking the warring nations to state their aims as a preliminary to the calling of a peace conference, it appeared that Bryan's prayers had at last been answered.[20]

The president's note, Bryan thought, could not fail to bring peace. Surely, he argued, "neither side will consent to assume responsibility for continuing the unspeakable horrors of this conflict, if any reasonable terms can be secured." To ensure the fulfillment of the U.S. mission of moral leadership without internal divisions, he urged Senator William E. Borah to sponsor a bipartisan Senate resolution applauding the president's course. Borah and other senators, however, were alarmed by a suggestion in Wilson's note that a postwar association of nations might help to keep the peace, and thus even an innocuous resolution of praise passed only narrowly.[21] Bryan, who had earlier criticized suggestions for a League to Enforce Peace, suppressed any doubts he might have had concerning Wilson's course, but not all isolationists were equally optimistic.

In fact, Bryan's view of America's world role was again changing. At the beginning of the war he was sure that the only interest of the United States in the conflict was to see it ended quickly. By the end of 1916, however, he had begun to believe that a stable and lasting peace was every bit as important as a speedy end to hostilities. Even American membership in a league of nations was conceivable if it would assure acceptance for the "reasonable" peace terms he wanted. Where the experience of the war tended to drive Borah and others deeper into a protective shell of isolationism, it pushed Bryan in the opposite direction toward a recognition that the United States might be able to play a part in averting such catastrophes in the future. As at other times in his career, a foreign crisis challenged Bryan to enlarge his definition of America's world role. The parting of the ways between Bryan and Borah that first appeared in their disagreement over Wilson's December 1916 peace proposal would be of importance in the future.

The peace proposal itself was ill fated, and Bryan, who had felt momentarily elated, found his hopes dashed. On December 26 the Germans called for a peace conference of belligerents, excluding neutrals. Four days later the Allies spurned this idea, and on January 10, 1917, they issued a list of preconditions for a meeting that destroyed any prospect of a conference. Wilson, now convinced that the situation was desperate, tried to avert disaster by suggesting peace terms himself in his January 22 "peace without victory" speech, but the Allies ignored his appeal, and the Germans announced on January 31 that they would begin unrestricted submarine warfare in a zone around the British Isles. Dismayed at the rapid deterioration of the situation, the president warned his private secretary, "This means war."[22]

Bryan feared the same thing. Although he had assured Wilson that the president's "peace without victory" speech would place him "among the Immortals," he soon recognized that it would not sway the mortals who governed the warring nations. If the United States was to avoid war, it must be by its own actions. Hence he issued an "Appeal to the American people" reiterating his familiar suggestions for postponing and avoiding conflicts and rushed to Washington to work with Senator Robert M. LaFollette in a frantic, futile, two-day effort to line up progressives of both parties to halt the slide toward war. On February 5, beaten, he went home. Two days later the Senate endorsed the president's severance of diplomatic relations with Germany by the overwhelming vote of 78 to 5.[23]

Now under attack by some politicians and segments of the press as a near-traitor, Bryan had little hope of being able to affect events. At the end of February he came again to Washington to encourage the "little group of willful men," as Wilson called those who were filibustering against the administration's Armed Ship Bill, and to lobby for a series of resolutions requiring a referendum before a declaration of war, but the publication of the Zimmermann telegram just as he arrived pretty well cut the ground out from under his efforts. After the president went ahead in mid-March on the basis of existing law to arm merchant ships even without the passage of the Armed Ship Bill, and after three American ships were sunk on March 18 and 19, Bryan was certain that war was inescapable. On March 28 he sent a final appeal to all congressmen and senators, urging them to support the application of his peace plan to the German dispute, to ban American travel on belligerent ships, to prevent passengers from traveling on ships carrying contraband, and to pass a bill calling for a referendum before a declaration of war. It was the same old program, and the legislators ignored it. On April 2 the president went before Congress to ask for a declaration of war.[24]

There was little in these hectic days to please Bryan, who struggled so long to keep the United States outside and above the European conflict, but, characteristically, he found evidence even at his darkest moment that America's example was being emulated. The overthrow of the Russian czar and the establishment of a republic demonstrated, he believed, the inevitable progress of democracy around the world.

Although his initial joy would later fade in the face of the Bolshevik takeover, for a moment he took the events in Russia as an omen that even war might produce progress.[25]

In deciding his own course during these dark moments Bryan accepted what he had been unable to prevent and hoped for the best. There was never any question in his mind; once war was declared, he pledged his fullest support to the government. "Gladly would I have given my life to save my country from war," he told a crowd on the day war was declared, "but now that my country has gone to war, gladly will I give my life to aid it." In keeping with this spirit, he telegraphed to the president his willingness to take on "any work I can do," including serving as a private in the army if necessary. He really thought, however, as he confessed to Josephus Daniels, that he was "too old to learn the art of war," but he was perfectly serious in wanting to serve. The administration, overwhelmed with volunteers who wanted to be generals, was delighted to find one who did not and promptly accepted his offer to do whatever was needed. Throughout the war he toured the country urging Americans to buy Liberty Bonds, conserve food, and raise larger crops. He entered into these drives wholeheartedly, particularly since he could, in advocating food conservation, advance the cause of prohibition at the same time by pointing out that vast quantities of grain were wasted in the production of alcohol.[26]

In addition to making speeches and donating to worthy causes like the Red Cross and the YMCA, Bryan also conducted a vigorous campaign for national unity. No matter what anyone had thought about the wisdom of entering the war, he argued, once the majority had decided, everyone must unite behind the government, support the Allies, and win the war. "Any discord or division, after the government has acted," he declared, "would prolong the war and increase its cost in money and men." And ever optimistic, he discerned hope in the future: "We must not only protect ourselves from those who are now our enemies, but we must find an opportunity for world service in aiding to arrange a permanent peace, built on justice, liberty and democracy."[27]

Believing that "freedom of speech is essential to representative government, and publicity is essential to honest administration," Bryan went slightly less far than some of his fellow patriots in demanding perfect conformity. Conscientious objectors were entitled to toleration, he thought, provided they accepted whatever limitations the government put on their behavior and did not try to influence others.

Likewise, ordinary citizens ought to refrain from divisive public debate, but they had a duty to make their opinions and wishes known to their representatives through the mail. And Congress had a positive obligation to discuss and debate policy fully; to give up this right would be to subject one branch of the government to another, to substitute despotism for democracy.[28]

Bryan sometimes found it hard to follow his own advice about avoiding public controversy. He criticized the new Bolshevik government in Russia even before it withdrew the Soviet Union from the war, he chastised the British and French for bombing German cities, and he demanded a fairer tax program at home that would put the burden of paying for the war on the wealthy and on those who stood to profit from it.[29] The truth was that though he was fully loyal, he was never really comfortable about the war. He applauded Wilson's Fourteen Points and tried to believe that the world would be reborn out of fire, but in his heart he still felt that example was a more effective and lasting teacher than force.

In supporting the war, Bryan undeniably violated some of his most basic principles. Beyond suppressing his doubts about the utility of force as an instrument of international policy, he acquiesced in excessive curtailments of national liberty undertaken in the name of patriotism. Respect for law became a demand for national conformity, and Bryan, whose whole career had been a testimony to the idea that reform requires endless debate of issues and education of the public to the necessity for change, now argued that there should be no national debate just at the crucial moment when war and peace policies that would affect the nation for years to come were being decided. Better than most people, he knew that governmental directions are not altered by letters to congressmen but by sustained public campaigns; yet driven by the desire to bring the killing to an end as soon as possible, he set his own experience aside for the duration of the war. In the interests of unity and efficiency he abdicated his duty to encourage debate and discussion of the vital issues facing the nation.[30]

The line between constructive debate and disloyalty always becomes blurred in nations at war, and even the most democratic governments usually err on the side of enforcing conformity rather than encouraging liberty. In choosing to gag himself, Bryan reflected prevailing national sentiment. In his mistakes as in his wisdom, he was a mirror of his followers. It is regrettable that he did not take a broader view in this case, but he would not have been the Commoner had he done so. He never realized that in following the public will so slavishly, he had perhaps done democracy a disservice. He might have served his country better by raising the issues that most Americans preferred not to think about during the war.

On the other hand, Bryan's antiwar arguments before 1917 challenged Americans to make difficult and important choices. He and Wilson agreed on the desirability of keeping the nation out of war, but the differences in the methods by which they would have pursued that aim were important. Only in retrospect did it become obvious that Bryan was right in believing that total war had so engulfed Europe that nothing the United States could do would compel the warring nations to respect American rights. The defense of American rights was incompatible with neutrality. If the nation really wanted to stay out of the war, Bryan's proposals, or some variation of them, offered the only available way.[31]

Whether the specific things Bryan proposed would have kept the nation out of war, and whether staying out would have been in the national interest, can only be questions for speculation. Since his loan ban was subverted, and his proposals to forbid American travel on belligerent ships or in the war zone, to prevent passenger ships from carrying contraband, and to require a referendum on a declaration of war were rejected, it is impossible to say what such policies might have accomplished. The fact that most controversies with the belligerents were over rights that Bryan would have given up suggests that strict adherence to his proposals might have been effective in minimizing incidents and reducing the friction that aroused the ire of Americans.

On the other hand, Bryan never came to grips with some of the more basic issues. He had no solutions to problems created by a pervasive pro-Allied sentiment among American leaders, no recommendations for dealing with the economic chaos that would have resulted from a complete embargo on trade with the belligerents, no real idea of whether or not the maintenance of a balance of power in Europe was important to the United States. Above all, Bryan never came to terms with his own and his nation's idealism. Neither he nor most of his countrymen could ever quite convince themselves that the bloody carnage in Europe did not concern them. As isolationists they aspired to perfect security, but in the end they found they did not want it if the price was the sacrifice of their ideals.[32]

Bryan constantly asserted that the outcome of the war was of no importance to Americans, but his eagerness to find examples of the progress of democracy in spite of war and his growing belief that a durable, fair peace was essential to world stability and long-range American interests contradicted his own arguments. As soon as he admitted to himself that it mattered who won, or that a certain sort of peace was desirable to the United States, it became difficult for him to maintain that the government should follow a course of noninvolvement. Nor could he really maintain that as a neutral the United States would have a moral influence on the belligerents; that was obviously not true. It was in fact a tacit admission that example had not been effective when he argued for the suspension of some rights, and it seems probable that in part a subconscious recognition that he cared about the outcome of the war and wanted to influence it eased the way for him to support the administration's policy after April 6, 1917.

If Bryan's proposals were ambiguous in conception, they were also practically unobtainable. When he resigned from the State Department, whether he knew it or not, he surrendered any real chance to influence policy. As a private citizen, despite a still substantial following, he could not overcome the political strength of the president and the hostility of most of the press, which depicted him as either a fool or a traitor. Bryan tried to be careful about his associations, but his connection with the Ford peace ship venture, his attacks upon a supposed conspiracy of the rich, his ill-informed diatribes against the Navy League, and his crusade for prohibition associated him with the lunatic fringe in many people's minds. Outside the structure of the two major parties, Bryan's proposals, whatever their merits, simply could not gain serious consideration.

Perhaps most difficult of all for Americans to understand and accept was the fact that the whole issue of war and peace was largely out of their control. Unless the United States was prepared to give up all its trade with Europe, which Bryan never suggested, the belligerents were free to treat the nation's ships as the exigencies of war dictated. What was more, Washington could offer mediation, but nothing compelled the belligerents to accept it, unless they thought it in their interest. Unable to protect its interests short of war or complete withdrawal from the world, and unable to force a peace on the frenzied combatants, the United States could only endure or fight. Bryan would have endured longer than some of his countrymen, but it was only a matter of degree, and in the end he must have been as relieved as everyone else when the president cut the Gordian knot by asking for a declaration of war.

On December 3, 1915, Bryan met with Henry Ford at the Waldorf-Astoria hotel in New York as Ford tried to persuade the Commoner that he should sail to Europe on Ford's peace ship. (Library of Congress.)

Below: Bryan and his wife, Mary, besieged by well-wishers and reporters at the Washington Naval Conference in 1922. Bryan was only an enthusiastic spectator, not a delegate. (Library of Congress.)

8

"OUT OF THE BLACK NIGHT OF WAR": 1918–1925

The experiences of World War I substantially changed and broadened Bryan's concept of America's world role. Before the war he had talked glibly about American obligations to lead the world toward peace and democracy, but as secretary of state he had accepted real commitments only in the Western Hemisphere, backing out of long-standing involvements in China and rejecting any responsibility for improving conditions in Europe. During the war, however, he began to realize that the peace and stability of the whole world were matters of concern for the United States. As a result, at a time when many Americans were turning their backs on the world and settling into comfortable isolationism, Bryan urged his countrymen to participate in and lead international efforts to avert conflicts and encourage cooperation. He was still no internationalist, but he now took account of the waning of the era of America's geographical security, thereby bringing his idealistic isolationism more into harmony with the realities of a changed world.

Before the war, Bryan was inclined to think that world peace could be assured through the application of some simple formula that would require a minimum of international cooperation and involvement. His own investigation treaty program fitted this definition, and he advanced extravagant claims for it as a panacea for the world's troubles. When the war began, he was sure not only that application of the investigation principle would solve America's conflicts with the belligerents but that the existence of a worldwide network of investigation treaties before the summer of 1914 would have prevented the war altogether.

Others who looked at the complex tangle of conflicts that led to hostilities in 1914 doubted that any such easy step would eliminate war. The internationalists, and even some nationalists, suggested that only an active commitment by peace-loving nations to enforcing the peace and settling clashes could be expected to have any real chance of maintaining world order. It was this belief that lay behind the founding of the League to Enforce Peace in June of 1915. The founders of the league, who included William Howard Taft, Theodore Marburg, Hamilton Holt, and other prominent Americans, drafted a proposal for the submission of all international disputes to an international tribunal for investigation and recommendation of solutions. Any nation that went to war without first submitting a dispute to investigation would be subject to collective economic or military sanctions by other members of the league.[1]

As a proponent of a different method of settling world conflicts, Bryan welcomed an opportunity in the autumn of 1915 to engage in a written debate with William Howard Taft on the proposals of the League to Enforce Peace. The main thing wrong with the league's program, he argued, was that it was based on the European doctrine of using force to compel peace, and it was thus contrary to the traditional American belief in leadership by moral example. By undertaking to "police Europe," he asserted, the United States would invite European nations to interfere in the Western Hemisphere, undermine the independence of Congress in deciding whether or not to declare war, and destroy America's ability to stand as an example to the world. There could be, he pointed out, no analogy between the use of police within a country to enforce the law and the use of international sanctions to maintain peace. Within a nation, the criminal was an individual who violated a commonly agreed upon moral and legal code; in the international sphere no such codes existed (indeed, Bryan suggested that none could exist because European values were so different from American ones), and the violator was a nation, against which enforcement almost certainly meant war—the very thing the league was supposed to prevent. He suspected, in fact, that the league's reliance upon force would encourage members to build up armaments—ostensibly to do the league's bidding—and thus actually increase rather than decrease the danger of conflict.[2]

Bryan's objections to the program of the league were a little overstated but not too far off the mark in light of subsequent world peace-keeping experience. The greatest weakness of his argument was that he had little constructive to offer in place of the league program. To move the discussion forward, he needed to offer some alternative to the league's proposals that would meet his objections to its ideas and give substance to his own idealistic vision of American world leadership. He seemed to sense this challenge in his debate with Taft, but he had not yet gone far enough beyond the simplistic formula of his investigation treaties to be able to give his hopes concrete form.[3]

During the debate with Taft, the best that Bryan could suggest was an effort to eliminate what he regarded as the causes of war. Hence he urged taking the power to declare war out of the hands of governments and putting it, by means of referenda, into the hands of the people, whom he thought naturally pacific; he recommended a general reduction of armaments to levels only sufficient for internal policing; he proposed bringing the influence of public opinion to bear on all disputes by submitting them to investigation; he suggested creating international guarantees of the integrity of small states; and he advised the promotion of the spirit of love and brotherhood as the only real solution to the problem of war. Himself the most peaceable of men, Bryan found it hard to imagine that anyone but monarchs and profiteers wanted war. The common people, who had to fight, die, and pay war taxes, must surely hate it. War, therefore, could be eliminated by Christianizing the world's people and by putting them securely in charge of all governments. To the extent that Christianity and democracy were accepted, war would tend to disappear.[4]

Although it would be hard to deny that universal obedience to Christ's principles would minimize conflict, Bryan's suggestions hardly illuminated a clear path to the goal he sought. His belief that democracy and Christianity would eliminate all conflicts was naive; his argument that force was necessary to maintain order within nations but could be eliminated in international relations was self-contradictory; and his assertion that democratic Christianity would wipe out war was more millennial than practical. At best, Bryan's prescription seemed likely to save the patient only after a very long and unpleasant illness.

Bryan was not oblivious to the fact that Christianity and democracy were long-range solutions to a problem that demanded immediate palliatives. In his debate with Taft he argued that his objection to the League to Enforce Peace was only partly to the organization's dependence on force; more specifically, it seemed to him that in the league the United States might be compelled by the votes of less democratic, less Christian nations to use force against its will. Admitting tacitly that force might have a place in keeping the peace, he suggested that instead of joining the proposed league the American people consider simply giving a promise that the United States would join in the "punishment of any nation which resorts to war without an excuse which to us seems sufficient." Such a policy he thought himself would be neither "wise nor necessary," but he pointed out that "it would have all the advantages conferred by membership of *[sic]* the proposed League without its dangers."[5] Although this particular proposal was so carefully hedged and qualified that it meant almost no modification of Bryan's original beliefs that force had no place in peacekeeping, and the United States no place in peace-keeping organizations, it was the first indication that he might be changing his ideas in response to new challenges.

During the months that followed the debate with Taft, Bryan apparently continued to think about alternatives to the program of the League to Enforce Peace, and in March 1916 he advanced another idea. The nations, he suggested, should create a court to which all disputes would be referred. Decisions of the court applying to the Western Hemisphere would then be entrusted for enforcement to the nations in that hemisphere, while those pertaining to other areas (Europe and Asia were those he cited) would be enforced by the nations in each area. As an additional safeguard, although the original decision would be reached in a court in which all the nations would take part, it would be enforced only if a majority of the nations in the appropriate area accepted it. In instances of disputes between nations in different regional groups, he believed that the time required for investigation and the dispassionate advice of uninvolved nations would be sufficient to assure a peaceful settlement without the need for enforcement.[6]

Bryan's suggestion was of course absurdly unrealistic and impractical, and he himself quickly abandoned it. Nevertheless, it deserves attention because it demonstrates the beginning of changes in the Commoner's attitudes that would eventually enable him to advocate ratification of the Treaty of Versailles. It shows a growing willingness on his part to think about associating the United States with other nations in a cooperative search for peace, and in combination with his suggested promise to the nations during the debate with Taft, it indicates a recognition on his part that force might be necessary to maintain peace. Gradually, under the pressure of war, Bryan was beginning to accept the idea that the United States could not evade the world's problems completely or solve difficulties only by unilateral example.

Since he had thought and talked so frequently about the ways to achieve peace, Bryan hoped that he might be included in the American peace delegation in 1918. Never one to let himself be overlooked when such an opportunity was at hand, he besieged the president with appeals to be considered for the post and begged all his friends to recommend him also. The president, inundated by letters recommending Bryan, had no intention of appointing him. Bryan, he told Secretary of the Navy Josephus Daniels, would be regarded by the public as too idealistic and too soft on Germany, and his appointment would displace closer advisers like House, or Lansing. Perhaps also lingering in the president's memory was Inauguration Day 1913, when the crowds along Pennsylvania Avenue had seemed to cheer Bryan as loudly and enthusiastically as the president. At this moment of triumph, Wilson wanted no potential rivals to overshadow him. When the American delegation sailed for Europe, a deeply disappointed Bryan remained at home.[7]

Undaunted by the president's rejection, Bryan offered his advice anyway. Applauding the Fourteen Points in general, he placed particular emphasis on the idea of eliminating secret treaties and on the reduction of armaments (with due regard for differing national needs). He was enthusiastic about the principle of self-determination but suggested that it might be more palatable if coupled with a requirement that new governments promise to purchase at fair market value the property of people who did not wish to live under the new regime. He also warned that any treaty which burdened Germany with excessive reparations would create an unstable situation in Europe, and he suggested that other possible causes of conflict among the nations be removed by making the Bryan investigation principle the heart of the peace and by requiring referenda before declarations of war. A plan to clarify his position further through another written debate with William Howard Taft had to be abandoned, however, when Bryan was laid up for a month with facial erysipelas.[8]

By the time Bryan recovered from his illness, the general shape of the proposed League of Nations was clear, and Wilson had returned to the United States briefly to find himself confronted by an uprising of Republican senators who informed him, in the so-called Round Robin of March 4, 1919, that they could not support the league without substantial modifications. Bryan seemed to share many of the feelings of these senators about the importance of amendments. Publicly, he suggested that the United States, the most powerful nation in the world in terms of population, wealth, and "moral influence," should have a greater vote; that entrance to the organization should require only a majority, not two-thirds support; that the Monroe Doctrine should be specifically protected; that no nation should be compelled to take mandates; that internal affairs be specifically excluded from league authority; that all nations be free to follow or ignore the recommendations of the league in regard to the use of economic sanctions or force; and that the league should be given the power to apportion among the overpopulated nations the "waste places of the earth," provided that the inhabitants of such areas were given an opportunity to sell their property to the new government and move out.⁹ It thus sounded as though all of the Commoner's objections to the League to Enforce Peace would be carried over to the League of Nations—and more besides.

The reasons for Bryan's suggested modifications to the League of Nations were essentially the same as the reasons for his objections to the League to Enforce Peace. He believed that peace must be based upon the winning of hearts, not upon coercion, and he was determined to protect American freedom of action. He was, therefore, perfectly willing to see amendments adopted which would limit the league's power to coerce miscreants, or which, at the very least, would permit the United States to stand aside from such actions if it disagreed with them. From both an isolationist and an idealistic point of view, he was inclined to favor amendments to the charter.¹⁰

Yet despite his doubts about the league, Bryan said flatly that it was "the greatest step toward peace in a thousand years" and proclaimed his intention to support it. Confounding those pundits who had anticipated his objections but not his conclusion, he declared that even if *none* of his proposed amendments were adopted, "the risks we take in accepting it are less than the risks we take if we reject it and turn back to the old ways of blood and slaughter." To his brother he admitted privately that he had overstated his objections to dramatize his insistence upon the importance of joining the league. The United States, he proposed, should ratify the treaty and then work from within the organization to improve it, just as twenty years earlier he had urged the nation to approve the treaty with Spain and then free the Philippines. The new treaty might be imperfect, but "our nation could not reject it without stultifying itself." It was, he thought, clear evidence of the triumph of American idealism: "The world moves forward, the United States leading the way." Joining with the president, he urged the Senate to approve the treaty without amendments.¹¹

There can be no doubt that Bryan's attitude toward the League of Nations in 1919 differed substantially from his approach to the League to Enforce Peace in 1915. Times had changed, and Bryan's ideas had changed too. The war had demonstrated that democracy and Christianity had not yet progressed far enough to eliminate conflict, and as early as 1916 he had begun to think that force might sometimes be necessary to maintain peace and order. In one sense his acceptance of the League of Nations was simply another step along a path he had begun to walk even before the United States entered the war. It was a path that wartime propaganda about fighting to make the world safe for democracy had made broader and smoother.

There were also some differences between the League to Enforce Peace and the League of Nations that seemed important to Bryan. Under the proposed charter of the League to Enforce Peace, the threat of force was employed to make disputants submit their conflicts to investigation, while under the League of Nations covenant the presumption was that the league itself could initiate investigation, and force would be used, if necessary, only to compel the nations to submit to the league's findings. This difference was, to Bryan's mind, crucial, because he thought that the investigative and deliberative functions of the league would almost always make the use of force unnecessary. Describing Article 10 (which called on members to act collectively against aggression) as "excess baggage," he emphasized that in his view the league was important not for its power to coerce but for its ability to focus public opinion and promote moral progress in the world. Unlike Wilson, who saw the league's primary importance as an instrument of collective security, Bryan hoped that its success in appealing to men's hearts would show the value of "substituting reason for force."[12] If one assumed that the League of Nations would exercise its influence mainly through deliberation and investigation rather than through coercion, there was an underlying consistency in Bryan's position between 1915 and 1919.

Bryan's view of the league as an investigative and deliberative body rather than a police organization meant that he did not really care about the details of the charter or worry about proposed Senate reservations to limit the organization's powers. Provided the league could investigate, he was quite willing to curtail any of its other functions. It seems likely, therefore, that his decision to support unconditional ratification of the Treaty of Versailles was more a gesture of loyalty to Wilson and the Democratic party than a matter of real conviction.

Nevertheless, having committed himself to unconditional ratification, Bryan struggled manfully for it. By the end of September 1919 the treaty fight was reaching a critical stage. Henry Cabot Lodge was delaying action in the Senate while public opposition gathered, and the president was stumping the country to arouse public support for the treaty. On September 24, Bryan met with fourteen Democratic senators in Washington to try to overcome some of their doubts. There was some evidence that he had been successful, but on the next day Wilson collapsed. Bryan expressed the hope that the Senate would react to the president's illness by passing the treaty at once and without reservations, but he knew better. Without Wilson's constant, vigorous leadership, Senate Minority Leader Gilbert Hitchcock warned Bryan, the prospects for the treaty looked pretty bleak.[13]

With Wilson ill and rejecting all of Hitchcock's suggestions for some compromise with Republican reservationists, leadership in the treaty struggle began to pass to Bryan. The turning point was the first test vote on November 19, 1919, which made it obvious that the Democrats could not command a two-thirds majority for unconditional ratification nor could the Republicans win ratification with reservations. When Wilson still refused to face facts and called upon Senate Democrats to hold out for unconditional ratification, Bryan decided the time had come to speak out publicly for compromise. The situation, he pointed out in a letter to Democratic senators, was dangerous not only because of the possibility that the United States would not join the league but also because failure to settle the issue before the 1920 election would force the Democrats to campaign on an indefensible position, make likely a bolt of reformers from the party, and thus assure the victory of Republican reactionaries.[14]

On January 8, 1920, at two Jackson Day dinners in Washington, Bryan openly challenged the president, capping a private campaign to work out compromises with a public call for recognition of the necessity of concessions to Republican strength. A few days later he sent telegrams to several senators urging immediate action, and thereafter he kept up steady pressure for ratification with whatever reservations were necessary to buy enough Republican votes to pass the treaty. It was a courageous and sensible position, but Wilson, even ill, was still the president and the head of the party, and he rejected all compromise and instructed Senate Democrats to stand firm. On March 19, Bryan's birthday, the treaty again came up for a vote, and with most Democrats insisting on an unamended treaty and almost all Republicans favoring Lodge's reservations, neither group was able to gain the necessary two-thirds majority. That evening, at a birthday dinner in New York, Bryan was uncharacteristically pessimistic; the political and economic situation was deteriorating in Europe, he said, and American failure to join the League of Nations might mean another major war.[15]

The Senate vote made it obvious that not only would the election of 1920 likely center on the league issue, but the Democratic convention was almost certain to be a battleground as well. The president, despite his illness, was pondering a third term and dreaming of electoral vindication. Bryan was not interested in the nomination himself, but he was determined to nominate a progressive and to commit the party to accepting reservations to the league covenant that would permit a compromise with the Republicans on that issue. To his mind, unconditional ratification was hopeless, and renewal of the party's reform commitment was vital.[16]

When Bryan carried his fight to the convention, he found that Wilson, although persuaded not to run himself, was solidly in control of the proceedings. Typically, the Commoner arrived with a slate of possible candidates and a complete platform draft, but he was able to win little more than a friendly hearing for his ideas. On the league issue the platform, as adopted, endorsed Wilson's "firm stand against reservations designed to cut to pieces the vital provisions of the Versailles Treaty." Bryan thought this suicidal and tried to get it altered, but the best he could do was to get a final clause added saying that the party did not "oppose the acceptance of any reservations making clearer or more specific the obligations of the United States to the League Associates." On other issues, including a recommendation that the party support a constitutional amendment to provide for Senate approval of treaties by a simple majority rather than two-thirds, he was completely defeated. And the nomination of James M. Cox, who endorsed ratification without amendments and opposed prohibition, seemed to Bryan a disaster. Despite Cox's pleas for support, for the first time in his political career Bryan sat out an election silently.[17]

The truth was that as Bryan became less active in party affairs, he was putting more stress on issues and less on partisan loyalty. More and more involved with such moral questions as woman suffrage, prohibition, and the antievolution crusade, he was finding men of similar views in both parties. Progressive Republicans like LaFollette, Borah, Hiram Johnson of California, and William S. Kenyon of Iowa were not only more attuned to his domestic political aims than many Democrats but shared some of his idealistic isolationism as well.

Temporarily estranged from Woodrow Wilson, whose obstinacy he blamed for the fiasco of 1920, Bryan was inclined to give even Warren Harding a chance to show what he would do. Soon after the election the Commoner suggested that Wilson resign early to clear the way for Harding to take office at once and get started organizing his proposed "association of nations." The proposal was ignored by Wilson of course, but Harding apparently appreciated the gesture and in mid-December invited Bryan to a conference in Ohio. Later the Bryans were hosts to the Hardings during a visit by the president-elect to Miami.[18]

It is hard to know how seriously Bryan took Harding's association of nations talk. Of course the idea of an international organization based entirely on investigation and moral suasion rather than on coercion appealed strongly to him. "Details" of such a plan, he argued enthusiastically, were unimportant. What was crucial was to lend American weight to an effort to reverse a world-wide trend toward rearmament and conflict.[19] At the very least, Bryan was willing to wait and see what the new president would do.

Before long it became obvious that Harding had no intention of doing anything. He would neither create a new organization nor join any existing one. Bryan was distressed by this attitude. He still had some doubts about the League of Nations, but he thought that developing tensions in Europe and Asia made it imperative for the United States to join "any . . . tribunal that is trying to promote peace," including the league and the World Court. He was now convinced, he told one correspondent, that "our country should throw its moral influence on the side of world peace, accepting invitations to every conference." The one condition he would set upon such cooperation with other nations, he added, was that the United States must reserve "independence of action" after it had conferred with others.[20]

The importance of Bryan's insistence upon reserving freedom of action may easily be overestimated. All but a tiny handful of Americans (and citizens of other nations as well) insisted upon such a guarantee. What is noteworthy about Bryan's position is that it was actually much closer to Wilson's internationalism than to Harding's ultranationalist isolationism. As had always been true during the most creative phases of Bryan's career, world crises challenged his isolationism and led him to discover more and more American obligations to the world community. Where many Americans preferred to forget about the world as much as possible or tried to convince themselves that the power of example was sufficient leadership, Bryan insisted upon a more strenuous duty of active service. He was doomed to failure but never to discouragement.

One international problem that most Americans hoped to ignore was the tangle of debts and reparations that had grown out of the war. The Versailles treaty had provided that the United States would be represented on the commission that was to set the amount of reparations to be required from Germany. It was generally assumed that the Americans would moderate the demands of the British and French, but of course when the Senate rejected the treaty, the United States did not take a seat on the reparations commission, which promptly set reparations at nearly $32 billion, plus interest. The reaction of most

Americans to this debacle was that the United States had opposed saddling Germany with such vast obligations, and hence the nation had no further concern with the matter. Certainly, they thought, there could be no connection between reparations and the debts owed by the Allied governments to the United States. These debts, amounting to a little over $10 billion, plus interest, were regarded as matters of honor, and there could be no question of linking them to the sordid reparations problem. It was, Americans generally agreed, up to the Allies to pay the debts, and if to do so they chose to squeeze the Germans for reparations payments, that was no affair of the United States.

Bryan refused to accept the convenient fiction that the United States had no interest in the reparations question. The peace and stability of Europe were endangered by it, he thought, and he urged the government to lend at least its "moral prestige and its disinterestedness" to efforts to resolve the problem reasonably. Actions such as the French occupation of the Ruhr, he argued presciently, only worsened the situation by undermining the stability of the German republic and antagonizing the Germans. Always an opponent of reparations, Bryan came to feel that exacting them had been one of the worst mistakes of the Treaty of Versailles.[21]

Since it seemed unlikely that the British or French would agree to give up reparations as long as the United States insisted upon having the debts paid, Bryan thought the situation offered an opportunity for America to make a substantial contribution to world peace. Noting that the debts would probably "never be paid," he proposed that the United States renounce them in return for Allied promises of disarmament. By so doing, he argued, America would deprive the Allies of their excuse for squeezing the Germans and promote the cause of disarmament. In the long run, he thought, a reduction of European tensions would permit the United States to reduce its own armaments and thus save more money than the debts were worth.[22]

The plan was too visionary for shuttered minds. Josephus Daniels, one of Bryan's most ardent admirers, objected that if the British were not compelled to pay up, they would use the money saved to buy oil concessions the United States needed, and President Coolidge myopically dismissed the idea with the remark, "It has not seemed moral to me to cancel obligations." Even Senator Borah, with whom Bryan often agreed on foreign policy isues, could not be persuaded of the value of this plan. Despite Bryan's enthusiastic persuasiveness, his proposal was ignored.[23]

Undiscouraged by his failure to convince others that the debts offered the best route to disarmament, Bryan urged that it be sought in other ways. "I am in favor of disarmament by agreement if we can get agreement," he told a correspondent, "by example, if we can not reach agreement. . . ." What better opportunity could there be for the United States to set an example for the rest of the world? "This," he argued, was "the time for the Christians of the world to unite with a view to building universal peace on the basis of friendship and cooperation," and he strongly urged the churches and church organizations of America to take an active part in committing the nation to such a policy. With an idealism that went beyond anything Wilson had suggested, he proclaimed that "Our motto should be: 'Disarmament—by agreement if possible, by example if necessary.' "[24]

Bryan's attitude toward disarmament in the 1920s suggests an important point about idealistic isolationism in general. Provided that he was not afraid of threats to national security, the idealistic isolationist might actually favor a *bolder, more active* foreign policy than the internationalist because he combined missionary zeal with a belief that the nation could change the world through its own unaided action. When not restrained by healthy fear, the idealistic isolationist verged on a faith in American omnipotence that could produce hare-brained schemes beyond the wildest dreams of an internationalist whose fantasies were bounded by the necessity of securing international agreement and cooperation. Bryan's unilateral disarmament proposal, his suggestion in the early 1900s that the United States renounce the use of force to collect debts in Latin America, his eagerness to withdraw from the loan consortium in China, and his efforts to remake the governments of various Caribbean nations were all examples of idealism unrestrained by any recognition of the necessity or desirability of international cooperation. For all its constructive role in setting unselfish goals of international service, idealistic isolationism was unstable. On one side it could tip toward panic and total withdrawal from the world, as it did for Bryan between 1915 and 1917, and on the other it could float over the rainbow to a land where reality was reshaped with a wish. Only when the two tendencies remained in a wobbly equilibrium did it offer anything like a reasonable basis for policy.

By the early 1920s, Bryan enjoyed a certain international reputation among men of goodwill who hoped that the world might somehow have been changed by the experience of World War I. The former American ambassador to Germany proposed the Bryan treaties as a viable alternative to American membership in the league; indeed, the idea of investigation was a fundamental part of the league itself, being embodied in Article 12 of the covenant. The plan was also included in the charter of the Permanent Court of International Justice (the World Court) when that was established in the late summer of 1920, and it was endorsed as a model conciliation plan by the assembly of the league in September 1922. At a Central American conference early in 1923 it formed a model for a program of international investigation of regional disputes, and it proved to be the only item upon which all of the participants in a league-sponsored disarmament conference in 1922 could agree. In addition, some newspapers suggested that the Bryan treaties played a role in reducing tensions arising from Anglo-Japanese-American rivalry in the Pacific, that they served as the model for bilateral treaties in various parts of the world, and that they were one of the sources of the multilateral Locarno treaties. Amid the chorus of international acclaim Bryan was only mildly disappointed that his plan failed to win the Bok Peace Prize when he entered the contest in 1925.[25]

Shortly before his death that same year, Bryan wrote a letter to the editor of the *Forum* summing up the direction his ideas about foreign policy were taking in a period when the United States seemed relatively safe from foreign threats. America, he wrote, should set an example for the rest of the world by unilaterally reducing its armaments, by supporting efforts to make war and conquest illegal, and by promoting the adoption of national referenda on war except in cases of actual invasion. As Dr. James Brown Scott, a distinguished American jurist and an expert on international law, later wrote, Bryan's ideas were in the vanguard of the peace movement of the 1920s, which culminated in the adoption of the Kellogg-Briand Pact of 1928, which declared war illegal.[26] Although the Commoner did not live to see it, the treaty was indeed a fitting monument to an idealistic isolationism that promised to change the world with a wish.

Wholeheartedly in favor of such broad schemes for the reformation of human behavior, Bryan was more guarded in his endorsement of the limited steps actually taken by the nations to resolve their differences. He favored the principle of disarmament, for example, but the actual disarmament agreements concluded at the Washington Naval Conference of 1921–1922 made him a little uneasy because they seemed to compromise the nation's freedom of action to some degree.

Growing out of Anglo-American-Japanese concern about a developing naval arms race and other frictions in the Pacific area, the Washington conference had its immediate genesis in a congressional resolution sponsored by Senator Borah in December 1920. Bryan joined the general applause for Borah's idea, and after the resolution was endorsed almost unanimously by both houses of Congress and accepted by other nations, he campaigned vigorously to be included in the American delegation. Again, as in 1918, he was unsuccessful, but he attended all of the sessions as a reporter and basked in the recognition of being invited to dine with such notables as H.G. Wells and Robert Laird Borden, former prime minister of Canada.[27]

Bryan was elated by the first session of the conference at which Secretary of State Charles Evans Hughes stunned the delegates and the world by proposing concrete disarmament plans. Believing the conference might be successful beyond initial expectations, Bryan went to every session, and when the delegates ran into trouble winning Japanese approval of disarmament proposals, he urged a compromise formula on the American delegation. His suggestion was not accepted, but he was relieved when other concessions to the Japanese eventually induced them to sign the Four-, Five-, and Nine-Power Treaties that were the major products of the conference.

Yet despite his general enthusiasm, such specific agreements made Bryan a little nervous. Was there not a danger, he wondered, that the Four-Power Treaty might bind the United States against its will to action desired by the other signatories? President Harding, himself no advocate of broad American commitments in the world, wryly assured the Commoner that there was no danger. The Senate, said Harding, "would be very unhappy if it did not have opportunity to write a reservation," and so it proved. Several reservations protecting the signatories' freedom of action were proposed in the Senate, and eventually one was adopted. Delighted, Bryan now urged Democrats to join with Republicans in approving all the treaties. The conference, he concluded, had not done all that idealists might wish in terms of limiting land as well as naval armaments, but what it had achieved marked, nevertheless, "the beginning of an epoch."[28]

The dawning epoch of 1922, the golden era of idealistic isolationism, lasted less than a decade, yet while it lasted, it was possible to believe that the world was growing better and better merely because Americans wished it to be so. Even the Bolshevik regime in Russia could not last, Bryan declared confidently, because it was neither democratic nor Christian, and hence it was out of phase with God's unfolding plan for the world.[29] In the absence of visible threats to American interests, dreams of world leadership expanded without limitation; isolationism and idealism did not seem to conflict at any point. Like most of his fellow countrymen, Bryan believed the great national illusion of the 1920s—that the nation's prosperity, security, and happiness were the inevitable rewards of superior virtue. The illusion would be rudely shattered in the 1930s by the Great Depression and the beginnings of World War II, but Bryan was not there to experience the revival of panicky fear so like his own between 1915 and 1917.

Confident that the world tide was running in America's favor in the early 1920s, Bryan laid special stress on the issues of moral regeneration that seemed to him the basis of the nation's domestic happiness and world standing. Although compelled by his own and his wife's declining health to pay special attention to making money in order to provide for his family's security, he nevertheless devoted the largest part of his time to the promotion of two great moral issues—prohibition and fundamentalism.[30] Thousands flocked to his weekly Sunday school classes, and thousands more looked to him for leadership in the struggles against liquor and religious modernism. A little tired but by no means discouraged, the Commoner did not see himself as fighting a rearguard action to protect a retreat but as leading the vanguard of a victorious host.

It was in that spirit that he came in the summer of 1925 to a hot courtroom in Dayton, Tennessee, to assist in the prosecution of John Thomas Scopes for the teaching of the theory of evolution in violation of Tennessee law. He did not feel he was defending a weak position, but rather he was confident that if the issues could be put before the American people, they would embrace the Christian view. For that reason he allowed himself to be put on the stand as an expert witness, secure as he had always been in the belief that "the example of an upright person, living a life of service according to the Christian ideal, is more eloquent than any sermon—it is the unanswerable argument in favor of our religion."[31]

Scopes's lawyer, Clarence Darrow, was not interested in the influence of Christianity upon the life of an individual or a nation. He was interested in winning his case even if to do so he had to humiliate and discredit the prosecution's most eminent witness, who happened to be an old friend. Bryan should have anticipated that and did not, but even more, he should have made it his main goal to demonstrate that fundamentalism and bigotry, intolerance, and reactionary politics were not inevitably linked. In failing to refute that implied correlation, Bryan not only undermined his case, but he allowed Darrow to wipe from public memory a distinguished thirty-year career of commitment to social justice at home and the promotion of peace in the world.[32] The real tragedy of Dayton for Bryan was not that he was ridiculed in the urban press—that was nothing new—but that having set out to show the example of a Christian life, he failed to make clear that Christian service was the cornerstone of his religion.

Throughout his life Bryan overestimated the influence and underestimated the ambiguity of example as a teacher. Already made painfully evident by the Dayton fiasco, that point was underlined with tragic irony a week after the end of the trial, when Bryan suddenly died. Seeking once again to set an example, the Commoner had asked that he be buried at Arlington National Cemetery. The request was honored, but the message of his example was not very clear, either to his contemporaries or to later biographers. "I think it is proper and fitting," said Mrs. Bryan, "for he battled for America, too, and he battled for the God of his fathers, courageously, unafraid," but others wondered why a near-pacifist should choose to lie in a national military cemetery.[33]

To me, the Arlington grave suggests not merely the paradox of a pacifist interred among soldiers but a more fundamental contradiction as well—Bryan's inability to recognize and reconcile the conflict between his missionary impulse to world service on the one hand and his desire for the security of perfect isolation on the other. When in balance, the two drives could provide the basis for a cautiously idealistic policy uniting service with self-interest, but the balance was always precarious, and at times one instinct or the other predominated in dangerous fashion. Like many Americans of his generation, Bryan was tempted by the opportunities offered by growing American power, yet at the same time he and they dreamed of the vanished security of an earlier, simpler age. They could not have it both ways, but unwilling to go back, they were still unable to commit themselves fully to go forward.

9

A LIFE OF CHRISTIAN SERVICE

In the thirty years of his public career Bryan never quite shifted all the way from the populist isolationism of his youth to Wilson's internationalism, but, as Wilson himself admitted, neither did most Americans. In foreign policy, as in so many other areas, the Great Commoner reflected widespread American attitudes.

The incompleteness of Bryan's change should not blind us to just how far he had come. In the 1890s he paid little attention to the outside world and regarded it, with the provincial suspicion of the "boy orator of the Platte," as dangerous and corrupting. Three decades later he supported American membership in the League of Nations, urged his countrymen to accept a permanent role in the affairs of Europe and Asia, and insisted that the United States could and should exercise world leadership. The same Christian idealism that led Bryan into public service in the 1890s also led him, step by step, to a commitment to world service by the 1920s.

The shifts of Bryan's attitudes over the years demonstrate his ability to change and grow in response to circumstances, as well as the mutability of American isolationism in general. Although isolationism is frequently thought of as the monolithic bedrock of American political sentiment in the late nineteenth and early twentieth centuries, Bryan's career suggests that this idea is too simple.

Isolationism was never monolithic. Isolationists agreed on very little except the basic principle that the United States should avoid entanglement in the ordinary vicissitudes of European politics. The application of that principle was, however, a matter of constant and frequently heated debate. A central theme of the debate appeared as early as 1793, when Jefferson and Hamilton disagreed about American policy toward the wars of the French Revolution. Both wanted neutrality, but their reasons for choosing that course, and their judgments about its feasibility, were revealingly different. Hamilton advocated neutrality to allow the nation time to develop its economic and political stability—in short, for practical, nationalistic, reasons. Jefferson recognized the importance of such practical interests but worried even more that the cause of republican government everywhere would be threatened if war led to an American defeat or to the adoption of an authoritarian government in the United States. On the other side, he argued that if the French invoked the alliance of 1778, the United States would be honor-bound to adhere to it. Both of his arguments were essentially idealistic. In this early debate were revealed basic issues that would constantly recur. Isolationists might take their stands for either nationalistic or idealistic reasons, and just as frequently, they might find in self-interest or idealism plausible reasons for modifying isolationism.

A century later the same patterns were still evident. Bryan, an idealistic isolationist, justified his opposition to American involvement in World War I in idealistic terms, but he also used very similar language to explain his support for American membership in the League of Nations. Henry Cabot Lodge, an ardent nationalist, espoused an aggressively imperialistic policy in the 1890s, but in 1919 he insisted that Wilson's proposed departure from isolationism was fraught with unnecessary dangers. Idealists tended to rationalize both their adherence to and their departures from isolationism in idealistic terms, while nationalists tended to rationalize both in terms of national self-interest.

Isolationism in the United States was always unstable because it was never absolute. Even the most ardent isolationists welcomed economic and cultural contacts with the outside world, and their attitudes toward that world were frequently ambiguous. They feared foreign intervention in the United States, but they believed also that American institutions were universally admired and envied. If envy made others want to undermine the nation, it was also true that people envy only the things they covet. Far from being hermits, most American isolationists had a strong missionary instinct.

Circumstances helped determine whether the missionary or the hermit would dominate. In the early nineteenth century, when the nation was weak and external dangers real, caution generally prevailed. After 1815 the foreign threat receded, but expansion, sectional conflict, and economic growth kept the nation's attention at home. At the same time, however, immigration, technological progress, rising production, and ideological shifts drew the nation gradually into more and more contacts with other countries, while the same process of growth made Americans more aware of their own strength. Almost a century of security made it easy to believe that growing national power was actually omnipotence. For the moment the fears of isolationists were lulled, while missionary ambitions were stimulated. It was easy to forget how dangerous the world had been and tempting to dream of how beautiful it might be.

The irony of the situation was that the basis of American confidence, geographical security, was diminishing at the very moment that the willingness to act from that secure base was growing. The result was a period of experimentation in foreign policy that produced, nearly all at once, imperialism, anti-imperialism, internationalism, and isolationism. Adding to the ferment was the domestic reform movement of the period. Supremely conscious of the virtues of their institutions and determined to perfect them, the reformers were particularly susceptible to fits of both fear and overconfidence in dealing with the outside world.

Between the 1890s and the 1920s, isolationism grew more conscious and more sharply focused but also narrower and less universal. On one side it was challenged by the development of new foreign policy ideas that declared that American interests were not as well served by isolationism as they would be by some other course—imperialism, Roosevelt's nationalist assertiveness, or Wilson's internationalism, for example. On the other side, idealists found their isolationism weakened by their feeling that their goals and values might be better served by experimenting with internationalism than by trying to remain detached from the world. In fact, the success of the United States in avoiding foreign dangers during the nineteenth century lulled isolationist fears and made it easy to believe that America could do pretty much as it liked in the world.

The imperialism of the 1890s was a direct challenge to isolationism, although to most Americans it did not at first appear to be a challenge. Up to that time, expansion had meant only continental growth, and accordingly there had been no conflict between expansion and isolation.[1] In the 1890s some people began to fear that when expansion moved overseas, that would no longer be true. Although reviving isolationism was not the only source of anti-imperialism, worries that foreign colonies would draw the nation into international rivalries and invite others to meddle in the Western Hemisphere were important elements in the thinking of the anti-imperialists. Most people, however, paid little attention to the warning. Tempted by the lure of world power, they preferred not to think about possible perils, and even the anti-imperialists, feeling the lure of temptation, hoped it would be possible to have the nation take a world role without too much danger.

Yet the warning was sound. The movement of the United States into the Caribbean and the Western Pacific drew the attention of other nations to the Americans as possible rivals and involved the country in issues and areas it had concerned itself with very little before the twentieth century. By 1907 even so dedicated an imperialist as Theodore Roosevelt admitted privately that the Philippines had become America's "heel of Achilles," and most of his countrymen lost their taste for imperialism in the same period. As its temptations receded, the dangers of imperialism became obvious, and the lure of isolationism reasserted itself.

Partially replacing imperialism as an alternative to isolationism was Wilsonian internationalism. Its great appeal was that, unlike imperialism, it offered both influence and idealism. It could reunite anti-imperialists like Bryan, who yearned for world power without colonies, with idealistic imperialists, who had felt that governing colonies really was "the white man's burden" of service to other races. The idea of creating a new world organization modeled on American principles that would offer both justice and peace to the nations was irresistibly appealing to Americans' vanity and idealism, while at the same time it was soothing to their consciences to think that they were doing all this with no desire for material gain.

The vision of America galloping to the rescue of the world on its white steed was shattered at the Paris Peace Conference. American ideals were only partly shared by Allied leaders, and the peace treaty that emerged from the negotiations bore disturbingly little resemblance to the dream in Wilson's mind. For Americans who thought that internationalism had promised a perfect world, hope gave way to bitterness, disillusionment, and cynicism. Wilson fought as hard as he could for the treaty, but in the end he was forced to admit that the American people had lost faith in it. "If we had joined the League when I asked for it," he said in 1924, "it would have been a great personal victory. But it would not have worked, because deep down in their hearts the American people didn't really believe in it."[2]

For various reasons, therefore, both imperialism and internationalism were at least temporarily discredited in many Americans' eyes by the 1920s. The result was a resurgence of isolationism, or perhaps more accurately, the desire to tend to business at home and let the rest of the world look after itself filled the vacuum left by the collapse of more activist policies. Yet even as they washed their hands of Europe's affairs, many Americans realized that World War I had upset the European balance of power which had stabilized the Western world during the nineteenth century; it had removed the protective shield of British naval supremacy behind which the United States had flourished for a century.[3] Expanding trade and investments around the world also made it difficult for American businessmen to believe that it made no difference what happened beyond the nation's borders. Americans thus felt the "isolationist impulse" in the 1920s, but having little fear of any other nation, they merely avoided the League of Nations while at another, private level they carried on active programs of economic expansionism that contradicted the official policy of isolation.

The roots of the policy of the 1920s were in the challenging, experimental period before World War I. Flexing its new industrial muscles, in that period the United States for the first time confronted both the opportunities and the dangers of world power. The temptations were strong, but the risks were great, and people who had given little or no thought to foreign policy before the turn of the century gradually began to realize that they could not have one without the other. On that basis they began, gradually, to define their positions. For the most part this choosing of sides was not a conscious, deliberate process. People's educations, where they lived, their economic interests, and their stands on other, more personally urgent issues shaped their attitudes toward foreign policy also.

Geography was probably more important than anything else in determining foreign policy alignments.[4] As might be expected, proximity to the coasts and to large metropolitan centers predisposed people to interest in foreign policy, while those who lived in the country, away from cities and coasts, tended to isolationism. These patterns, frequently pointed out in regard to the 1930s, were equally and perhaps even more notable in the days of slower transportation and more limited communications before World War I. The South and West were bastions of anti-imperialism and opposition to American involvement in World War I. Not only did Bryan lead the antipreparedness and anti-involvement fights, but Bryanite Democrats from the South and West were leaders in opposing naval appropriations bills in 1915 and 1916, led the struggle to pass the Gore-McLemore Resolutions in 1916, and cast most of the few votes against the war resolution in 1917, to cite only a few examples.[5] Concentrations of German-Americans in the West further strengthened an already evident regional pattern.[6]

In addition to their physical remoteness from foreign policy issues, many rural Americans of the early twentieth century shared an individualistic, Jeffersonian philosophy that stressed a simple, limited government and depicted Europe as corrupt, hostile, and militaristic.[7] Such people were intellectually as well as physically distant from foreign policy concerns. They were fearful and suspicious of the outside world by conviction as well as because it was unfamiliar, and they were hostile to the development of a strong, centralized federal government that could conduct a dynamic foreign policy. Suspicious that all power was corrupting, such neo-Jeffersonians were especially disturbed by foreign policy because it evoked for them a fear of a military and professional elite unresponsive to democratic control. Any army larger than absolutely necessary "to maintain law and order in time of peace and to form the nucleus of such an army as may be required when the military establishment is placed upon a war footing" tended to "place force above reason in the structure of our government," declared Bryan.[8]

Geography was not an infallible predictor of foreign policy positions in the Bryan period, however. Because foreign policy was not usually very important to rural people in the South and West, they sometimes took inconsistent positions if by so doing they could gain an immediate, tangible benefit for their area. Although committed to anti-imperialism in 1900, southern Democrats supported the imperialist Platt and Spooner amendments in 1901 in exchange for other advantages for their section and divided acrimoniously over the Panama treaty in 1903 when it appeared that southern ports would benefit from the construction of an Isthmian canal. Only in times of crisis and threat did the regional isolationist impulse become really conscious, and then it could be formidable indeed, as Wilson found out in 1916 when he tried unsuccessfully to shake the commitment of southern and western Democrats to the Gore-McLemore Resolutions. In the election that autumn the president tacitly recognized the strength of southern and western isolationism by stressing the slogan, "He kept us out of war," and by sending Bryan to campaign for him in the region.

Partisanship also played a role in determining foreign policy positions for both parties during Bryan's period. Since the presidents from Roosevelt to Wilson pursued active foreign policies, the opposition party in each case was inclined to isolationism. The Democrats' anti-imperialism, for example, or the Republicans' attacks on Wilson's Mexican policy and on the Treaty of Versailles, were at least partly the result of partisanship. Bryan was certainly not immune to the temptations of partisanship, as he demonstrated in his attacks on the Hay-Pauncefote Treaty of 1901 and in his uninformed criticisms of Taft's dollar diplomacy.

Since the majority of Democrats who served in Congress before World War I came from the South and West, their partisan and sectional interests normally coincided on matters of foreign policy. During and after World War I, however, this situation began to change. Wilson pushed the Democrats toward internationalism, while the Republicans moved into isolationism. The result of this shift was the opening of something of a gap between Democratic political leaders and their followers in the South and West. Bryan obviously felt some strain as a result of this situation, and his eagerness to restore harmony with his supporters helps to account for his resignation from the State Department and for the fervor of his subsequent antiwar campaign.

Yet the Commoner found that he could not drop his party loyalties completely nor forget the things he had learned in Washington. Once the nation entered the war, he was drawn back to support of the president, and after 1920 both his own experience and his partisan instincts made him somewhat uneasy with the Harding administration's extreme isolationism. Because in this period he concentrated on prohibition and the evolution controversy, potential differences with his followers were little visible, but they existed nonetheless. Had he lived a few more years, when foreign problems again became acute, he might have found himself in an uncomfortable position.

Aside from his experience as a national leader, Bryan's divergence from his followers' attitudes toward foreign policy stemmed mainly from an important difference between him and them. Bryan was the poor man's candidate, but he was not poor; he was the champion of the uneducated and unsophisticated, yet he was fairly well educated himself, and over the years he became an experienced and knowledge-able politician; he was the spokesman of those who never quite captured the American dream, yet he was a successful self-made man. His tie to his followers was not that he was one of them but that he empathized with them. Largely because of his deep Christian princi-ples, he felt the needs of the less fortunate as if they were his own—but they were not.

In domestic affairs Bryan's greater experience and sophistication helped him articulate his followers' desires and needs more effectively than they could, but in foreign policy that did not always work. Essentially, Bryan's followers—the poorly educated, the politically unsophisticated, the poor, the culturally deprived, those outside the mainstream of American life—were those whom political psycholo-gist Herbert McCloskey has identified as most inclined to isola-tionism.[9] Bryan started from the same point as many of them and initially shared their prejudices, but he changed, and they did not. His political experience, as well as the very Christian principles which made him the champion of the less fortunate, pushed him toward a belief that the United States could not remain entirely isolated and must take a constructive, continuing role in world affairs.

In the 1890s, before he became more sophisticated, Bryan's views were essentially the same as those of his followers. He and they took a typically populist approach to foreign policy, arguing that foreign involvement of any kind would delay and impede domestic reform. Feeling themselves the oppressed victims of Wall Street capitalists, they sought to level privilege and restore democracy. A part of this process was to strike out not only against economic privilege but against a European culture and style of life to which they thought the eastern upper class aspired. "Their isolationism," one scholar argues, "expressed both their estrangement from Europe and their anxiety about the forms of American life."[10] Their goals of domestic reform and isolationism in foreign policy were in harmony, and in fact their attitude toward foreign policy was completely determined by their domestic objectives. One of the main objections Bryan expressed to what he described as an "English" policy of imperialism in 1900 was the fear that foreign involvement would interfere with domestic reform. Convinced that foreigners harbored malevolent intentions of subverting the American political system, the populists of the 1890s could not imagine anything but an isolationist foreign policy.

In the 1920s a quasi-populist attitude again seems to have become prevalent among western and southern farmers as the boom times of the prewar and wartime period gave way to a time of relative deprivation. Better off than their fathers in the 1890s, farmers of the 1920s nevertheless felt themselves less well treated than they deserved. The result of this situation was a revival of rural hostility to urban and "alien" values that seemed to threaten the traditional ways. This sense of threat motivated the prohibition and fundamentalist movements in which Bryan was so prominent, and it was the same distrust of metropolitan ways that lay behind the regional isolationism of the 1920s.[11] The political and economic issues espoused by the populists had given way to moral reformism, but the rural reformers of both the 1890s and the 1920s held attitudes toward domestic reform which identified foreign policy activism with threatening urban ideas and which strengthened isolationism.

Not all domestic reformers approached foreign policy the same way as the populists of the 1890s or the farmers of the 1920s. An entirely different attitude was exemplified by Republican progressives like Theodore Roosevelt and Albert Beveridge. Their interest in reform resulted less from sympathy with the downtrodden of America than from a desire to make the nation strong internationally. If the United States was not united and efficient, it would not have the world influence they wanted it to wield. They favored a strong, Hamiltonian government as the best means to achieve both the international standing and the domestic streamlining they thought desirable. They found imperialism and balance of power politics perfectly congenial, and they had no use for isolationism.[12]

Between the Roosevelt progressives and the conservatives like Henry Cabot Lodge the line was rather indistinct. Lodge and Roosevelt thought much alike on matters of foreign policy, differing only in their judgment about the desirability of domestic reform. So close were the two in many ways that it is quite possible that their differences can be attributed to nothing more than variations in personality and background.[13] Indeed, many conservative Republicans admired and followed Roosevelt's magnetic personality and dynamic foreign policy, finding those qualities so appealing that they could suppress doubts they may have felt about his domestic programs.

The great weakness of both the populist and the Roosevelt-Lodge approaches to foreign policy was that despite moralistic rhetoric, neither was really idealistic in its goals. The populist reformers paid lip service to idealism, suggesting that America could save the world by example, but they focused all their energies on domestic reform and obviously had no real interest in the outside world. Roosevelt and Lodge insisted stridently on the moral virtue of their policies, but what they did owed more to *Realpolitik* than idealism. Neither the populists nor Roosevelt and Lodge really offered much to Americans for whom idealistic principles were basic determinants of foreign policy.

It was this gap that could be filled by Bryan's idealistic isolationism or by Wilson's internationalism. Just as there were no vast differences between Lodge and Roosevelt, so there was much that Bryan and Wilson agreed on also. Emphasizing service as the main duty of government, they made little distinction between service at home and service abroad. Like Roosevelt and Lodge, their different backgrounds led them to differences of emphasis and focus, but both stressed an idealism that awakened a strong response in Americans for whom a sense of religious and political mission had always formed a major basis of foreign policy.[14]

A generation of Americans raised on the argument that "moralism" in foreign policy is bad and "realism" good may be unaware of the substantive, constructive influence of idealism on American policy over the years. If idealists were sometimes guilty of self-righteous meddling in others' affairs, they also set broad and generous goals for America in the world. The idealists' aims—peace, human rights, and the orderly resolution of conflicts—promoted the general welfare while, in a broad sense, they also served the national interest. After a generation of American leaders in the post–Civil War period who were mainly concerned with nationalistic and materialistic interests, Wilsonian internationalist idealism touched a responsive and neglected chord in American hearts. Like many other people, Wilson and Bryan were subject to the errors that men make when they try to translate great visions into practical policy, but their dreams had a rejuvenating and invigorating power nonetheless.

The difference between the Roosevelt-Lodge and Wilson-Bryan approaches to foreign policy was more than just a matter of superficial appearances. It reflected fundamental philosophical differences. Roosevelt had little faith in man's perfectibility and doubted the efficacy of sweeping solutions to human problems. He believed that in government only skilled, committed individuals had the resourcefulness to deal with problems as they came up. Imbued with pragmatism, he stressed goals rather than methods and depended more on tough, honorable men than on legal and constitutional reforms.[15] Wilson and Bryan, on the other hand, were shaped by a prepragmatic nineteenth-century liberal tradition which was reinforced by evangelical Protestantism. Thus they were more optimistic about solving basic problems through broad reforms than was Roosevelt. Edmund Burke and Thomas Jefferson, not John Dewey and William James, were the thinkers who shaped Wilson's and Bryan's ideas. With no apparent awareness of a contradiction, they combined an eighteenth-century faith in man's rationality and in the efficacy of constitutional and legal reforms with a romantic vision of the purity of the human heart and the inevitability of progress. Not only did they believe that they really could alter the world with the means then at hand, but they felt that time was on their side in so doing.

Yet for all their confidence in progress, Bryan and Wilson suffered attacks of impatience and frequently resorted to the use of force to make others do what they thought ought to be done. So common was this pattern, in fact, that it raises the question of whether something in their ideas justified and made likely the use of force.

Bryan summed up his attitude with the remark, " 'Go ye into all the world and preach the gospel to every creature,' has no gatling gun attachment."[16] He was never enthusiastic about the use of force, even in a good cause, as his attitude toward intervention in Mexico showed, and he was also realistic in his understanding that in some parts of the world, such as East Asia, the United States could not make much use of force even if it wanted to do so. Above all, he was always eager to find peaceful means for settling *all* disputes; force was never his first choice in any situation.

But if Bryan was reluctant to turn to the use of force, he never ruled it out flatly. No pacifist, he suffered no qualms of conscience about supporting the government during the Spanish-American War or World War I, and as secretary of state he authorized and even advocated the use of force in Latin America on several occasions.

Some of the contradictions in Bryan's ideas, in fact, tempted him toward the very forceful methods he abhorred. His confidence in the intrinsic superiority of American institutions and values made him sure that other peoples would want to imitate the American example and, paradoxically, made it easy for him to rationalize imposing those values on others. Had he been less sure that America was the promised land, he might have been less the militant missionary. Americans, he argued, were not only superior to those whom they were coercing, which of course warranted treating them roughly, but the people who were put under pressure would in the long run benefit from being forced to improve themselves. In time they would doubtless even be grateful.

Bryan's commitment to democracy also helped him rationalize the use of force. Although he opposed war before the conflicts of 1898 and 1917, once they were inevitable he argued that when the public will had been recorded, it was everyone's duty to rally round the flag. In 1917 in particular he would have liked an explicit expression of public sentiment in the form of a national war referendum, but even without that he acceded to the best available expression of the public's desires, the congressional resolution.

In his concern for the public will, Bryan was likely to fall into a trap. Not only was he constantly striving to read the American people's wishes, but in dealing with other nations he was tempted to try to discern their citizens' wishes as well. At its mildest the conviction that Americans knew better than the government of another country what its people wanted led to nonrecognition of a government deemed unpopular, as in Mexico. Where such limited pressures did not work, more extensive intervention was easily rationalized, as in Haiti or the Dominican Republic.

The two principles which generally governed Bryan's willingness to use force were that the goal in view had to be morally justifiable and that the security of the United States must not be endangered by the action to be taken. Fear was always a powerful restraint on Bryan's missionary impulses, but we should not underestimate the importance of moral restraints as well. He was always opposed to intervention in Latin America on what he described as "purely business grounds"; he advocated the abandonment of the practice of having the navy enforce the payment of loans owed to Americans by foreign borrowers; and he was less worried about such security-related matters as the safety of the Panama and Nicaragua canal routes than Roosevelt and Taft had been. He did not reject completely the possibility of using force to protect either commercial or security interests, but he felt far more comfortable about acting when he was satisfied that the people of the other nation would really benefit in the long run from the American action.[17] Suspicious of the aims of special interests at home and abroad, Bryan found in idealism an alternative basis for diplomacy. Although by no means infallible as a guide to action, his ideals served both to inspire a desire to serve others and to restrain the tendency for service to become dictation.

The number of the Wilson administration's interventions in Latin America, however, as well as Bryan's ability to rationalize support of intervention in World War I, demonstrate that idealism did not infallibly mean nonintervention. Both intervention and nonintervention could usually be defended in moral terms, and the Wilson record suggests that idealists may have been about as likely to come down on the side of intervention as nonintervention. I do not wish to suggest that Bryan's or Wilson's moral arguments were therefore hypocritical. They may well have been perfectly sincere. I merely wish to point out that the terms in which an argument is stated inevitably shape the action to be taken. Stating a problem in idealistic terms meant that its solutions had to be perfect; compromise became more difficult than when less apocalyptic issues seemed to be at stake. Intervention undertaken for idealistic reasons tended to produce efforts to reconstruct the society which was the focus of attention, and anything less than complete success in that effort seemed like failure. Such projects became open-ended and likely to involve profound emotional commitments on both sides. The very idealism of the Wilson administration raised special risks of intervention and made it likely that, once begun, intervention would be pushed to extremes beyond those sought by a less idealistic administration.

The central question about Wilson-era diplomacy, therefore, is not why such moralists were so willing to use force, but rather why they were as restrained in its use as they were. In Bryan's case the principal restraint was his isolationism. Where that was not a major concern, as in the Western Hemisphere, he could be flagrantly interventionist, whereas in Asia and Europe, regions traditionally off limits to American isolationists, he was much more cautious. Wilson, who felt the curb of isolationism less than his secretary of state, was equally willing to meddle in Latin American affairs but was also bolder in dealing with Asia and considerably more willing to involve the United States in European affairs. Until the war began, however, these differences were not apparent. The president and secretary were in almost perfect agreement about foreign policy up to that point. Their harmony resulted less from deliberate choice than from a lack of temptation to become involved in Europe or Asia and from the fact that they, like most Americans, paid very little attention to *any* foreign policy questions. Both delighted in setting Latin Americans' feet onto the paths of virtue, but they seldom looked beyond the hemisphere. The war changed all that. Wilson sensed in it new opportunities, while for Bryan it aroused old fears. The difference in their reactions led to disagreement and eventually to the secretary's resignation. Once the United States actually entered the war, however, the gap between the two men again shrank. The worst having happened, Bryan's fears receded, and his idealism brought him back into harmony with the president.

Throughout his public career Bryan approached foreign policy as he did domestic issues—in an intuitive rather than an analytical way. His attitudes and programs were shaped by a combination of Christian principles and his sympathetic understanding of the fears and desires of his followers. Derived from these two sources, his proposals were often inconsistent, sometimes self-contradictory, and rarely logically rigorous, yet they had great appeal because they were so often true to the feelings and moods of his supporters. Their logic was emotional rather than intellectual. Hope joined with fear, hostility with benevolence, anxiety with confidence, ambition with timidity, just as they did in the lives of the people who voted for Bryan in election after election.

Bryan's ability to express these mixed feelings in terms of both domestic and foreign policy was both a strength and a weakness. His approach assured him of the devoted support of millions of Americans over a three-decade public career, but it made him a much better advocate of causes than an administrator, and it subjected him to the ridicule of the analytically minded. For a candidate or critic, emotional consistency was more important than logical rigor, but as secretary of state, and again at Dayton, Tennessee, in 1925, he faced situations where logic and analytical ability were more important than intuitive harmony with his followers, and in those cases he was not very successful. For all his faith in the universal language of the heart, he had little success in persuading those whose mental methods were different from his.

The substance of Bryan's foreign policy reflected its tangled origins. Embodying on the one hand an evangelical Christian zeal for service and on the other a fear of the dangers and corruptions of the world, it sought both to reach out to others and to avoid being touched by them. The idea of missionary isolationism was satisfying to Bryan and to many of his followers, but it was almost impossible to translate into workable policy. It made the most sense when it was expressed in terms of America's mission to uplift the world simply by the power of example, and that theme recurred frequently in Bryan's statements throughout his career. In stressing America's exemplary role, Bryan reconciled isolationism with idealism and fitted foreign policy into the framework of domestic reform. The Puritan concept of a perfect society serving as an example for the world—the "city on a hill"—was as appealing to Bryan as to John Winthrop.

Yet circumstances seldom permitted the nation to adhere strictly to the balanced, harmonious vision of beneficent influence exerted from afar. As Bryan found while secretary of state, American strength tempted him to intervention, and the world's troubles frequently intruded into the streets of the hilltop city. Missionary isolationism proved to be unstable, as one element or the other predominated. Nevertheless, it endured, not because it was logical, but because its basic elements of faith and fear were so deep-rooted in American attitudes. No leader could reconcile the two feelings completely, and many preferred not to try, choosing instead one or the other. The public desire to have both persisted, however, and Bryan, less analytical than some politicians, felt that desire keenly without being intellectually aware of the impossibility of attaining it. In this as in so much else during his long career, the Great Commoner was less effective than he might have been as a political leader had he been willing and able to proceed from philosophy rather than intuition, but he was unmatched as a prophet of American confusion, uncertainty, and basic optimism as the nation stood poised on the brink of a new world of industrialism, urbanization, and world power.

Notes

[1]Louis W. Koenig, *Bryan: A Political Biography of William Jennings Bryan* (New York, 1971), 24.

[2]William Jennings Bryan and Mary Baird Bryan, *The Memoirs of William Jennings Bryan* (Chicago, 1925), 35.

[3]Ibid., 17–18.

[4]Borah quoted in James M. Cox, *Journey Through My Years* (New York, 1946), 409.

[5]Bryan, *Memoirs*, 25.

[6]Bryan explained his religious views in some detail at a world missionary conference in Scotland in June 1910. See *Commoner,* 10 (Aug. 19, 1910), 1. For a helpful analysis of his ideas, see Paolo E. Coletta, *William Jennings Bryan*, III, *Political Puritan, 1915–1925* (Lincoln, Neb., 1969), 205–8. Deeply committed to the ideal of service, Bryan admitted frankly that he had a good deal of trouble with the Presbyterian doctrine of "election," or predestination. He claimed to accept it, but in fact he leaned perilously close to the idea of salvation through works.

[7]Quoted in Coletta, *William Jennings Bryan,* III, 207. Bryan's commitment to the social gospel made him unusual among fundamentalists, most of whom tended to political as well as religious conservatism. About this, see Lawrence W. Levine, *Defender of the Faith: William Jennings Bryan, The Last Decade, 1915–1925* (New York, 1965), 260–6, 349; Willard H. Smith, "William Jennings Bryan and the Social Gospel," *Journal of American History* 53 (June 1966), 41–60.

[8]William Jennings Bryan, *The First Battle: A Story of the Campaign of 1896* (Chicago, 1896), 548; *Commoner* 15 (Oct. 1915), 1.

[9]Milton Plesur, *America's Outward Thrust: Approaches to Foreign Affairs, 1865–1890* (DeKalb, Ill., 1971), 74–86. Plesur is one of very few diplomatic historians to recognize and document the enormous importance of American missions and missionaries to foreign policy.

[10]The influence of missionaries on the Wilson administration's China policy is discussed in Ch. 6, below.

[11]Richard L. Metcalfe, comp., *The Real Bryan: Being Extracts from the*

Speeches and Writings of "a Well-Rounded Man" (Des Moines, Iowa, 1908), 174–5.

[12]Bryan, *Memoirs,* 456.

[13]Metcalfe, *Real Bryan,* 176–7.

[14]Ibid., 177–8, 174–5.

[15]Quoted in Levine, *Defender of the Faith,* 106; see also 121–2.

[16]*Commoner* 21 (Aug. 1921), 3; ibid. 16 (July 1916), 5; ibid. 22 (Nov. 1922), 3; Bryan to James R. Anthony, Feb. 10, 1923, BP.

[17]Bryan to William Jennings Bryan, Jr., June 17, 1922, NBP; *Commoner* 11 (Aug. 11, 1911), 6; ibid. 15 (Oct. 1915), 1.

[18]Paxton Hibben and C. Hartley Grattan, *The Peerless Leader: William Jennings Bryan* (New York, 1929), 217. For a more temperate but similar assessment, see Richard Challener, "William Jennings Bryan, 1913–1915," in Norman Graebner, ed., *An Uncertain Tradition: American Secretaries of State in the Twentieth Century* (New York, 1961), 79–100.

[19]Bryan, *Memoirs,* 34.

[20]*Commoner* 1 (Jan. 23, 1901), 1; Bryan, *Memoirs,* 204, 320, 12.

[21]Bryan, *Memoirs,* 12; *Commoner* 1 (Feb. 22, 1901), 1; ibid. 2 (Feb. 7, 1902), 3; ibid. 9 (Dec. 26, 1909), 5; ibid. 22 (July 1922), 5; Bryan to F.C. Howe, May 17, 1910, NBP; William Jennings Bryan, *Speeches of William Jennings Bryan, Revised and Arranged by Himself* (New York, 1911), II, 100–1; Levine, *Defender of the Faith,* 230–6.

[22]Bryan, *Memoirs,* 505; Metcalfe, *Real Bryan,* 100.

[23]Bryan, *Memoirs,* 261; Metcalfe, *Real Bryan,* 35.

[24]Selig Adler, *The Isolationist Impulse: Its Twentieth Century Reaction,* (New York, Collier ed., 1961), 15–23.

[25]Lodge quoted in Robert Beisner, *From the Old Diplomacy to the New, 1865–1900* (Arlington Heights, Ill., 1975), 13; Richard Olney, "International Isolation of the United States," *Atlantic Monthly* 81 (1898), 578–9.

[26]Adler, *Isolationist Impulse,* 20; John M. Cooper, Jr., *The Vanity of Power: American Isolationism and the First World War, 1914–1917* (Westport, Conn., 1969), 5n2.

[27]Quoted in Manfred Jonas, *Isolationism in America, 1935–1941* (Ithaca, N.Y., 1966), 10. See also ibid., 4–7; Cooper, *Vanity of Power,* 2–3.

[28]Adler, *Isolationist Impulse,* Ch. 1.

[29]Justus Doenecke, *Not to the Swift: The Old Isolationists in the Cold War Era* (Lewisburg, Pa., 1979), 21–2. Doenecke argues that recent scholarship has demonstrated that economic and geographical factors were more important in determining isolationism than ethnic ones. See also Scott Greer, "Urbanization, Parochialism, and Foreign Policy," in James N. Rosenau, ed., *Domestic Sources of Foreign Policy* (New York, 1967), 253–61.

[30]See William Appleman Williams, *The Roots of the Modern American Empire: A Study of the Growth and Shaping of Social Consciousness in a Marketplace Society* (New York, 1969).

[31]Paul Seabury, *The Waning of Southern "Internationalism"* (Princeton, N.J., 1957), 4–10. Seabury traces the roots of southern "internationalism" to

the post-Civil War period but notes that Anglophilia, which he suggests was the basis of later internationalism, was essentially an upper-class phenomenon, while Bryan's support, of course, came largely from poorer farmers. Their attitudes were more Anglophobic and certainly more provincial. See C. Vann Woodward, *Origins of the New South, 1877–1913* (Baton Rouge, La., 1951), 369–71. Even less work has been done on southern foreign policy attitudes of the late nineteenth century than on those of the rest of the country, but see the cautious and suggestive article by Alexander DeConde, "The South and Isolationism," *Journal of Southern History* 24 (1958), 332–46. Isolationism in the South, says DeConde, was "in many ways . . . more deep-rooted than its 'internationalism.' "

[32]For a discussion of the attitudes of southern Democratic congressional leaders after 1900, see below, ch. 3.

[33]Cooper, *Vanity of Power*, 3–4. Anglophobia in the silver campaign is discussed in ch. 2, below. Lodge's skepticism about America's ability to remake the world had deep New England roots. See William C. Widenor, *Henry Cabot Lodge and the Search for an American Foreign Policy* (Berkeley, Calif., 1980).

[34]Alexander DeConde, "On Twentieth Century Isolationism," in Alexander DeConde, ed., *Isolation and Security: Ideas and Interests in Twentieth-Century American Foreign Policy* (Durham, N.C., 1957), 4–5.

[35]Bernard Fensterwald, "The Anatomy of American 'Isolationism' and Expansionism," *Journal of Conflict Resolution* 2 (1958), 117–19.

[36]Koenig, *Bryan*, 25–9, 39–40.

[37]Arthur S. Link, John Wells Davidson, David Hirst, eds., *The Papers of Woodrow Wilson*, IX, *1894–1896* (Princeton, N.J., 1966), vii, 508n1.

[38]Paul Glad, *The Trumpet Soundeth: William Jennings Bryan and His Democracy* (Lincoln, Neb., 1960).

[39]Paolo E. Coletta, *William Jennings Bryan*, I, *Political Evangelist, 1860–1908* (Lincoln, Neb., 1964), 316, gives the circulation figure for the *Commoner*, which Bryan started just after the election of 1900. It was very much his voice, though his younger brother, Charles, and editor Richard L. Metcalfe also contributed unsigned editorials. It is difficult to get accurate circulation figures for the paper, because Bryan gave away literally thousands of free subscriptions, as well as free copies of individual issues.

[40]Metcalfe, *Real Bryan*, 36.

NOTES TO CHAPTER 2

[1]Quoted in Coletta, *William Jennings Bryan*, I, 75. See also Paolo E. Coletta, "Greenbackers, Goldbugs, and Silverites: Currency Reform and Policy, 1860–1897," in H. Wayne Morgan, ed., *The Gilded Age: A Reappraisal* (Syracuse, N.Y., 1963), 111–39.

[2]Walter T.K. Nugent, *The Money Question During Reconstruction* (New York, 1967), 105.

3Bryan, *The First Battle,* 407.

4Ibid., 337.

5William Jennings Bryan, "Foreign Influence in American Politics," *Arena* 19 (April 1898), 438.

6Bryan, *First Battle,* 337.

7Walter Millis, *The Martial Spirit: A Study of Our War with Spain* (Boston, 1931), 44–50, 80; Ernest R. May, *Imperial Democracy: The Emergence of America as a Great Power* (New York, 1961), 3–111; Margaret Leech, *In the Days of McKinley* (New York, 1959), 115–16.

8Eugene H. Roseboom, *A History of Presidential Elections* (New York, 1959), 311; Stanley L. Jones, *The Presidential Election of 1896* (Madison, Wis., 1964), 173.

9Richard Hofstadter, *The Age of Reform: From Bryan to F.D.R.* (New York, Vintage Books, 1960), 90; Hofstadter, *The Paranoid Style in American Politics and Other Essays,* (New York, Vintage Books, 1967), 184–5. A similar theory may be found in Paul S. Holbo, "The Convergence of Moods and the Cuban-Bond 'Conspiracy' of 1898," *Journal of American History* 55 (June 1968), 54–72. Holbo refers to "Bryanites," but his examples are almost all silver Republicans or Populists (e.g., p. 58), not Democrats. Holbo's theory is that "Bryanites" suspected the Republicans of opposing war because Republican leaders supposedly held Spanish bonds.

10J. Rogers Hollingsworth, *The Whirligig of Politics: The Democracy of Cleveland and Bryan* (Chicago, 1963), 134; Coletta, *William Jennings Bryan,* I, 221. The idea that Bryan was jingoistic gained currency soon after his death. See, for example, Merle E. Curti, *Bryan and World Peace,* Smith College Studies in History, vol. XVI, nos. 3–4 (Northampton, Mass., 1931), 116–19.

11Bryan, *First Battle,* 628–9; Arthur Sewall to Bryan, Dec. 3, 1896, B.P. Sewall was the Democratic vice-presidential candidate in 1896.

12*New York Times,* Feb. 27, 1897, p. 3.

13"The Trans-Mississippi Congress," *Literary Digest* (Aug. 7, 1897), 428; "Annexation Policies," *American Monthly Review of Reviews* 15 (Aug. 1897), 135; Julius Pratt, *Expansionists of 1898: The Acquisition of Hawaii and the Spanish Islands* (Chicago, Quadrangle ed., 1964), 224. The idea of recognizing Cuban belligerence was popular among partisans of Cuban independence in both parties. They seemed to think it would assist the Cubans, but probably it would have had the opposite effect by tightening the requirements of the neutrality laws and thus cutting off supplies from the rebels. It might also have permitted the Spanish to refuse to pay claims for damages done by rebels to American property in Cuba. Both Cleveland and McKinley regarded the passage of any congressional resolution recognizing belligerence as an infringement on executive prerogatives.

14Wayne C. Williams, *William Jennings Bryan* (New York, 1936), 206–7; *New York Times,* Feb. 26, 1898, p. 2.

15Coletta, *William Jennings Bryan,* I, 220–2; May, *Imperial Democracy,* 149.

16See, for example, the *New York World,* Apr. 1, 1898. Paul S. Holbo,

"Presidential Leadership in Foreign Affairs: William McKinley and the Turpie-Foraker Amendment," *American Historical Review* 72 (July 1967); Holbo argues that by April 1, McKinley had decided that the Spanish were not negotiating in good faith with the United States.

[17]*New York World,* Apr. 1, 1898, p. 3. Only late editions of the paper carried the speech, and then it was pushed to page 3 by the news of the crisis and Washington's reaction to it.

[18]*New York Times,* Apr. 14, 1898, p. 6. Hollingsworth, *Whirligig,* 134, says that Bryan appeared at the April 13 Jefferson Day dinner waving a Cuban flag in one hand and an American one in the other. I cannot confirm this even in the more sensational account of the speech printed in the *New York World,* Apr. 14, 1898, p. 8.

[19]C. Vann Woodward, *Tom Watson, Agrarian Rebel* (New York, Galaxy Books, 1963), 334–5.

[20]Senator James K. Jones to Bryan, Apr. 29, May 9, 1898, BP; Hollingsworth, *Whirligig,* 131–2; Holbo ("Convergence of Moods," 59) cites the expressed hopes of silverites but does not mention their recognition of the impossibility of the dream.

[21]For a detailed study of this myth, see Holbo, "Convergence of Moods."

[22]*New York Times,* Apr. 17, 1898, pp. 1, 2.

[23]Holbo, "Presidential Leadership," 1322–5.

[24]Ibid., 1328–9.

[25]Ibid., 1330–2; *New York Times,* Apr. 19, 1898, p. 1; *New York World,* Apr. 15, 17–19, 1898. For the debates and votes, see *Congressional Record,* 55th Cong., 2nd sess. (1898), pp. 4004–12, 4017–19, 4023, 4027–40, 4069, 4073–84. The motives behind the Teller Amendment remain obscure. Teller himself was an expansionist who later voted for the annexation of the Philippines. His own explanation of the amendment was that it was designed to head off possible European intervention in the Spanish-American War. See Paul Varg, "The United States a World Power, 1900–1917: Myth or Reality?" in John Braeman, Robert H. Bremner, and David Brody, eds., *Twentieth Century American Foreign Policy* (Columbus, Ohio, 1971), 324–5. Other explanations include pressures from the American sugar lobby, who wanted to keep Cuban sugar outside the tariff wall, and the idealism prevalent at the outset of the war. See Thomas A. Bailey, *A Diplomatic History of the American People,* 8th ed. (New York, 1969), 463. Still another possible theory is that Teller, a silverite, feared that if the United States annexed Cuba, it would have to pay the $400 million worth of bonds issued by the Spanish government. See Holbo, "Convergence of Moods," 69.

[26]*New York Times,* June 15, 1898, p. 3.

[27]Hollingsworth, *Whirligig,* 141, 146–7. Brian P. Damiani, "Advocates of Empire: William McKinley, the Senate and American Expansion, 1898–1899" (Ph.D. diss., Univ. of Delaware, 1978), makes clear that positions on the treaty were largely determined by party lines, with McKinley putting great pressure on the Republicans to support it despite the doubts many of them felt.

[28]Finley Peter Dunne, *Mr. Dooley in Peace and in War* (Boston, 1899), 85; J.R. Johnson, "William Jennings Bryan, the Soldier," *Nebraska History* 31 (Sept. 1950), 95–106; Bryan to adjutant general, United States of America, Dec. 10, 1898, and adjutant general to Bryan, Dec. 12, 1898, B.P.

[29]E. Berkeley Tompkins, *Anti-Imperialism in the United States: The Great Debate, 1890–1920* (Philadelphia, 1970), 120–39. A detailed and sophisticated study of the political issues of the period is Göran Rystad's *Ambiguous Imperialism: American Foreign Policy and Domestic Issues at the Turn of the Century* (Stockholm, 1975).

[30]Bryan to Andrew Carnegie, Jan. 30, 1899, BP. See also Bryan to W.R. Hearst, Feb. [?] 1899, ibid.

[31]William Jennings Bryan et al., *Republic or Empire? The Philippine Question* (Chicago, 1899), 13–15; *New York Times,* Dec. 14, 1898, p. 6; H.M. Teller to Bryan, Jan. 20, 1899, James K. Jones to Bryan, Jan. 24, 1899, B.P.

[32]Bryan, *Memoirs,* 120–1; Bryan to Andrew Carnegie, Jan. 13, 1899, and Carnegie to Bryan, Dec. 26, 1898, BP; Bryan, *Republic or Empire,* 28–9, 53–4.

[33]Bryan, *Republic or Empire,* 18–22, 23–5, 29–32, 53–9; Bryan to Carnegie, Jan. 13, 30, 1899, and Bryan to William Randolph Hearst, Feb. [6 or 7], 1899, BP.

[34]Hollingsworth, *Whirligig,* 150–1; Bryan, *Republic or Empire,* 13–15, 24, 29–32; Bryan, *Memoirs,* 120–2.

[35]Bryan, *Memoirs,* 121. It is tempting to speculate on what might have been. The chief weaknesses of Bryan's program were its complexity, which made it hard to win popular support for it, and its failure to command the backing of other anti-imperialists, which divided the opposition and made McKinley's task easier. It may be that the idea of attaching to the treaty a reservation promising independence, an idea suggested by some anti-imperialists but never followed up, would have been better than Bryan's approach. Bryan spurned the suggestion in the mistaken impression that it would have compelled renegotiation of the whole treaty.

[36]Bryan's role in the passage of the treaty remains controversial. An examination of the motives of the nineteen Democrats, silver Republicans, and Populists who voted for the treaty (and whose votes Bryan might be supposed to have influenced) convinces me that he did not control, and probably did not much influence, any of them. For the details of my analysis, see Kendrick A. Clements, "William Jennings Bryan and Democratic Foreign Policy, 1896–1915" (Ph.D. diss. Univ. of California, Berkeley, 1970), appendix. A thorough study of this problem (it reaches the same conclusion) is José S. Reyes, *Legislative History of America's Economic Policy toward the Philippines,* Columbia University Studies in History, Economics and Public Law, vol. CVI (New York, 1923).

[37]*Congressional Record,* 55th Cong., 3rd sess., 1838. In place of the Bacon Resolution, the Senate passed the harmless McEnery Resolution, which promised self-government but not independence. Even this insipid substitute never came to a vote in the House, however, a fact that points out yet one more weakness in Bryan's strategy. It was unlikely that the Bacon Resolution

would have passed the House, and even had it done so, that McKinley would have approved it.

[38]Rystad, *Ambiguous Imperialism,* 242-4, 246-8, 308-9; Charles DeBenedetti, *The Peace Reform in American History* (Bloomington, Ind., 1980), 74–5.

[39]Carnegie to Bryan, Dec. 26, 1898, "Confidential," and Bryan to Carnegie, Dec. 24, 1898, BP; Andrew Carnegie, *Autobiography* (Boston, 1920), 364; R.F. Pettigrew, *Triumphant Plutocracy: The Story of American Public Life from 1870 to 1920* (New York, 1921), 273; Rystad, *Ambiguous Imperialism,* 240–2.

[40]Bryan, *Republic or Empire,* 23, 63, 73–9. Bryan insisted on restating the 1896 silver plank over the objections of not only gold Democrats but some silverites as well. See *New York Times,* May 11, June 14, July 1, 3, 6, 1900. Some gold Democrats, already hostile to Bryan on the silver issue, were inclined to favor imperialism as well on the ground that the economy needed foreign markets. See Waldo Lincoln Cook, "Present Political Tendencies," *Annals of the American Academy of Political and Social Science* 18 (Sept. 1901), 14–15.

[41]A representative sample of Bryan's arguments can be found in Bryan, *Republic or Empire.*

[42]Franklin Modisett, ed. (material selected by William Jennings Bryan, Jr.), *The Credo of the Commoner* (Los Angeles, 1968), 79, 127.

[43]Ibid., 73; Bryan, *Republic or Empire,* 13–15, 24.

[44]Thomas A. Bailey, "Was the Election of 1900 a Mandate on Imperialism?" *Mississippi Valley Historical Review* 24 (June 1937), 43–52. Most anti-imperialists found neither Bryan nor McKinley very appealing. See E. Berkeley Tompkins, "Scylla and Charybdis: The Anti-Imperialist Dilemma in the Election of 1900," *Pacific Historical Review* 36 (1967), 143–61.

[45]Rystad, *Ambiguous Imperialism,* 310.

NOTES TO CHAPTER 3

[1]*Commoner* 1 (June 7, 1901), 1–12; ibid. (Aug. 2, 1901), 6.

[2]The platform's plank on "Imperialism" can be found in Democratic National Committee, *The Campaign Text Book of the Democratic Party of the United States, 1904* (New York, 1904), 17–18. Compare this with the similar, though stronger, draft in BP, box 48. See also Bryan, *Memoirs,* 146, 149, 155–7; draft of form letter to Indiana Democrats, 1904, in BP, box 27; William Jennings Bryan, "The Future of the Democratic Party: A Discussion of Moral Issues in Pending Questions," *Outlook* 78 (Dec. 10, 1904), 926–7; Harold Baron, "Anti-Imperialism and the Democrats," *Science and Society* 21 (Summer 1957), 237–9.

[3]William Jennings Bryan, *The Old World and Its Ways* (St. Louis, 1907), 191–2, 196; Bryan to Charles W. Bryan, Jan. 20, [1906] NBP.

⁴*Commoner* 7 (July 19, 1907), 2–3; William Jennings Bryan, "The Democratic Party's Appeal," *Independent* (Oct. 15, 1908), 872–5; William Jennings Bryan, "Why the Philippines Should Be Independent," *Everybody's Magazine* 19 (Nov. 1908), 640d–f; William Jennings Bryan, "Colonialism: How Could the United States, If Necessary, Give Up Its Colonies?" *World To-Day* 14 (Feb. 1908), 151–4.

⁵William Jennings Bryan, "The United States in Porto Rico," *Independent*, (July 7, 1910), 20–3.

⁶Democratic National Committee, *Democratic Campaign Book, Presidential Election, 1900* (Washington, D.C., 1900), 9; *Commoner* 1 (Mar. 15, 1901), 1; ibid. (Feb. 13, 1901), 1; ibid. 3 (Aug. 7, 1903), 3; Bryan, *Old World*, 299, 305–6.

⁷For the text of the Spooner Amendment, see *Congressional Record*, 56th Cong., 2nd sess. (1901), p. 3050. Democratic objections to it were expressed by Senators Tillman of South Carolina, Lindsay of Kentucky, Culberson of Texas, and Mallory of Florida. See ibid., 3128–32.

⁸Ibid., 3035, 3116–25, 3134. The main provisions of the Platt Amendment, which was later embodied in the Cuban constitution (June 1901) and in a Cuban-American treaty (May 1903), were as follows: the Cubans promised never to impair their own independence or to assume an excessive debt; the United States was allowed to maintain bases in Cuba and was given the right to intervene to preserve life, liberty, and property on the island; all acts of the American military government were validated; the Cubans promised to carry out the sanitation programs begun by Americans; the status of the Isle of Pines was left for future determination.. See David F. Healy, *The United States in Cuba, 1898–1902: Generals, Politicians and the Search for Policy* (Madison, Wis., 1963), 163–4.

⁹Ibid., 166–7; *Commoner*, 1 (Feb. 6, 1901; Mar. 8, 15, 1901).

¹⁰For the debates, see *Congressional Record*, 56th Cong., 2nd sess. (1901), pp. 3025–152. The *New York Tribune* charged that expediency dictated Democratic votes: see Healy, *United States in Cuba*, 166. Other considerations that may have had some share in determining Democrats' votes were reluctance to delay the Army Appropriations Bill and racism. See Hollingsworth, *Whirligig*, 197–9; John B. Wiseman, "Racism in Democratic Politics, 1904–1912," *Mid-America* 51 (Jan. 1969), 38–58. The expedient policy followed by the Democrats in this and other cases casts some doubt on Göran Rystad's contention that the Democratic party emerged from the election of 1900 united as the party of anti-imperialism. See Rystad, *Ambiguous Imperialism*, 309.

¹¹W. Stull Holt, *Treaties Defeated by the Senate: A Study of the Struggle between President and Senate over the Conduct of Foreign Relations* (Baltimore, 1933), 185–95; *Commoner* 1 (Feb. 22, 1901), 3; ibid. (Mar. 22, 1901), 2, 4; ibid. (Jan. 10, 1902), 1.

¹²For a more charitable view of Gorman's role in this affair, emphasizing his moral aversion to Roosevelt's methods, see John R. Lambert, *Arthur Pue Gorman* (Baton Rouge, La., 1953), 297–308.

[13]*New York Times,* Nov. 11, Dec. 16, 1903. Excused from obedience to the rule were all who were bound by a prior campaign pledge, by instructions from state legislatures, or by scruples of conscience. If all 90 senators voted, 61 would have been needed to pass the treaty; the Democrats had 33 votes, the Republicans (not including vacancies) 57. Thus the Republicans needed only 4 Democrats to make the necessary 61. In the vote, 52 Republicans and 14 Democrats supported the treaty.

[14]*Commoner* 3 (Nov. 13, 1903), 4.

[15]*Congressional Record,* 58th Cong., 2nd sess. (1904), pp. 1243–6, 1661–7, 2260–1. Fourteen Democrats opposed the treaty, but southerners in particular found it hard to oppose a treaty that promised such benefits to the South.

[16]This was done at least partly at the direction of the president. See Roosevelt to Senator Shelby M. Cullom, Jan. 26, 1904, In Elting E. Morison, ed., *The Letters of Theodore Roosevelt,* 8 vols. (Cambridge, Mass., 1951–4), III, 710. For the discomfort of the Democrats, see *Congressional Record,* 58th Cong., 2nd sess. (1904), pp. 426, 473–4, 613–14, 700, 795, 1036, 1303.

[17]In general the American party system does not encourage the development of clearly defined foreign policy alternatives. Because the parties, of necessity, must be broad coalitions, a premium is put upon defining policies in terms that include rather than exclude any possible members of the coalition. In this situation the "outs" find it simpler and better to criticize the "ins" than to suggest possibly controversial alternatives. For perceptive general evaluations of the role of American parties, see Theodore J. Lowi, "Party, Policy, and the Constitution in America," and Walter Dean Burnham, "Party Systems and the Political Process," both in William Nisbet Chambers and Walter Dean Burnham, eds., *The American Party Systems: Stages of Political Development* (New York, 1967), 238–77, 277–307. The roots of the chaos prevailing in the Democratic party during this period are traced by R. Hal Williams, " 'Dry Bones and Dead Language': The Democratic Party," in H. Wayne Morgan, ed., *The Gilded Age,* rev. ed. (Syracuse, N.Y., 1970), 129–48.

[18]*Commoner* 1 (Dec. 6, 1901), 5; William Jennings Bryan, *First Battle,* 412; Metcalfe, *Real Bryan,* 154.

[19]*Commoner* 3 (Feb. 20, 1903), 1.

[20]Ibid. 2 (Dec. 19, 1902), 3.

[21]Ibid. 5 (Jan. 20, 1905), 4; ibid. (Mar. 17, 1905), 3; ibid. (Mar. 24, 1905), 2; Bryan, *Speeches,* II, 67.

[22]Grace Bryan Hargreaves, "Notes on Foreign Travel," manuscript biography of William Jennings Bryan, I, BP.

[23]Metcalfe, *Real Bryan,* 248–9. See also the *Commoner* 10 (Jan. 4, 1910; Feb. 5, 1910), for Bryan's speeches in Havana and Lima.

[24]Modisett, *Credo of the Commoner,* 91. See also Metcalfe, *Real Bryan,* 44–5, 174–9. At least one Japanese boy, Yachichiro Yamashita, took the Commoner more literally than he had expected. Yamashita appeared on Bryan's doorstep one day in 1898 with the announced intention of being educated by the great man. Bryan took him in, and he lived with the family for five years while

.

he went, at Bryan's expense, all the way through the University of Nebraska. See Bryan, *Memoirs*, 282.

[25]*Commoner* 10 (Mar. 11, 1910), 2; ibid. 11 (Feb. 10, 1911), 1.

[26]Ibid. 7 (Jan. 1907; Feb. 1907); ibid. (July 17, 1907), 1; ibid. 8 (May 8, 1908), 1–2; Bryan, *Old World*, 55, 491; William Jennings Bryan, *Letters to a Chinese Official, Being a Western View of Eastern Civilization* (New York, 1906), 70, 79. Bryan's belief that Americans in Asia had a duty to Americanize the Orient is representative of an important though frequently overlooked aspect of the Open Door policy. See Jerry Israel, " 'For God, for China and for Yale'—The Open Door in Action," *American Historical Review* 75 (Feb. 1970), 796–807.

[27]Metcalfe, *Real Bryan*, 171–4.

[28]For a Latin American reaction to Bryan, see Stanley R. Ross, "A Cuban View of William Jennings Bryan," *Nebraska History* 40 (Sept. 1959), 223–6.

[29]Bryan, *First Battle*, 379–80, 412; Bryan to Senator Francis G. Newlands, Aug. 27, 1916, BP.

[30]*Commoner* 5 (Feb. 17, 24, 1905; Sept. 15, 1905); Bryan to Harry Walker, Jan. 20, 1915, BP; Paolo E. Coletta, "William Jennings Bryan's Plans for World Peace," *Nebraska History*, 58 (Summer 1977), 193–7.

[31]Metcalfe, *Real Bryan*, 80; William Jennings Bryan, *The Forces That Make for Peace*, World Peace Foundation Pamphlet Series, vol. 3, no. 7, pt. 3 (Boston, 1912), 3; Bryan, *Letters to a Chinese Official*, 32; *Commoner* 4 (Feb. 5, 1904), 14–15; American Peace Congress, *Proceedings of the National Arbitration and Peace Congress, New York, April 14th to 17th, 1907* (New York, 1907), 40, 358–9.

[32]Bryan, *The Forces That Make for Peace*, 4–11.

[33]Bryan, *Old World*, 418–19, 566; Bryan, *The Forces That Make for Peace*, 11–13; Bryan, *Speeches*, II, 230–1; American Peace Congress, *Proceedings, 1907*, 393–4; *Commoner* 8 (June 12, 1908), 1–2; ibid. 15 (Dec. 1915), 3; Bryan to P.W. Maer, May 29, 1912, BP.

[34]Bryan, *Speeches*, II, 65–6.

[35]Hargreaves, "Notes on Foreign Travel"; *Commoner* 6 (July 27, 1906), 14; ibid. (Nov. 30, 1906), 7; ibid. 9 (Nov. 19, 1909), 3; ibid. 10 (July 8, 1910), 1–3; ibid. 19 (Aug. 1919), 7; Bryan, *Speeches*, II, 65–6, 227–9; American Peace Congress, *Proceedings, 1907*, 356–7; American Peace Congress, *Proceedings of the Second National Peace Congress, Chicago, May 2 to 5, 1909* (Chicago, 1909), 486– 7 (Bryan was now a vice-president of the organization).

[36]Bryan to William Howard Taft, June 29, 1910, BP.

[37]George E. Mowry, *The Era of Theodore Roosevelt, 1900–1912* (New York, 1958), 278.

[38]During a speech in Lincoln, Nebraska, in the autumn of 1911, Taft gave Bryan credit for the investigation principle. See Charles Moreau Harger, "William J. Bryan on the Political Situation: An Authorized Interview," *Outlook* (Jan. 6, 1912), 28. To Taft's great pleasure, Bryan strongly supported

the president's tariff reciprocity agreement with Canada. See Archibald Butt, *Taft and Roosevelt: The Intimate Letters of Archie Butt, Military Aide* (Garden City, N.Y., 1930), II, 610–11; Bryan to Harry Walker, Jan. 20, 1915, BP.

³⁹William Howard Taft, "The Arbitration Treaties," *National Geographic Magazine* 22 (Dec. 1911), 1165–72; *Congressional Record*, 62nd Cong., 2nd sess. (1911), pp. 643–5, 2874, 2934–40; Isidor Rayner, "The Great Arbitration Treaties," *Independent* (Feb. 8, 1912), 290–4; Philip C. Jessup, *Elihu Root* (New York, 1939), II, 274–5.

⁴⁰Theodore Roosevelt, "The Arbitration Treaty with Great Britain," *Outlook* (May 20, 1911), 97–8; Roosevelt, "Arbitration: Pretense and Reality," ibid. (Nov. 4, 1911), 565–7; Roosevelt to Senator Coe Isaac Crawford, June 12, 1911, in Morison, *Letters of Theodore Roosevelt*, VII, 283.

⁴¹*Commoner* 11 (June 2, 1911), 1; ibid. (Aug. 11, 1911), 6; ibid. (Aug. 18, 1911), 2; ibid. (Oct. 13, 1911), 2; ibid. (Dec. 22, 1911), 1; William Jennings Bryan, *The Hopeful Outlook for Peace*, World Peace Foundation Pamphlet Series, vol. 2, no. 7, pt. 3 (Boston, 1912), 13–14; William Howard Taft, "Why Not Arbitrate Everything?" *Independent* (Mar. 16, 1914), 380.

⁴²See, for example, *Congressional Record*, 62nd Cong., 2nd sess. (1911), pp. 2826, 2865–77, 2943–50; Richard Olney, "The New Arbitration Treaty with Great Britain," *Independent* (Sept. 21, 1911), 622–4; "The New Arbitration Treaty," *Independent* (May 25, 1911), 1125–6; "The Arbitration Compromise," *Nation* (Jan. 18, 1912), 50.

⁴³Bryan's aim in this odd interchange was, he said, "to act as peacemaker between you two [Roosevelt and Taft] in the interest of universal peace." He tried, but failed, to get supporters of the treaties to agree to changes that Roosevelt wanted. See Bryan to Roosevelt, Nov. 4, 13, 1911, Roosevelt to Bryan, Nov. 10, 1911, NBP.

⁴⁴Metcalfe, *Real Bryan*, 249.

⁴⁵Bryan, *Letters to a Chinese Official*, 75, 79.

⁴⁶*Commoner* 10 (Aug. 19, 1910), 1.

NOTES TO CHAPTER 4

¹Bryan expressed some of his doubts to Charles M. Rosser. See Rosser, *The Crusading Commoner: A Close-Up of William Jennings Bryan* (Dallas, 1937), 208–10. For Wilson's feelings, see Ray Stannard Baker, *Woodrow Wilson, Life and Letters*, III, *Governor, 1910–1913* (Garden City, N.Y., 1931), 442–3. For other perspectives, see James Kerney, *The Political Education of Woodrow Wilson* (New York, 1926), 287–8; Bryan, *Memoirs*, 187; Edward M. House Diary, Dec. 21, 1912, I, 39, in House Papers, Sterling Memorial Library, Yale University, New Haven, Conn.

²Although Bryan influenced Wilson's views over the years and certainly could claim credit for making the Democratic party progressive, he was not a kingmaker at Baltimore. See Arthur S. Link, *Wilson: The Road to the White*

House (Princeton, 1947), 106–22, 126–7, 459, 463–4 (hereafter cited as Link, *Wilson,* I); Paolo E. Coletta, *William Jennings Bryan,* II, *Progressive Politician and Moral Statesman, 1909–1915* (Lincoln, Neb., 1969), chs. 2, 3. Colonel House understood Bryan's importance in the party and urged Wilson to woo him; House Diary, Sept. 25, 1912, I, 1; ibid., Oct. 14, 1912, 21; ibid., Nov. 14, 1912, 20; ibid. Dec. 18, 19, 1912, 36, 38; House to Wilson, Nov. 28, 1912, House Papers. Charles Seymour, *The Intimate Papers of Colonel House* (Boston, 1926), I, 48–62.

³Bryan released Wilson publicly from any obligation. See *Commoner* 13 (Jan. 10, 1913), 1. He confessed to his brother a desire to be secretary of agriculture, however: Bryan to Charles W. Bryan, Dec. 12, [1912], NBP. But when Wilson offered him the secretaryship of the State Department, Bryan accepted because he believed that "the principles upon which foreign questions must be dealt with are precisely the same as those which govern in dealing with internal questions." William Bayard Hale, "Mr. Bryan," *World's Work* 26 (June 1913), 160–1.

⁴George Fitch, "Bryan—Democracy's Goat," *Collier's* (Apr. 17, 1915), 18.

⁵Bryan, *Memoirs,* 187–9. Outside of the big cities, much of the American press supported Bryan. "Mr. Bryan's Grape-Juice Banquet," *Literary Digest* (May 17, 1913), 1128–9. Bryan's mail also ran very heavily in favor of his decision not to serve alcohol. Representative letters, and a form letter Bryan drafted to answer them, are in BP.

⁶Fitch, "Bryan—Democracy's Goat," 18.

⁷*New York Times* (July 14, 1913), 1. Wilson explicitly granted Bryan permission to continue his twenty-year tradition of summer Chautauqua lecturing. See Wilson to Bryan, Jan. 16, 1913, BP.

⁸*New York Times* (July 14, 1913), 1; Bryan to Josephus Daniels, July 27, [1916], Josephus Daniels Papers, Manuscripts Division, Library of Congress, Washington, D.C. Other cabinet members supported Bryan's complaint about the heavy expenses of the State Department: "The Secretary of State on the Lecture Platform," *Literary Digest* (July 26, 1913), 116; Coletta, *William Jennings Bryan,* II, 104–7.

⁹Woodrow Wilson to William L. Marbury, Feb. 5, 1914, Woodrow Wilson Papers, Manuscripts Division, Library of Congress, Washington, D.C. The letter was published in the *New York Times* (Feb. 7, 1914) and other newspapers. Bryan's earlier argument that cabinet officers should "observe the simplicity that befits a republic" now came back to haunt him. See the *Commoner* 5 (July 28, 1905), 2–3. For samples of the public outcry, see the *New York Times* (July 16, 1913), 1; "Public Office and Public Duty," *Outlook* 104 (July 26, 1913), 646–7; "Secretary Bryan and the Chautauqua Lectures: A Poll of the Press," ibid. (Aug. 2, 1913), 746–8; "The Bryan Scandal," *Nation* (Sept. 18, 1913), 256–7.

¹⁰*New York Times* (Jan. 16, 1915), 6; Bryan, *Memoirs,* 12. The "deserving Democrats" letter (Aug. 20, 1913) was written to the collector of customs in the Dominican Republic, W.W. Vick. It was widely published in 1915. See,

for example, *North American Review* 201 (Feb. 1915), 285. Although critical of Bryan's State Department, Rachel West *(The Department of State on the Eve of the First World War* [Athens, Ga., 1978]) does not mention the letter or the Sullivan scandal.

[11]Katherine Crane, *Mr. Carr of State: Forty-Seven Years in the Department of State* (New York, 1960), 151–3, 156–7; Richard Hume Werking, *The Master Architects: Building the United States Foreign Service, 1890–1913* (Lexington, Ky., 1977), 239–40, 245–6.

[12]Wilson professed support for civil service but bowed to political realities in selecting most of his cabinet members and major ministers for political reasons. See Link, *Wilson,* I, 98–103. The three mission chiefs he kept were all career men. Werking, *Master Architects,* 246–7. For the changes Bryan was able to make within the department, see Coletta, *William Jennings Bryan,* II, 111.

[13]For Osborne's career, see *Commoner* 3 (Oct. 2, 1903), 3; Robert Lansing, *War Memoirs* (Indianapolis, 1935), 361. Osborne exercised almost no visible influence on policy. For Adee's 38-year career (1886–1924) as second assistant, see Crane, *Carr,* 37–47. Malone served only briefly, from April to November of 1913, when he resigned to become collector of the Port of New York. See *Commoner* 13 (Apr. 18, 1913), 15; Wilson to Malone, Nov. 25, 1913, Wilson Papers. Phillips was House's particular choice: House Diary, Nov. 11, 25, 1913, III, 354, 368. Bryan was a little intimidated by his Harvard background: House Diary, Jan. 16, 1914, IV, 11–12, 15; William Phillips, *Ventures in Diplomacy* (Boston, 1952), 3, 5–6, 59–63. As it turned out, Bryan and Phillips got along very well.

[14]Arthur S. Link, *Wilson: The New Freedom* (Princeton, 1956), 98 (hereafter cited as Link, *Wilson,* II), points out that Moore had initial misgivings about working with Bryan but got on well with the secretary and resigned early in 1914 as the result of a disagreement with the president, not Bryan. Lansing, son-in-law of former Secretary of State John Foster and prominent in international law, was a natural choice for the post when Moore resigned. See Judge George Gray (3rd Circuit Court of Appeals) to Bryan, Mar. 7, 1914, Bryan to Wilson, Mar. 10, 1914, Wilson to Bryan, Mar. 12, 1914, all in ABP; White House memorandum, Mar. 10, 1914 (citing endorsement of Lansing by Judge Gray and James Brown Scott), Wilson Papers; Lansing to Senator James A. O'Gorman, Mar. 8, 1913, Robert Lansing Papers, Manuscripts Division, Library of Congress, Washington, D.C.

[15]For Putney, see Coletta, *William Jennings Bryan,* II, 111. Williams was certainly the missionaries' candidate: Bishop J.W. Bashford (Methodist bishop in Peking) to Bryan, Oct. 10, 1913, no. 711. 93/36, State Department Decimal Files, National Archives, Washington, D.C. (hereafter cited as DF, with file number); Paul Reinsch, *An American Diplomat in China* (Garden City, N.Y., 1922), 50. For Long's appointment, see Koenig, *Bryan,* 505–6. Long was poorly qualified for the post, business-oriented, and decidedly out of sympathy with the administration's aims; his appointment partially ex-

plains the ease with which some business interests were subsequently able to manipulate departmental policy, especially in the Dominican Republic and Haiti. See below, ch. 5.

[16]Coletta, *William Jennings Bryan*, II, 100–3, 112; Baker, *Woodrow Wilson*, IV, 41. Two able diplomats then serving in junior posts later testified that they were surprised not to be fired by Bryan: Joseph C. Grew, *Turbulent Era, A Diplomatic Record of Forty Years, 1904–1945* (Cambridge, Mass., 1952), I, 119; Lewis Einstein, *A Diplomat Looks Back,* ed. Lawrence E. Gelfand (New Haven, 1968), 28–9.

[17]The best contemporary evaluation of the Democratic appointments is by George Harvey, "The Diplomats of Democracy," *North American Review* 199 (Feb. 1914), 161–71. Harvey concludes that the worst losses to the service were probably in Latin America but that on the whole the new diplomats were less bad then frequently depicted. A much more critical view is "The Thud of the Spoilsman's Axe Is Heard in Washington," *Literary Digest* (Feb. 1914), 91–92. A careful modern evaluation which concludes that, on the whole, Democratic appointments were probably "average" is Coletta, *William Jennings Bryan,* II, 112–19. West, in *Department of State,* is very critical of the Bryan State Department. She judges Bryan's and Wilson's appointees against modern standards of professional competence and finds them amateurish and ignorant. The charge is substantially accurate but beside the point. Without saying so directly, West leaves the impression that the Republicans had appointed and promoted diplomats only for professional merit, which was not true, and she displays no understanding of Wilson's desire to have new policies carried out by new men loyal to him. Moreover, she implies that American diplomatic amateurism contributed to the advent of World War I, or at least to American involvement in the war. That notion will not bear close inspection, and in fact West advances little evidence to show that the failings of Wilsonian diplomats undermined American policies anywhere.

[18]Not until Christmas of 1914 did the administration begin an official investigation. See Bryan to senator-elect James Phelan, Dec. 23, 1914, James D. Phelan Papers, Bancroft Library, Univ. of California, Berkeley. For the press exposé that led to the official investigation, see *New York World* (Dec. 7–11, 13, 1914); *New York Times* (Dec. 9, 12, 1914; Jan. 13–17, 19–23, 26–29, 1915; Feb. 10, 1915; July 27, 1915). The July 27 issue carries a summary of the official investigation report subsequently published as *Santo Domingo Investigation, Copy of the Report, Findings, and Opinion of James D. Phelan, Commissioner Named by the Secretary of State, with the Approval of the President, to Investigate Charges Against the United States Minister to the Dominican Republic* (Washington, D.C., 1915). Documents bearing on the Sullivan case are in the State Department files, no. 123Su51. Bryan originally had doubts about Sullivan but unwisely suppressed them when O'Gorman and Tumulty pushed the appointment. See Bryan to Wilson, June 9, 1913, Wilson Papers.

[19]Rumors of Sullivan's incompetence and improprieties began to reach the

State Department in early December 1913 (DF 123Su51/13B, 14 [2 telegrams], 15), but Wilson and Bryan resisted any investigation (Wilson to Bryan, Apr. 21, 1914, Wilson Papers) until the *New York World* broke the scandal publicly in December 1914. The press unfairly blamed Bryan for choosing Sullivan, but he might properly have been blamed for failing to investigate his appointees adequately and for trying to cover up the scandal. See "San Domingo and Secretary Bryan: A Poll of the Press," *Outlook* (Feb. 3, 1915), 267–70; "Secretary Bryan and the San Domingo Spoils," ibid. (Jan. 27, 1915), 163–5; "Prince of Job Hunters," *Nation* (Jan. 21, 1915), 69; " 'To Reward Deserving Democrats,' " *Literary Digest* (Jan. 30, 1915), 179–80; "High Politics and High Finance," *World's Work* 29 (Mar. 1915), 492–3.

[20]Relations with the press were a serious problem for Bryan. He tried to be open but felt that reporters abused his confidence and hence he became increasingly secretive. Coletta, *William Jennings Bryan,* II, 98–100, and Koenig, *Bryan,* 506–7, examine this problem. The special agent system and its reasons and effects are examined in Link, *Wilson,* II, 105, 112–13. House loved the cloak-and-dagger games involved in being a special agent and played up the system as well as his own role in it. See House Diary, Feb. 19, 1913, I, 105; ibid., Dec. 3, 1914, V, 237–8; Seymour, *Intimate Papers,* I, 115. For an excellent study of the way the system worked in Mexico, see Larry D. Hill, *Emissaries to a Revolution: Woodrow Wilson's Executive Agents in Mexico* (Baton Rouge, La., 1973). For the sake of departmental morale, Bryan should probably have objected to the special agent system, but because it did not bother *him* to be bypassed, he ignored it. Concerned more about substance than form, he ignored even House's domination of the peacemaking efforts in Europe until, in the spring of 1915, it became obvious that House and Wilson were following a course he thought erroneous. West, *Department of State,* 52.

[21]Bryan, *Memoirs,* 300–2. Patrick Devlin *(Too Proud to Fight: Woodrow Wilson's Neutrality* [New York, 1975] 144–5, 155) describes Bryan as lovable but extremely naive and ignorant of the outside world.

[22]Bryan, *Memoirs,* 187; Coletta, "William Jennings Bryan's Plans for World Peace," 197–206.

[23]See original draft of treaty plan, with marginal notes of cabinet opinions, and "President Wilson's Peace Proposal: Supplementary Memorandum by the Secretary of State," BP.

[24]E. David Cronon, ed., *The Cabinet Diaries of Josephus Daniels, 1913–1921* (Lincoln, Neb.,1963), 35; *New York Times* (Apr. 23, 24, 1913); *Commoner* 13 (May 2, 1913), ll; U.S. Department of State, *Papers Relating to the Foreign Relations of the United States, 1913* (Washington, D.C., 1920), 8–10 (hereafter cited as *For. Rels., 1913)*; Bryan to Wilson, Aug. 1, 1913, ABP; Bryan to Wayne C. Williams, Jan. 26, 1923, BP; Wilson to Senator William J. Stone, Aug. 13, 1914, Wilson Papers; Clara Ontell Kisch, "Bryan and the 'Cooling Off' Treaties of 1913–1914," (M.A. thesis, Univ. of California, Berkeley, 1955), 74–7 and passim.

[25]Edwin Borchard, Joseph P. Chamberlain, and Stephen Duggan, trustees of John Bassett Moore Fund, *The Collected Papers of John Bassett Moore* (New Haven, 1944), VII, 344; William Howard Taft, "Why Not Arbitrate Everything?" (Mar. 16, 1914), 380; Curti, *Bryan and World Peace*, 151–3; Andrew Carnegie to Bryan, Oct. 5, 1914, BP; Coletta, *William Jennings Bryan,* II, 249.

[26]Wilson doubted that "moral sanctions alone" would be enough to secure peace: Coletta, *William Jennings Bryan,* II, 240. Others were equally skeptical or, like Theodore Roosevelt and Henry Cabot Lodge, openly hostile. See "How Mr. Bryan's Peace Plan Is Received," *Current Opinion* 54 (June 1913), 451–2; "A Pacifist in Charge of Our Foreign Relations," *Literary Digest* (May 31, 1913), 1207–8; Morison, *Letters of Theodore Roosevelt,* VII, 809, 828; Karl Schriftgeisser, *The Gentleman from Massachusetts: Henry Cabot Lodge* (Boston, 1944), 260. For subsequent applications of the investigation principle, see Coletta, *William Jennings Bryan,* II, 249.

[27]Ambassador Cecil Spring Rice to Bryan, Jan. 17, Oct. 6, 1914, Ambassador Walter Hines Page to Bryan, Mar. 17, Sept. 1, 1914, BP; Wilson to Bryan, Jan. 19, 1914, ABP; U.S. Department of State, *Papers Relating to the Foreign Relations of the United States, 1914, Supplement* (Washington, D.C. 1928), 4, 11 (hereafter cited as *For. Rels., 1914, Supp.*); Kisch, "Bryan and the 'Cooling Off' Treaties," 73–4, 91–2. Bryan thought the treaties his most important achievement; perhaps that was naive, and perhaps it is merely a comment on how difficult it is to achieve *any* progress toward peace.

[28]Baker, *Wilson,* IV, 62; John Wells Davidson, ed., *A Crossroads of Freedom: The 1912 Campaign Speeches of Woodrow Wilson* (New Haven, 1956), 43, 288; House Diary, Jan. 24, 1913, I, 84; Cronon, *Cabinet Diaries,* 35–7, 44–5.

[29]Arthur S. Link, David W. Hirst, and John E. Little, eds., *The Papers of Woodrow Wilson,* XXVII, *1913* (Princeton, N.J., 1978), 221–3, 310–11, 357–8, 482, 533–5; ibid., XXIX, *December 2, 1913–May 5, 1914* (Princeton, N.J., 1979), 34–5, 162, 203–4, 217–18, 231–3, 418–20; U.S. Department of State, *Papers Relating to the Foreign Relations of the United States, 1914* (Washington, D.C., 1922), 317–18 (hereafter cited as *For. Rels., 1914*).

[30]The McAdoo and Burleson Papers, both in the Manuscripts Division, Library of Congress, Washington, D.C., provide a detailed picture of the progress of the repeal fight. For Bryan's role, see Hibben and Grattan, *Peerless Leader,* 333–4; *Commoner* 14 (Apr. 1914), 1; Bryan to Charles W. Bryan, May 20, [1914], NBP; William Gibbs McAdoo to Bryan, Apr. 10, 1914, McAdoo Papers.

[31]The *New York Times* (Feb. 7, 1914) published a letter from Wilson to William L. Marbury, Feb. 5, 1914; Stephen Gwynn, ed., *The Letters and Friendships of Sir Cecil Spring Rice: A Record* (Boston, 1929), II, 201–2. There is no evidence that Wilson made or offered any sort of bargain to repeal the tolls exemption in return for British support of his Mexican policy. Indeed, he was publicly on record as favoring repeal before the Mexican situation became acute. See William S. Coker, "The Panama Canal Tolls Controversy: A

Different Perspective," *Journal of American History* 55 (Dec. 1968), 555–64; Link, *Wilson*, II, 304–14. By contrast, see Coletta, *William Jennings Bryan*, II, 157. For documents bearing on the issue, see Link et al., *Papers of Woodrow Wilson*, XXVII, 543–5; ibid., XXIX, 34–5, 162.

[32]Emilio Aguinaldo y Famy to Bryan, Nov. 15, 1912, BP.

[33]Bryan to Aguinaldo, Jan. 2, 1913, Wilson to Bryan, Jan. 16, 1913, BP; Emilio Aguinaldo and Vicente Albano Pacis, *A Second Look at America* (New York, 1957), 161; Kerney, *Political Education of Woodrow Wilson*, 165; Davidson, *A Crossroads of Freedom*, 31; Josephus Daniels, *The Wilson Era: Years of Peace, 1910–1917* (Chapel Hill, 1944), 169; William C. Redfield, "Glimpses of Our Government: Toilers by Land and Sea," *Saturday Evening Post* (May 10, 1924), 175; Francis Burton Harrison, *The Corner-Stone of Philippine Independence: A Narrative of Seven Years* (New York, 1922), 70.

[34]Baker, *Woodrow Wilson*, IV, 217; Roy Watson Curry, "Woodrow Wilson and Philippine Policy," *Mississippi Valley Historical Review* 41 (Dec. 1954), 436–8.

[35]Wilson to Bryan, Aug. 13, 20, 1913, Bryan to Wilson, Aug. 16, 1913, Wilson Papers; Manuel Quezon to Bryan, Aug. 16, 1913, Wilson to Bryan, Aug. 18, 1913, ABP; Harrison, *Corner-Stone*, 3, 50; Curry, "Woodrow Wilson and Philippine Policy," 439–40.

[36]W. Cameron Forbes (Taft's governor-general of the Philippines) to Charles S. Hamlin, Apr. 14, 1914, Charles S. Hamlin Papers, Manuscripts Division, Library of Congress, Washington, D.C.; Harrison, *Corner-Stone*, 51–7, 76–85; "Filipino Freedom Dawning," *Literary Digest* (Oct. 18, 1913), 668–9; *Commoner*, 13 (Dec. 1913), 3; Curry, "Woodrow Wilson and Philippine Policy," 441–50.

[37]Baron Shidehara to Bryan, with enclosures, Mar. 7, 1913, Shidehara to Ransford S. Miller, Mar. 15, 1913, DF 811.52/32, 33. The land law controversy has attracted much attention from historians. See Elmer C. Sandmeyer, "California Anti-Chinese Legislation and the Federal Courts: A Study in Federal Regulations," *Pacific Historical Review* 5 (Sept. 1936), 189–211; Spencer C. Olin, Jr., "European Immigrant and Oriental Alien: Acceptance and Rejection by the California Legislature of 1913," ibid. 35 (Aug. 1966), 303–15; Roger Daniels, "Westerners from the East: Oriental Immigrants Reappraised," ibid. (Nov. 1966), 373–83; Thomas A. Bailey, "California, Japan, and the Alien Land Legislation of 1913," ibid. 1 (Mar. 1932), 36–59; Roy Watson Curry, *Woodrow Wilson and Far Eastern Policy, 1913–1921* (New York, 1957), 43–65; Paolo E. Coletta, " 'The Most Thankless Task': Bryan and the California Alien Land Legislation," *Pacific Historical Review* 36 (May 1967), 163–87.

[38]*Commoner* 1 (Oct. 18, 1901), 3; ibid. (Dec. 6, 1901), 1; ibid. 7 (Aug. 16, 1907), 5: Bryan to James D. Phelan, May 6, 1907, Phelan Papers; Link, *Wilson*, II, 290; *For Rels., 1913*, p. 625; Coletta, " 'The Most Thankless Task,' " 165. Adding to the problems of the administration was the fact that such prominent California Democrats as Phelan strongly favored restrictions

on Orientals. See, for example, Phelan to William F. McCombs, Mar. 6, 1912, Phelan to Woodrow Wilson, Apr. 20, 1912, Phelan to Bryan, Apr. 5, 1913, Phelan Papers.

[39]Link, *Wilson*, II, 290–1. The Japanese would have accepted this small concession as sufficient. See *For. Rels., 1913,* p. 639; Link et al., *Papers of Woodrow Wilson,* XXVII, 293–4, 318–21. For an analysis of Japanese governmental attitudes by an unusually well-informed Westerner, see A. M. Pooley, *Japan's Foreign Policies* (New York, 1920), 123–6.

[40]Link, *Wilson,* II, 291–5.

[41]Franklin Hichborn *(Story of the Session of the California Legislature of 1913* [San Francisco, 1913], 254–5) indicates that there was substantial opposition to aspects of the bill. The *Sacramento Bee,* however, like other opponents of the bill, changed its attitude apparently as a result of Bryan's intervention. The *Bee* ignored the pending legislation in the crucial period between April 1 and 22 and endorsed the idea of some sort of limitation on Oriental landownership only in an editorial on April 22 (p. 6) with the specific recommendation that the law be drawn so as not to offend the Japanese. On April 25, however, after Bryan's trip was announced, a strong editorial endorsed the pending law (p. 6). The *New York Times* (Apr. 26, 1913), reported that the Japanese were pleased by the trip.

[42]The correspondence between the secretary and president during Bryan's trip is in the Wilson Papers. A full transcript of the supposedly secret April 28 sessions, entitled "Executive Joint Conference of the Senate and Assembly of the State of California at Sacramento, California, April 28, 1913," is in BP. Some of Bryan's suggestions to the legislators of less offensive ways to phrase a law are in William Jennings Bryan and State Senator Lee C. Gates, *Farewell Remarks of Secretary of State William Jennings Bryan and State Senator Lee C. Gates before the California Legislature of 1913, upon the Departure of Our Secretary for Washington* (no publisher, no date), p. 3. I believe that Paolo Coletta is in error in saying that Bryan was not authorized to offer alternatives to the pending law (Coletta, " 'The Most Thankless Task,' " 171–2). See also Eldon Penrose, " 'Grape Juice Diplomacy and a Bit of Political Buncombe,' " *Pacific Historical Review* 37 (May 1968), 160–2. A full report on Johnson's answer to Bryan, as well as complete details on what Bryan had said and an editorial in favor of a land law, appeared in the *Sacramento Bee* within two hours after the end of the session: *Bee* (April. 28, 29). The Japanese were extremely upset about the passage of the Webb Act: see John Bassett Moore (acting secretary) to Wilson, Apr. 29, May 1, 1913, with enclosures of memoranda of conversations with the Japanese ambassador, in Wilson Papers.

[43]*For Rels., 1913,* pp. 629–31. For Japanese opinion, see "The Japanese Press on California," *Literary Digest* (May 3, 1913), 1002–3; "Japan and the Land Law," ibid. (May 31, 1913), 1214–15; "The Japanese Press and the California Crisis," *Current Opinion* 54 (June 1913), 448–9.

[44]Daniels, *Wilson Era,* 163–5; Cronon, *Cabinet Diaries,* 52–8, 64–8.

[45]Bryan to Wilson, May 18, June 19, 1913, Wilson Papers. Bryan's sugges-

tion was embodied in a note to the Japanese on July 16: *For Rels., 1913,* pp. 641–5.

⁴⁶Borchard et al., *Collected Papers of John Bassett Moore,* VII, 21; Ambassador Guthrie to Bryan, Aug. 19, 1913, enclosing treaty draft, DF 811.52/189. Exactly how this treaty was negotiated is rather obscure. Moore recalled many years later that he had been in charge of talks with the Japanese during the summer of 1913, but details of those talks are apparently lost. See also Coletta, " 'The Most Thankless Task,' " 180.

⁴⁷John Bassett Moore, memorandum of conversation with Japanese ambassador, Aug. 29, 1913, DF 811.52/110; Guthrie to Bryan, Sept. 23, 25, Oct. 13, Nov. 20, 1913, DF 811.52/198, 199, 214, 205; Chinda to Bryan, Dec. 13, 1913, DF 811.52/204; Bryan, memorandum of conversation with Japanese ambassador, Jan. 23, 1914, DF 811.52/209; Bryan to Wilson, Sept. 17, 30, 1913, and Wilson to Bryan, Sept. 9, 11, 1913, Jan. 15, 1914, Wilson Papers; Arthur S. Link, David W. Hirst, and John E. Little, eds., *The Papers of Woodrow Wilson,* XXVIII, 1913 (Princeton, N.J., 1978), 282–3, 305–6, 314–15. British ambassador Spring Rice reported on February 3 that Wilson was seriously concerned about a possible Japanese threat to the Philippines and even about a joint attack by Japan and Mexico. See ibid., XXIX, 217–18.

⁴⁸Wilson to Bryan, Jan. 15, 1914, Bryan to Wilson, Sept. 17, 1913, Wilson Papers; Bryan to Wilson, Jan. 23, 1915, Wilson to Bryan, Jan. 27, 1915, ABP; Guthrie to Bryan, Jan. 29, 1914, June 15, 1914, DF 811.52/213, 236; *For Rels., 1914,* pp. 426–34; Arthur S. Link, David W. Hirst, and John E. Little, eds., *The Papers of Woodrow Wilson,* XXX, *May 6–September 5, 1914* (Princeton, 1979), 169–70, 273–4. With the demise of the treaty proposal in January 1915, Bryan proposed what Coletta correctly calls a "harebrained plan" (Coletta, *William Jennings Bryan,* II, 214) to solve the problem by dispersing the Japanese around the country; Wilson vetoed the suggestion. See Bryan to Wilson, Mar. 8, 1915, Wilson to Bryan, Mar. 8, 1915, BP.

NOTES TO CHAPTER 5

¹Bryan, *Memoirs,* 365. Bryan's ideas were not new: see ch. 3, above. Wilson shared his opinions on this subject: Harley Notter, *The Origins of the Foreign Policy of Woodrow Wilson* (Baltimore, 1937), 187–90, 195, 197; Ray Stannard Baker and William E. Dodd, eds., *The New Democracy: Presidential Messages, Addresses and Other Papers, 1913–1917* (New York, 1926), I, 67.

²*Commoner* 13 (Nov. 1913), 2; Bryan, *Memoirs,* 364–6. In November 1913, Wilson told Sir William Tyrrell, private secretary to British foreign secretary Sir Edward Grey, that he was determined "that those Republics should have fairly decent rulers," and that he saw an opportunity in the Mexican case "to teach these countries a lesson." Link et al., *Papers of Woodrow Wilson,* XXVIII, 544.

³"Dinner of the Pan American Society," *Bulletin of the Pan American Union* 36 (June 1913), 816; interview with Bryan in the *St. Louis Post-Dispatch* (Apr.

20, 1913), quoted in Barton J. Bernstein and Franklin A. Leib, "Progressive Senators and American Imperialism, 1898–1916: A Reappraisal," *Mid-America* 50 (July 1968), 187; "Mr. Bryan Puts Conscience into Diplomacy and Business," *New York World* (Apr. 20, 1913); *For. Rels., 1913,* p. 7. A marginal note on a draft of the press release in BP says, "The reference to gov't by the consent of the governed was put in at my suggestion." American businessmen were doubtful about the administration's promises of support, suspecting correctly that governmental backing for their activities would be limited. See Coletta, *William Jennings Bryan,* II, 194.

⁴Coletta, *William Jennings Bryan,* II, 184, 193; Bryan to Wilson, June 14, 1913, Wilson Papers. The protection of traditional interests in Latin America during the Wilson administration deserves a more careful examination than I have given it in the context of this study; it is obvious, however, that neither Wilson nor Bryan thought that the advancement of strategic and economic interests would conflict with their moralistic intentions. Such naivete infused their whole policy.

⁵Coletta, *William Jennings Bryan,* II, 189; Bryan to Wilson, July 17, 1913, BP; Bryan to Wilson, Aug. 6, 16, 1913, Wilson Papers; Bryan to Wilson, Feb. 21, 1914, ABP; House Diary, Oct. 29, 1913, III, p. 331; *Commoner* 15 (June 1915), 15; ibid. 17 (July 1917), 3; Wilson to Bryan, Mar. 20, 1914, quoted in Baker, *Woodrow Wilson,* IV, 434. Frank Vanderlip, president of the National City Bank of New York, endorsed Bryan's proposal as "daring," a "really brilliant conception," which was also "extremely sound business." See the *Commoner,* 15 (June 1915), 26; Frank A. Vanderlip to Mrs. Bryan, Jan. 26, 1917, BP. Bryan proposed a variation of his scheme in 1920: that the United States take over the debts owed by Allied governments to the United States. *Commoner* 20 (Mar. 1920), 4.

⁶Bryan to Wilson, Nov. 5, 1913, Wilson to Bryan, Nov. 7, 1913, Wilson Papers; Baker, *Woodrow Wilson,* IV, 285; Seymour, *Intimate Papers,* I, 207–19, 221–3; Mark T. Gilderhus, "Pan-American Initiatives: The Wilson Presidency and 'Regional Integration,' 1914–1917," *Diplomatic History* 4 (Fall 1980), 409–23.

⁷Paolo E. Coletta, "William Jennings Bryan and the United States–Colombia Impasse, 1903–1921," *Hispanic American Historical Review* 47 (Nov. 1967), 486–501, covers the Colombian negotiations in detail. The treaty was very much Bryan's personal project. State Department Counselor Robert Lansing, who succeeded Bryan as secretary in June 1915, wrote to Wilson that "Mr. Bryan handled the matter without discussing it with me." Arthur S. Link, David W. Hirst, and John E. Little, eds., *The Papers of Woodrow Wilson,* XXXIV, *July 21–September 30, 1915* (Princeton, N.J., 1980), 49.

⁸Link, *Wilson,* II, 331–4; *For. Rels., 1913,* pp. 1040–2.

⁹Charles A. Douglas (Nicaragua's Washington lawyer) to Bryan, June 9, 11, 1913, DF 817.812/38, 39; memorandum of Latin American Division of State Department giving treaty draft, June 19, 1913, DF 817.812/34; Bryan to Wilson, June 16, July 31, 1913, Wilson to Bryan, June 19, 1913, Wilson Papers; *New York World* (July 20, 27, 1913; Aug. 3, 1913); *New York Times*

(July 21, 22, 1913; Aug. 3, 1913). The provisions of the Platt Amendment are outlined in note 8, ch. 3, p. 164.

[10]Dana G. Munro, *Intervention and Dollar Diplomacy in the Caribbean, 1900–1921* (Princeton, N.J., 1964), 393–6; President Adolfo Díaz to Wilson, Feb. 3, 1914, Wilson Papers; Bryan to Wilson, Feb. 6, 1914, ABP. The Nicaraguan request was not inspired by Washington. Wilson thought of suggesting that Nicaragua request the Platt Amendment, but not until after Díaz had already done so (Wilson had apparently overlooked Díaz's letter). Wilson to Bryan, Feb. 20, 1914, DF 817.812/182.

[11]Coletta, *William Jennings Bryan,* II, 191–3.

[12]On at least two points Wilson disagreed to some extent with Bryan but left him a free hand: the first was when the secretary thought Central American protests about the proposed protectorate less important than Wilson did; the second was when Wilson accepted the protectorate proposal only with reluctance. See Wilson to Bryan, Jan. 20, June 13, 1914, Wilson Papers.

[13]Link, *Wilson,* II, 342–6.

[14]Arthur S. Link, *Wilson: The Struggle for Neutrality, 1914–1915* (Princeton, N.J., 1960), 499–500 (hereafter cited as Link, *Wilson,* III); Selig Adler, "Bryan and Wilsonian Caribbean Penetration," *Hispanic American Historical Review* 20 (May 1940), 218.

[15]*For. Rels., 1913,* pp. 424–7; undated memorandum from Bryan to Wilson, DF 839.00/961½.

[16]*For. Rels., 1913,* pp. 428–53; Baker, *Woodrow Wilson,* IV, 444–5.

[17]*For. Rels., 1914,* pp. 199–200, 206–7, 214–22. For the mechanics of the receivership arrangement, see Melvin M. Knight, *The Americans in Santo Domingo* (New York, 1928), 56. By this time Bryan was beginning to have serious doubts about Sullivan. See ch. 4, above.

[18]*For. Rels., 1914,* pp. 222–5; Bryan to Wilson, Apr. 4, 1914, Wilson to Bryan, Apr. 4, 1914, DF 839.00/1141, 1136.

[19]*For. Rels., 1914,* pp. 225–47; Bryan to Wilson, undated (about July 20, 1914), Wilson Papers; memoranda by Jordan Stabler (assistant chief of Latin American Division), July 9, 17 (two), 20, 1914, and by Boaz Long, July 31, 1914, DF 839.00/1424, 1425, 1451, 1458, 1510.

[20]Bryan to Wilson, Dec. 12, 1914, ABP; William Jennings Bryan, memorandum, "San Domingo," July 27, 1914, Wilson Papers; *For. Rels., 1914,* pp. 246–61. At least one author thinks that despite American supervision, fraud pervaded the elections. See Sumner Welles, *Naboth's Vineyard: The Dominican Republic, 1844–1924* (New York, 1928), 745–7.

[21]U.S. Department of State, *Papers Relating to the Foreign Relations of the United States, 1915* (Washington, D.C., 1924), 279–80, 283–4 (hereafter cited as *For. Rels., 1915); For. Rels., 1914,* p. 261.

[22]For the background of the Haitian problem, see Hans Schmidt, *The United States Occupation of Haiti, 1915–1934* (New Brunswick, N.J., 1971), 19–42.

[23]Link, *Wilson,* III, 517; *For. Rels., 1914,* pp. 334–5, 341.

[24]Schmidt, *United States Occupation,* 49–54; Farnham to Bryan, Jan. 22,

31, 1914, DF 838.00/901, 793; Boaz Long to Bryan, Jan. 23, 1914, DF 817.812/616; Jordon Stabler to Bryan, Feb. 3, 1914, DF 838.00/894.

[25]*For. Rels., 1914*, pp. 339–41; two memoranda dictated by R.L. Farnham in Latin American Division, Mar. 5, 6, 1914, DF 838.51/335, 328; Farnham to Bryan, Mar. 13, 1914, DF 838.51/329; Minister Smith to Bryan, Mar. 16, 18, 19, June 9, 1914, DF 838.51/331, 332, 334, 340; French ambassador to Bryan, Mar. 12, 1914, DF 838.51/345; Walker W. Vick to Bryan, received May 2, 1914, DF 838.51/339; Jordon H. Stabler to Bryan, May 13, and undated, 1914, DF 838.00/1667, 1668; Boaz Long to William Phillips, May 16, 1914, DF 838.00/1669; Vice-Consul Ross Hazeltine to Bryan, July 6, 1914, DF 838.345/20; Bryan to Wilson, Mar. 24, 1914, DF 838.51/395a. The Germans approached the Haitian government rather than the Americans with their request.

[26]*For. Rels., 1914*, pp. 347–59; memorandum by Farnham, June 23, 1914, DF 838.51/494; two memoranda of conversations between Jordan Stabler and Farnham, Aug. 14, 31, 1914, DF 838.51/346, DF 838.516/83.

[27]*For. Rels., 1914*, pp. 359–64, 370–1; Bryan to Wilson, Dec. 12, 1914, Wilson Papers; Bryan to Wilson, Dec. 18, 1914, ABP.

[28]*For. Rels., 1914*, pp. 365–82; Bryan to Wilson, Jan. 7, 1915, Wilson Papers; memorandum of telephone call from Roger Farnham, Dec. 7, 1914, DF 838.51/494; Coletta, *William Jennings Bryan*, II, 205.

[29]Bryan to Wilson, Jan. 7, 1915, Lansing to Wilson, Oct. 29, 1914, Wilson Papers.

[30]Wilson to Bryan, Jan. 13, 1915, Wilson Papers; Bryan to Wilson, Jan. 15, Feb. 25, Mar. 27, Apr. 2, 8, 1915, Wilson to Bryan, Mar. 21, Apr. 6, 8, 1915, ABP; Bryan to Wilson, Mar. 23, 1915, BP; Bryan to Wilson, enclosing note from French ambassador, Feb. 25, 1915, Wilson to Bryan, Feb. 26, 1915, Bryan to Farnham, Mar. 25, 1915, DF 838.51/385, 385½, 394a; Bryan to Paul Fuller, Jr., May 6, 1915, DF 838.00/1393a; Fuller's report, June 14, 1915, DF 838.00/1197; *For. Rels., 1915*, pp. 464–8. For the beginning of the American occupation, see Link, *Wilson*, III, 532–8. Schmidt's *United States Occupation* is a detailed and extremely critical study of the occupation.

[31]For the background of the Mexican Revolution, see Charles C. Cumberland, *The Mexican Revolution: Genesis Under Madero* (Austin, 1952). I have examined and documented American policy toward Mexico during the Bryan era more fully in three articles: " 'A Kindness to Carranza': William Jennings Bryan, International Harvester, and Intervention in Yucatan," *Nebraska History* 57 (Winter 1976), 479–90; "Emissary from a Revolution: Luis Cabrera and Woodrow Wilson," *Americas* 35 (Jan. 1979), 353–71; "Woodrow Wilson's Mexican Policy, 1913–1915," *Diplomatic History* 4 (Spring 1980), 113–36.

[32]Link, *Wilson*, II, 347–55, 366–77; Coletta, *William Jennings Bryan*, II, 147–51, 154–9. For a detailed study of the Anglo-American difficulties over Mexico, see Peter Calvert, *The Mexican Revolution, 1910–1914: The Diplomacy of Anglo-American Conflict* (Cambridge, 1968). Calvert concludes that the friction between the two powers was largely the result of misunderstanding.

By the end of November 1913, British policy was closely aligned with Washington's wishes. See Link et al., *Papers of Woodrow Wilson*, XXVIII, 34, 467–9, 543–5, 561–2, 573–5.

[33]Link, *Wilson*, II, 355–61; Coletta, *William Jennings Bryan*, II, 150–4. George Stephenson's *John Lind of Minnesota* (Minneapolis, Minn., 1935), is a good, sympathetic biography.

[34]Hill, *Emissaries to a Revolution*, 96–8, 110–20; Hale to Bryan, Nov. 14, 15, 16, 17, 1913, Bryan to Hale, Nov. 16, 1913, John Lind to Bryan, Nov. 15, 1913, DF 812.00/9735, 9759, 9769, 9789, 9759, 9760; House Diary, Dec. 12, 1913, III, 392–3, and Jan. 16, 1914, IV, 11–12, 15; Phillips, *Ventures in Diplomacy*, 3, 5–6, 59–63.

[35]Ambassador Spring Rice to Sir Edward Grey, Feb. 6, 1914, Link et al., *Papers of Woodrow Wilson*, XXIX, 228.

[36]Link, *Wilson*, II, 389–91; Walter V. Scholes and Marie V. Scholes, "Wilson, Grey, and Huerta," *Pacific Historical Review* 37 (1968), 153–4; Samuel G. Blythe, "Mexico: The Record of a Conversation with President Wilson," *Saturday Evening Post* (May 23, 1914), 3–4, 71; Robert Quirk, *An Affair of Honor: Woodrow Wilson and the Occupation of Vera Cruz* (Lexington, Ky., 1962), 1–33. Wilson was not normally willing to let military men influence national policy, but in this case he let Admiral Mayo's ultimatum to Huerta stand even though the admiral had apparently exceeded his authority in sending it without first consulting Washington. In January, General Leonard Wood told Ambassador Spring Rice that the United States had no plan for intervention in Mexico beyond that for sending a relief expedition to Mexico City if conditions for foreigners became intolerable there. Link et al., *Papers of Woodrow Wilson*, XXIX, 168–9. There is no reason to believe that the situation was different in April.

[37]*For. Rels., 1914*, pp. 452–6, 477, 479, 481, 483–7, 489; Coletta, *William Jennings Bryan*, II, 162–3; Wilson to M.W. Jacobus, Apr. 29, 1914, Wilson Papers; House Diary, Apr. 28, 1914, IV, 60; Link, *Wilson*, II, 401–7. The only Mexican leader to applaud the Vera Cruz intervention was Pancho Villa, whose apparent pro-Americanism simply reflected his hope of securing American help in wresting revolutionary leadership away from Carranza.

[38]Link, *Wilson*, II, 407–16; Hill, *Emissaries to a Revolution*, 177–260. The British foresaw that foreigners would suffer in the factional strife and urged Wilson to take steps to protect them. See, for example, Link et al., *Papers of Woodrow Wilson*, XXIX, 348; ibid., XXX, 29, 33, 59.

[39]Hill, *Emissaries to a Revolution*, 261–90, 314–21; *For. Rels., 1915*, pp. 659–61, 824, Consul John R. Silliman to Bryan, Mar. 14, 1915, DF 612.1123/118.

[40]Bryan to Wilson, Mar. 5, 1915, Wilson to Bryan, Mar. 5, 1915, ABP; Bryan to Wilson, Mar. 13, 1915, BP. Wilson downplayed the seriousness of the situation in public. He told a press conference that his notes to Carranza were only to "represent our views," not to convey an ultimatum, and he emphasized to the British ambassador his determination "not to allow intervention on a large scale." Arthur S. Link, David W. Hirst, and John E.

Little, eds., *The Papers of Woodrow Wilson,* XXXII, *January 1–April 16, 1915* (Princeton, N.J., 1980), 342–3. Had Carranza reacted more hostilely, Wilson's confidence in his ability to control the situation might have evaporated.

[41]Bryan to Father Francis C. Kelley, Mar. 20, 1915, Wilson Papers; Bryan to John Lind, Apr. 18, 1915, Bryan to Wilson, May 22, 26, June 2, 1915, Wilson to Bryan, May 23, 27, June 2, 1915, ABP; *New York Times* (Apr. 20, 1915), 1, 7, (Apr. 30, 1915), 7; *For Rels., 1915,* pp. 689–92, 649–95; David F. Houston, *Eight Years with Wilson's Cabinet, 1913 to 1920* (Garden City, N.Y., 1926), I, 133–5.

[42]Paolo E. Coletta, ed., "Bryan Briefs Lansing," *Pacific Historical Review* 27 (Nov. 1958), 393.

NOTES TO CHAPTER 6

[1]Coletta, *William Jennings Bryan,* II, 254, 258–9, 316. See also, ch. 1, above.

[2]Link, *Wilson,* III, 49–56; Ray Stannard Baker, *Woodrow Wilson, Life and Letters,* V, *Neutrality, 1914–1915* (Garden City, N.Y., 1932), 212–15; Ernest R. May, *The World War and American Isolation, 1914–1917* (Chicago, Quadrangle Books, 1966), 34–7; Cooper, *Vanity of Power,* 32–9; Devlin, *Too Proud to Fight,* 144.

[3]Coletta, *William Jennings Bryan,* II, 277.

[4]*For. Rels., 1914, Supp.,* 547–52. The idea behind Wilson's speech seems to have been suggested by Counselor Robert Lansing. See U.S. Department of State, *Papers Relating to the Foreign Relations of the United States: The Lansing Papers, 1914–1920,* 2 vols (Washington, D.C., 1939), I, 151–2 (hereafter cited as *For. Rels., Lansing*). Wilson's speech may be found in Baker and Dodd, *New Democracy,* I, 157–8. For examples of Bryan's rigid interpretation of neutral duties, see Link, *Wilson,* III, 58–60; Coletta, *William Jennings Bryan,* II, 266–8. Despite Wilson's call for strict neutrality, Ambassador Spring Rice told Foreign Secretary Sir Edward Grey, "I am sure we can at the right moment depend on an understanding heart here." Arthur S. Link, David W. Hirst, John E. Little, eds., *The Papers of Woodrow Wilson,* XXXI, *September 6–December 31, 1914* (Princeton, 1979), 13–14; ibid., XXX, 472.

[5]For Bryan's first enunciation of the idea, see American Peace Congress, *Proceedings, 1907,* 313; *Commoner* 7 (Apr. 26, 1907), 4–5. As it was stated in a letter to J.P. Morgan and Co., Aug. 15, 1914, see *For. Rels., 1914, Supp.,* 580; Bryan to Wilson, Aug. 10, 1914, BP. For Lansing's views and the authorization of credits, see *For. Rels., Lansing,* I, 137–40. Lansing had succeeded John Bassett Moore in the spring of 1914. For Wilson's desire to do everything possible to further trade, see Link et al., *Papers of Woodrow Wilson,* XXXII, 87.

[6]Joseph V. Fuller, "The Genesis of the Munitions Traffic," *Journal of Modern History* 4 (Sept. 1934), 285; *For. Rels., Lansing,* I, 131–7, 141, 144; *For. Rels., 1914, Supp.,* vii–xiv.

[7]American Peace Congress, *Proceedings, 1907,* 313; Baker and Dodd, *New*

Democracy, I, 50. Repeated rejections of the arms embargo can be found in Bryan to William G. McAdoo, Aug. 8, 1914, McAdoo Papers; *For. Rels., 1914, Supp.,* x, 274–8, 573–4; *For. Rels., Lansing,* I, 113, 116. Reasons for this position can be found in Bryan to Wilson, Jan. 6, Mar. 1, 1915, Wilson to William Bayard Hale, Mar. 31, 1915, Wilson to Bryan, Jan. 7, 1915, Wilson Papers. See also Clifton J. Child, "German-American Attempts to Prevent the Exportation of Munitions of War, 1914–1915," *Mississippi Valley Historical Review* 25 (Dec. 1938), 351–68; Ruth Warner Towne, *Senator William J. Stone and the Politics of Compromise* (Port Washington, N.Y., 1979), esp. chs. 13–15.

[8]For the negotiations, see *For. Rels., 1914, Supp.,* 216–20; Richard W. Van Alstyne, "The Policy of the United States Regarding the Declaration of London, at the Outbreak of the Great War," *Journal of Modern History* 7 (Dec. 1935), 434–47. Basic provisions of the declaration, which at the outbreak of the war had been approved by all the signatories except England, were that blockade must be effective to be legal; contraband was to be limited, and cotton and raw materials were never to become contraband; continuous voyage applied only to absolute contraband; conditional contraband was subject to seizure only if destined directly for a belligerent; and belligerent-owned merchant vessels could not be transferred to neutral flags. See U.S. Department of State, *Papers Relating to the Foreign Relations of the United States, 1909* (Washington, D.C., 1914), 320–33 (hereafter cited as *For. Rels., 1909*).

[9]*For. Rels., 1914, Supp.,* 225–58; *For. Rels., Lansing,* I, 255–6; House Diary, Sept. 27, 28, 1914, V, 176–9; Link, *Wilson,* III, 109–14, 124–5, 129–31; John M. Cooper, Jr., *Walter Hines Page, The Southerner as American, 1855–1918* (Chapel Hill, N.C., 1977), 290–6; Link et al., *Papers of Woodrow Wilson,* XXXI, 96–8, 100, 110, 117–18, 133–6, 189–92, 229–30.

[10]Coletta, *William Jennings Bryan,* II, 282; Daniel M. Smith, "Robert Lansing and the Formulation of American Neutrality Policies, 1914–1915," *Mississippi Valley Historical Review* 43 (June 1956), 75.

[11]*For. Rels., 1914, Supp.,* 372–5; U.S. Department of State, *Papers Relating to the Foreign Relations of the United States, 1915, Supplement* (Washington, D.C., 1928), 299–302 (hereafter cited as *For. Rels., 1915, Supp.*); *For. Rels., Lansing,* I, 259–66; "Our Warning to Great Britain," *Literary Digest* (Jan. 9, 1915), 37–9; "The Rights of Neutral Nations and Our Protest to Great Britain," *Current Opinion* 58 (Feb. 1915), 73–6.

[12]Wilson to Bryan, Jan. 16, Feb. 21 [11?], 17, 1913, BP; House Diary, Jan. 17, 1913, I, 71; ibid., Apr. 4, 1913, II, 174; Coletta, *William Jennings Bryan,* II, 114.

[13]*For. Rels., 1913,* pp. 145–71; Bryan, *Memoirs,* 362–3; Link, *Wilson,* II, 284–6; Charles Vevier, "The Open Door: An Idea in Action, 1906–1913," *Pacific Historical Review* 24 (Feb. 1955), 49–62; Tien-yi Li, *Woodrow Wilson's China Policy, 1913–1917* (New York, 1952), 35–46.

[14]Bryan to Dr. Wu Ling-lang, Jan. 1, 1912, BP; Li, *Woodrow Wilson's China Policy,* 66–9; Meribeth E. Cameron, "American Recognition Policy toward

the Republic of China, 1912–1913," *Pacific Historical Review* 2 (June 1933), 214–30; *For. Rels., 1913,* pp. 96–115, 132; Notter, *Origins,* 243; Baker, *Woodrow Wilson,* III, 417–18; *Commoner* 13 (Apr. 18, 1913), 1.

[15]Paolo E. Coletta, "Bryan, Anti-Imperialism and Missionary Diplomacy," *Nebraska History* 44 (Sept. 1963), 183–4; Link, *Wilson,* II, 271–3; Li, *Woodrow Wilson's China Policy,* 116–19.

[16]*For. Rels., 1914, Supp.,* 162–70; Curry, *Woodrow Wilson and Far Eastern Policy,* 104–5; Charles Nelson Spinks, "Japan's Entrance into the World War," *Pacific Historical Review* 5 (Dec. 1936), 297–309; Ernest R. May, "American Policy and Japan's Entrance into World War I," *Mississippi Valley Historical Review* 40 (Sept. 1953), 284–90; Burton F. Beers, *Vain Endeavor: Robert Lansing's Attempt to End the American-Japanese Rivalry* (Durham, N.C. 1962), 19–20.

[17]Bryan to Wilson, [ca. Aug. 18, 1914], Oct. 2, 1914, Wilson Papers; *For. Rels., 1914, Supp.,* 164–209; Reinsch, *An American Diplomat in China,* 123, 161–2; Link, *Wilson,* III, 267–8.

[18]*For. Rels., 1915,* pp. 79–81, 159–61; Reinsch to Bryan, Feb. 1, 1915, Wilson Papers; Smimasa Iditti, *The Life of Marquis Shigenobu Okuma, A Maker of New Japan* (Tokyo, 1940), 381–3; Reinsch, *American Diplomat,* 129–32; E.T. Williams, "Japan's Interest in Manchuria," *University of California Chronicle* 34 (Jan. 1932), 12–13; Noel Pugach, *Paul S. Reinsch, Open Door Diplomat in Action* (Millwood, N.Y., 1979), 141–57.

[19]The first full and accurate list of the demands came from Reinsch on Feb. 1, 1915. The Japanese did not confirm this list until Feb. 21, but the Americans had been working on the basis of their own information before that. Wilson decided to protest on Feb. 25, but Lansing did not provide the draft until Mar. 12. His delay is not entirely explainable. He at first opposed any protest and later suggested that the United States accept the demands in return for Japanese concessions on the land law problem. Wilson and Bryan rejected this approach. *For. Rels., 1915,* pp. 82–98; Wilson to Bryan, Jan. 27, 1915, E.T. Williams to Bryan, Feb. 26, 1915, ABP; Reinsch to Bryan, Feb. 1, 1915, E.T. Williams to Bryan, Feb. 2, 1915, Wilson to Bryan, Feb. 8, 1915, Wilson Papers; E.T. Williams memorandum, "The Crisis in China," Jan. 27, 1915, DF 793.94/211; *For. Rels., Lansing,* II, 405–7. Wilson reversed himself on the wisdom of a protest between Feb. 8 and 25, presumably because of the receipt of fuller information about exactly what the Japanese were demanding in China.

[20]*For. Rels., 1915,* pp. 105–11; Wilson to Bryan, Mar. 10, 12, 1915, Bryan to Wilson, Mar. 22, 1915, DF 793.94/240 (two), 258a; memorandum from Japanese ambassador, Mar. 22, 1915, ABP.

[21]*For. Rels., Lansing,* II, 409–11, 413–15; *For. Rels., 1915,* pp. 115–22, 126; Reinsch, *American Diplomat,* 138–44. On Mar. 25 the Okuma Ministry won overwhelming support in Japanese national elections; the victory seems to have allowed the government to tone down its bellicosity in China. See Thomas La Fargue, *China and the World War,* Hoover War Library Publications, no. 12 (Stanford, Calif. 1937), 48.

[22]*For. Rels., Lansing,* II, 411; Wilson to Bryan, Apr. 14, 16, 1915, ABP. Pugach *(Reinsch,* 153–6) credits Reinsch with stiffening Wilson's resolve.

[23]*For. Rels., Lansing,* II, 56, 417–22; *For. Rels., 1915,* pp. 127–31, 143; Reinsch to Bryan, Apr. 14, 24, 1915, DF 793.94/292, 309; Bryan to Wilson, Apr. 28, May 4, 1915, Wilson to Bryan, Apr. 28, May 4, 1915, Bryan's memorandum to Japanese ambassador, Apr. 27, 1915; Bryan to Chinda, May 4, 1915, ABP; Bryan to Wilson, May 5, [1915], Wilson Papers; Link, *Wilson* III, 298.

[24]*For. Rels., 1915,* pp. 130–1, 141–5; *For. Rels., Lansing,* II, 422–3; Curry, *Wilson and Far Eastern Policy,* 128. Since the Chinese had already given in to almost everything the Japanese demanded in the "ultimatum" of May 7, it is hard to see why it was sent—unless it was merely to give the appearance of a final, showy triumph with which to cap the negotiations. In fact, the so-called ultimatum actually demanded *less* than some previous Japanese notes, and hence the Chinese were quite pleased to accept it.

[25]*For. Rels., Lansing,* II, 424, 426; *For. Rels., 1915,* p. 146. Lansing had taken two weeks to draft the note of Mar. 13, with which he did not agree, but he produced this one in one day, despite the *Lusitania* crisis.

[26]*For. Rels., 1915,* pp. 156–7; Link, *Wilson,* III, 308. When the United States entered the war in 1917, the Japanese seized the opportunity to secure what they regarded as American acceptance of their gains in the form of the Lansing-Ishii exchange.

[27]Three different mediation proposals were made during the autumn of 1914. The first was suggested by Bryan and made by the president on August 4 and 5, 1914: *For. Rels., 1914, Supp.,* 18–20, 29, 37, 42, 45; Bryan to Wilson, [Aug. 4, 1914], Wilson Papers. The second was instigated by Oscar Straus, a retired American diplomat, in September and October: *For. Rels., 1914, Supp.,* 98–104; Oscar S. Straus to Bryan, Sept. 8, 16, 1914, BP; Oscar S. Straus, *Under Four Administrations, from Cleveland to Taft* (Boston, 1922), 378–86. The third was a proposal for joint mediation made by other neutrals and spurned by Bryan and Wilson, who seemed unwilling to share world leadership with anyone else: *For. Rels., 1914, Supp.,* 53, 65, 130; *For. Rels., Lansing,* I, 9–11; Wilson to Bryan, Oct. 8, Dec. 10, 1914, Bryan to Wilson, Dec. 9, 17, 1914, Wilson Papers. In retrospect, none of these projects had much chance of success. Link et al., *Papers of Woodrow Wilson,* XXXI, 10, 15–16, 140–1, 540–1.

[28]For a penetrating analysis of the House-Wilson relationship, see Alexander L. George and Juliette L. George, *Woodrow Wilson and Colonel House: A Personality Study* (New York, 1956). House's diary during the autumn of 1914 records a series of unsuccessful efforts to get peace talks started, but not until mid-December did there seem to be much hope: House Diary, Dec. 16, 1914, V, 249; House to Wilson, Jan. 8, 1915, Wilson Papers; Seymour, *Intimate Papers,* I, 321–53. Self-effacing in public, House gave himself unstinting praise in private, and it is thus necessary to be cautious in the use of both his diary and Seymour's authorized biography. For a judicious evaluation of House, see Devlin, *Too Proud to Fight,* 462–3.

[29]Seymour, *Intimate Papers,* I, 346–467; *For. Rels., 1915, Supp.,* 5–17, 107–56; May, *World War and American Isolation,* 82–109; Link et al., *Papers of Woodrow Wilson,* XXXII, 13, 107–10, 124, 254–7, 264–5, 283–4, 333–4, 351, 361–3, 462.

[30]*For. Rels., 1915, Supp.,* 94. For the background of the German decision, see May, *World War and American Isolation,* 113–22; Link, *Wilson,* III, 312–20.

[31]*For. Rels., 1915, Supp.,* 98–101; Lansing's draft of the note, with penciled changes, Feb. 6, 1914, Wilson Papers; Link, *Wilson,* III, 320–4; Smith, "Robert Lansing," 75–6.

[32]*For. Rels., 1915, Supp.,* 95–7, 112–18, 358; *For. Rels., Lansing,* I, 365–6, 372; Bryan to Wilson, Mar. 23, 1915, ABP; "When the Torpedo Kills Non-Combatants," *Literary Digest* (Apr. 10, 1915), 789–91; Link, *Wilson,* III, 326–31.

[33]*For. Rels., Lansing,* I, 366–77; *For. Rels., 1915, Supp.,* 359–60, 364–5.

[34]*For. Rels., Lansing,* I, 11–12, 378–80.

[35]Ibid., 13, 377–85; *For. Rels., 1915, Supp.,* 157–8, 160–2, 378; Link, *Wilson,* III, 355–9, 365; Bryan to Wilson, Apr. 27, May 5, 1915, House to Wilson, May 7, 1915, Wilson Papers; Seymour, *Intimate Papers,* I, 461–7. Part of the reason Bryan was able to carry the day at this point was because Lansing was still uncertain of what to do and thus exercised little influence on policy. See Lansing's private memoranda, May 3, 25, 1915, Robert Lansing Papers, Manuscripts Division, Library of Congress, Washington, D.C. Lord Devlin faults Wilson for never really discussing the issues fully with his advisers. *Too Proud to Fight,* 468–9.

[36]*For. Rels., 1915, Supp.,* 384; *For. Rels., Lansing,* I, 386–8; Bryan to Wilson, May 1, 9, 1915, Wilson Papers; "America's Response to Germany's Challenge," *Literary Digest* (May 22, 1915), 1197–9; "Where the German-Americans Stand," ibid., 1200–1; "The 'Lusitania' Torpedoed," ibid. (May 15, 1915), 1133–4.

[37]*For. Rels., 1915, Supp.,* 387, 389, 393–6. The note was sent on May 13.

[38]Someone leaked an extremely accurate account of the meeting to the press. See clipping, May 12, 1915, from *Washington Post,* in Bryan to Wilson, May 12, 1915, Wilson Papers. See also *For. Rels., Lansing,* I, 392–404. The draft of the "tip," written by the president on his own typewriter, is in the Wilson Papers. For the decision not to issue it, see Lindley M. Garrison to Ray Stannard Baker, Nov. 12, 1928, Ray Stannard Baker Papers, Manuscripts Division, Library of Congress, Washington, D.C.

[39]*For. Rels., Lansing,* I, 296–7, 404–7, 411–13, 416; *For. Rels., 1915, Supp.,* 400–1, 406, 416–17; Bryan to Wilson, May 16, 1915, Wilson to House, May 18, 20, 1915, House to Wilson, May 25, 1915, Wilson Papers; Wilson to Bryan, May 20, 1915, ABP.

[40]*For. Rels., 1915, Supp.,* 396–403, 407–9, 419; Constantin Dumba, *Memoirs of a Diplomat* (Boston, 1932), 232–5; Bryan to Wilson, May 17, 1915, Bryan to Dumba, May 24, 1915, Dumba to Bryan, May 24, 1915,

Ambassador Gerard (in Berlin) to Bryan, Mar. 13, 1923, Wilson to Bryan, Dec. 17, 1917, BP; Wilson to Bryan, May 20, 1915, ABP.

[41]May, *World War and American Isolation*, 206–9; Link, *Wilson*, III, 406–9; *For. Rels., 1915, Supp.*, 419–21.

[42]*For. Rels., Lansing*, I, 417, 419–21, 426; Bryan to Wilson, June 3, 1915, Wilson to Bryan, June 2, 1915, ABP; Wilson to Bryan, June 2 (two letters), 5, 1915, Bryan to Wilson, June 5, 1915, BP; memorandum (unsigned, probably Lindley M. Garrison), June 1, 1915, Wilson Papers; Ambassador Gerard to House, June 1, 1915, House Papers; Houston, *Eight Years*, I, 132–9.

[43]*For. Rels., 1915, Supp.*, 436–8. Three drafts of the note, written on Wilson's own typewriter and bearing his corrections, are in the Wilson Papers. For the cabinet meeting, see Houston, *Eight Years*, I, 139–40; Bryan, *Memoirs*, 419–23.

[44]Bryan, *Memoirs*, 423–5; Bryan to Wilson, June 7, 1915 (two letters), ABP; Bryan to Wilson, June 9, 1915, Wilson Papers; Wilson to Bryan, June 9, 1915, BP; Houston, *Eight Years*, I, 141–7. Bryan neither expressed nor seemed to feel the slightest bitterness toward Wilson—not even any embarrassment at subsequent meetings. Wilson maintained an outward show of cordiality to prevent Bryan's supporters from depicting the resignation as the president's fault, but privately he alternated between expressions of wonder at the Commoner's "naivete" and agreement with Edith Bolling Galt's invariable description of Bryan as "that Traitor." Arthur S. Link, David W. Hirst, and John E. Little, eds., *The Papers of Woodrow Wilson*, XXXIII, *April 17–July 21, 1915* (Princeton, N.J., 1980), 366, 422; ibid., XXXIV, 172, 192, 288, 486, 493, 510–11.

[45]For various reactions, see especially the many letters in BP, as well as a synopsis of press comments in box 30 of the BP. For Bryan's analysis of the press reaction, see the *Commoner* 15 (July 1915). A few articles showed surprising insight into the real issues in dispute between Wilson and Bryan: "The Retirement of Mr. Bryan," *New Republic* (Mar. 13, 1915), 139; Albert Shaw, "Wilson, Bryan, and Our German Correspondence," *American Monthly Review of Reviews* 52 (July 1915), 13–19; George F. Milton, "Mr. Bryan's Position," ibid. (Aug. 1915), 213–16; Gregory Mason, "How Washington Views the Crisis with Germany," *Outlook* (June 16, 1915), 360–2. Ironically, one of those who best understood the consistency of Bryan's position, though he disagreed totally with it, was Henry Cabot Lodge, who pointed out to the Commoner in a letter on June 7 that Wilson and the American public were seeking contradictory goals when they demanded a firm stand against Germany yet refused to take any steps toward preparedness. Widenor, *Henry Cabot Lodge*, 218.

[46]*New York Times* (June 9, 10, 11, 13, 1915); Bryan, *Memoirs*, 408–12.

[47]Colin Simpson (*The Lusitania* [Boston, 1973]) argues that Wilson knew (and deliberately concealed the information) that the *Lusitania* was armed and carried contraband. Appealing though such an argument is to the conspiratorially minded, the Simpson book has been thoroughly refuted by

Thomas A. Bailey and Paul B. Ryan, *The Lusitania Disaster* (New York, 1975).

[48]Bryan, *Memoirs,* 404, hints at this but does not state it clearly. Lord Devlin observes that ironically Wilson never insisted on the terms of the *Lusitania* notes, and Bryan's resignation was thus unnecessary. The president's position changed, not because he feared war as Bryan did, but because he was beginning to get a higher vision of himself as a world peacemaker, and he therefore held himself above such "petty" quarrels. Devlin, *Too Proud to Fight,* p. x.

[49]William Jennings Bryan, "The Path to Peace," *Independent* (Aug. 30, 1906), 489.

NOTES TO CHAPTER 7

[1]*Commoner* 16 (Aug. 1916), 11. I have reversed the order of these phrases.

[2]Ibid.; ibid. 15 (July 1915), 6–7; ibid. (Aug. 1915), 5; ibid. 16 (Mar. 1916), 9; Bryan to Josephus Daniels, [Feb.] 22, [1916], Daniels Papers; Levine, *Defender of the Faith,* 28–9, 60, 262. Wilson pointed out a major danger in Bryan's tendency to state issues in such moral terms: "He suffers from a singular sort of moral blindness and is as passionate in error as in the right courses he has taken." Wilson to Edith Bolling Galt, June 8, 1915, in Link et al., *Papers of Woodrow Wilson,* XXXIII, 366.

[3]*Commoner* 15 (July 1915), passim; ibid. (Sept. 1915), 2; ibid. (Nov. 1915), 7; Bryan to [?] Walker, Aug. 28, [1915], Bryan to [?] Weisman, Aug. 27, [1915], BP; Bryan, *Memoirs,* 425–34; Curti, *Bryan and World Peace,* 223–8; Coletta, *William Jennings Bryan,* III, 7–10, 20; Levine, *Defender of the Faith,* 31–5.

[4]*Commoner* 15 (Sept. 1915), 4–5; Levine, *Defender of the Faith,* 54–5; Coletta, *William Jennings Bryan,* III, 20; Gwynn, *Letters and Friendships,* II, 298.

[5]*Commoner* 15 (Sept. 1915), 4; Coletta, *William Jennings Bryan,* III, 10, 21–2; Gwynn, *Letters and Friendships,* II, 280–1.

[6]Arthur S. Link, *Wilson: Confusions and Crises, 1915–1916* (Princeton, N.J., 1964), 15–22 (hereafter cited as Link, *Wilson,* IV); Morison, *Letters of Theodore Roosevelt,* VIII, 894; William L. Neumann, *America Encounters Japan: From Perry to MacArthur* (Baltimore, 1963), 146–7.

[7]*Commoner* 16 (Mar. 1916), 3–4; ibid. 15 (Aug. 1915), 1; ibid. (Sept. 1915), 1. The geographical security of the United States was a familiar theme with Bryan; see his often repeated Chautauqua lecture, "The Price of a Soul," quoted in Genevieve Forbes Herrick and John Orgien Herrick, *The Life of William Jennings Bryan* (Chicago, 1925), 301. Bryan praised the South and West as "safe and sane" on preparedness: *Commoner* 15 (Nov. 1915), 3; ibid. (Dec. 1915), 3; Bryan to Claude Kitchin, Sept. 10, 1915, BP. For an analysis of the sources of western and southern isolationism, see DeConde, "On Twentieth Century Isolation," 10–25; DeConde, "The South and Isolation-

ism," 333–4; Ray Allen Billington, "The Origins of Middle Western Isola-tionism," *Political Science Quarterly* 60 (Mar. 1945), 44–56. For an essay by an eminent scholar which questions the isolationism of Bryanite-Populist areas, see C. Vann Woodward, "The Populist Heritage and the Intellectual," *American Scholar* 29 (Winter 1959–1960), 55–72.

    [8]*Commoner* 15 (Nov. 1915), 1, 2, 4; ibid. (Dec. 1915), 6; ibid. 16 (Jan. 1916), 2; ibid. (Feb. 1916), 1; ibid. (May 1916), 3. The idea of a conspiracy among armaments interests to foment war was not new to Bryan: ibid. 13 (May 9, 1913), 1; ibid. (May 30, 1913), 1. On the Navy League controversy, see Bryan to [Jacob McG.?] Dickinson, Sept. 9, 1915, BP; Coletta, *William Jennings Bryan*, III, 10–11; Armin Rappaport, *The Navy League of the United States* (Detroit, 1962), 52–60.

    [9]Bryan, *Letters to a Chinese Official*, 27–8, 31–3; *Commoner* 15 (Jan. 1915), 6–7; John R. Dunlap to Woodrow Wilson, Jan. 16, 1916, Wilson Papers.

    [10]*Commoner* 16 (May 1916), 1–2; Wilson to Frank Glass (editor of the *Birmingham News*), Nov. 10, 1915, Wilson Papers. Bryan denied any person-al animosity between him and Wilson: *Commoner* 16 (Feb. 1916), 1. He also suggested physical education as an alternative to military training, a reflection of his naive faith in the efficacy of a militia system for defense: William Jennings Bryan, "Citizenship in a Republic," *School and Society* 4 (July 15, 1916), 86–8.

    [11]*Commoner* 15 (July 1915), 2; ibid. (Aug. 1915), 5; ibid. 16 (Feb. 1916), 6; ibid. (Dec. 1916), 8; ibid. 17 (Feb. 1917), 1; John Bassett Moore, "Peace, Law, and Hysteria," in Borchard et al. *Collected Papers of John Bassett Moore*, VII, 242; Levine, *Defender of the Faith*, 55–6; Coletta, *William Jennings Bryan*, III, 43.

    [12]*Commoner* 15 (Sept. 1915), 2; ibid. (Nov. 1915), 6; ibid. (Dec. 1915), 5; Link et al., *Papers of Woodrow Wilson*, XXXIV, 478.

    [13]*Commoner* 16 (Jan. 1916), 1–2, 5, 25; ibid. (Feb. 1916), 2; George F. Sparks, ed., *A Many-Colored Toga: The Diary of Henry Fountain Ashurst* (Tucson, Ariz., 1962), 47; Ray Stannard Baker, *Woodrow Wilson, Life and Letters*, VI, *Facing War, 1915–1917* (Garden City, N.Y., 1937), 166n1. Wilson tried for an indirect compromise that would have labeled armed merchant ships warships but was unable to gain the belligerents' agreement to this proposal. See Gwynn, *Letters and Friendships*, II, 316. For a surprisingly frank statement of the president's role in the struggle in Congress, which admits that Wilson sought a "showdown," see Democratic National Commit-tee and Democratic Congressional Committee, *The Democratic Text Book, 1916* (New York, 1916), 117–18; see also Ray Stannard Baker to William G. Fletcher, Nov. 16, 1937, House Papers. Predictably, Theodore Roosevelt regarded the Gore-McLemore Resolutions as "yellow; of the deepest yellow." Morison, *Letters of Theodore Roosevelt*, VIII, 1136. See also Curti, *Bryan and World Peace*, 237; Levine, *Defender of the Faith*, 39–45; Link, *Wilson*, IV, 193–4; and an exceptionally clear analysis of the whole complicated business in Coletta, *William Jennings Bryan*, III, 25–9.

    [14]*Commoner* 16 (Mar. 1916), 1. Another experienced western politician,

Henry Cantwell Wallace, believed that Bryan was misreading personal affection for him as political support on these issues. Hearing Bryan speak against preparedness at Tacoma, Wallace reported to Colonel House, "He fully believed he had his audience with him. I do not think so. I have observed for twenty years that he mistakes applause for sympathy and conviction." Link et al., *Papers of Woodrow Wilson*, XXXIV, 135.

[15]Bryan to Mary Baird Bryan, undated (about Apr. 20, 1916), BP; *Commoner* 16 (May 1916), 7; Charles S. Hamlin Diary, Mar. 25, 1916, III, 214, in Charles S. Hamlin Papers, Manuscripts Division, Library of Congress, Washington, D.C.; Coletta, *William Jennings Bryan*, III, 30–3; Levine, *Defender of the Faith*, 46–8; Link, *Wilson*, IV, 228.

[16]Bryan to Josephus Daniels, Feb. 4, 1916, Daniels Papers; *Commoner* 15 (Oct. 1915), 7; ibid. 16 (Oct. 1916), 1; ibid (Nov. 1916), 2; Bryan to Wilson, Nov. 10, 1916, Wilson to Bryan, Sept. 27, 1916, Wilson Papers; Wilson to Bryan, Nov. 17, 1916, BP; Bryan, *Memoirs*, 440–7. Bryan's opposition to war included strong opposition to conflict with Mexico and led him to recommend the withdrawal of the Pershing expedition. See *Commoner* 15 (Jan. 1915), 6–7; ibid. (Sept. 1915), 1; Bryan to William Gibbs McAdoo, June 27, 1916, McAdoo Papers; Bryan to Josephus Daniels, June 24, July 2, July 4, 1916, Daniels Papers; A.S. Burleson to Bryan, July 1, 1916, [Claude Kitchin?] to Bryan, July 6, 1916, BP.

[17]Coletta, *William Jennings Bryan*, III, 20–1. Colonel House and Walter Hines Page, American ambassador to Britain, agreed that Bryan's proposed trip in the summer of 1915 would do no harm and would leave Bryan, as House told Wilson, "a sadder, if not wiser, man." Seymour, *Intimate Papers*, II, 21; Burton J. Hendrick, *The Life and Letters of Walter Hines Page* (Garden City, N.Y., 1926), II, 12–17. Bryan's admirers continued to believe, however, that he could do much in Europe. Richard Bartholdt to Bryan, Oct. 9, 1915, BP.

[18] F.L. Seely to Bryan, Dec. 7, 1915, Bryan to Henry Ford, undated telegram [Dec. 1915], Bryan to Ford Peace Party, Stockholm, undated [early Jan. 1916], BP; Bryan to Charles W. Bryan, Dec. 25, 1915, NBP; *Commoner* 15 (Dec. 1915), 2; Coletta, *William Jennings Bryan*, III, 23–5; Levine, *Defender of the Faith*, 38–9.

[19]Baker, *Woodrow Wilson*, VI, 390–1. The president had begun to consider a new peace offer in October but delayed it because of the American election, a cabinet change in England, and uncertainty about whether the belligerents (especially the Allies) would accept a proposal. He had tightened up on credit to the Allies to put pressure on them, but this policy took time to work, and Wilson was not quite ready when Bryan forced his hand. For a detailed account of this peace effort, see Arthur S. Link, *Wilson: Campaigns for Progressivism and Peace, 1916–1917* (Princeton, N.J., 1965), 165–219 (hereafter cited as Link, *Wilson*, V); Coletta, *William Jennings Bryan*, III, 43–7.

[20]Bryan to David Lloyd George, Dec. 13, 1916, Bryan to Count von Bernstorff, Dec. 15, 1916, Bryan to Cecil Spring Rice, Dec. 15, 1916, Spring

Rice to Bryan, Dec. 17, 1916, John Barrett (director-general of the Pan American Union) to Bryan, Dec. 17, 1916, Josephus Daniels to Bryan, Dec. 17, 1916, Bernstorff to Bryan, Dec. 18, 1916, Congressman Claude Kitchin to Bryan, Dec. 19, 1916, Charles S. MacFarland (general secretary, Federal Council of Churches) to Bryan, Dec. 20, 1916, BP. The ambassadors were cordial in their replies to Bryan, but Lloyd George never answered.

²¹Bryan to Wilson, [Dec. 21, 1916], Borah to Bryan, Dec. 29, 1916, Senator Henry F. Hollis to Bryan, Jan. 16, 1917, BP; *Commoner* 17 (Jan. 1917), 2.

²²Coletta, *William Jennings Bryan,* III, 47–9; Link, *Wilson,* V, 220–89.

²³Bryan to Wilson, Jan. 26, 1917, Wilson to Bryan, Feb. 2, 1917, Congressman Warren Worth Bailey to Wilson, Feb. 3, 1917, Wilson Papers; *Commoner* 17 (Feb. 1917), 2; George W. Kirchway (president, American Peace Society) to Bryan, Feb. 10, 1917, BP. The BP have a number of letters and telegrams supporting Bryan's stand, but as he lamented to his brother, the response was disappointing. By this time he was so sure that war was inescapable that he told Charles "to kill editorials that may seem like criticisms of [the] administration." Bryan to Charles W. Bryan, Feb. 6, 1917, NBP; *Commoner* 17 (Feb. 1917), 3. Such restraint was wise, as Washington was already abuzz with rumors that he would not support the government in the event of war. See Charles S. Hamlin Diary, Feb. 12, 1917, IV, 84.

²⁴Bryan, *Memoirs,* 447; Alton B. Parker to Bryan, Mar. 4, 1917, copy of interview given by Bryan to *New York Herald,* Mar. [5?], 1917, Congressman George Huddleston to Bryan, Feb. 13, 1917, Senator Blair Lee to Bryan, Feb. 29, 1917, Bryan to W.P. Trent, Mar. 22, 1917, Bryan to members of the Senate and House, Mar. 28, 1917, Senator James K. Vardaman to Bryan, Mar. 31, Apr. 2, 6, 1917, Bryan to Congressman B.C. Hilliard, Apr. 3, 1917, BP; Levine, *Defender of the Faith,* 86–90; Coletta, *William Jennings Bryan,* III, 51–3; Curti, *Bryan and World Peace,* 242–6.

²⁵*Commoner* 17 (Apr. 1917), several articles; draft letter by Bryan, "Prepared for Judge Pierce to send to Russia," [1917], Bryan to Wilson, Jan. 15, 1918, BP.

²⁶Herrick and Herrick, *Life of William Jennings Bryan,* 299; Bryan to Wilson, Apr. 6, 1917, Wilson to Bryan, Apr. 7, 1917, Wilson Papers; Bryan to Daniels, Apr. 8, 1917, Daniels Papers; Daniels to Bryan, Apr. 11, 1917, W.G. McAdoo to Bryan, Sept. 17, 18, 1917, David F. Houston to Bryan, Apr. 24, 1917, BP; Coletta, *William Jennings Bryan,* III, 59–60.

²⁷Herrick and Herrick, *Life of William Jennings Bryan,* 308; *Commoner* 17 (Apr. 1917), 3; ibid. (July 1917), 1; ibid. (Sept. 1917), 3. See also Bryan to Charles W. Bryan, Mar. 31, 1917, NBP; George Foster Peabody to Bryan, Apr. 23, 1917, Arthur D. Call to Bryan, June 6, 1917, Bryan to William Jennings Bryan, Jr., undated, Bryan to George Sylvester Viereck, Mar. 15, 1921, BP.

²⁸*Commoner* 17 (Oct. 1917), 1; Coletta, *William Jennings Bryan,* III, 58.

²⁹*Commoner* 17 (Nov. 1917), 3; Levine, *Defender of the Faith,* 97–100.

³⁰Historians have tended to concentrate on the question of whether Bryan

was or was not a pacifist and to slight the equally important problems of whether or not he violated other political principles. See, for example, Hibben and Grattan, *Peerless Leader,* 357; Coletta, *William Jennings Bryan,* III, 57–8; Levine, *Defender of the Faith,* 90–2.

[31]For the president's aims and the policies of the warring nations, see Link, *Wilson,* IV and V; May, *World War and American Isolation;* Devlin, *Too Proud to Fight.* All three point out that crucial European decisions affecting the neutrals were made with minimal concern about American reactions.

[32]At least one historian thinks that Bryan's program would have averted war: Curti, *Bryan and World Peace,* 228–34. On the other hand, for a conclusion that American entrance into the war was fundamentally a result of economic ties, popular support for the Allies, and a concern for the European balance of power—all forces which Bryan's suggestions would have affected very little if at all—see Coletta, *William Jennings Bryan,* III, 55.

NOTES TO CHAPTER 8

[1]Provisions of the proposed charter of the League to Enforce Peace are given in William Howard Taft and William Jennings Bryan, *World Peace, A Written Debate* (New York, 1917), xii–xiii. For a detailed and highly sympathetic study of the league, see Ruhl H. Bartlett, *The League to Enforce Peace* (Chapel Hill, N.C., 1944).

[2]*Commoner* 15 (July 1915), 1, 8–9; Taft and Bryan, *World Peace,* 27–30, 36–41, 49–53, 85–90, 98–103, 112–14, 138–41.

[3]Coletta *(William Jennings Bryan,* III, 45) points out that there were some contradictions in Bryan's argument and that it tended to support isolationism. Ruhl Bartlett *(League to Enforce Peace,* 72) goes much further to assert, "Possibly at no time in his career was Bryan less the master of his subject than in these debates with Taft." Since Bartlett wrote, however, the validity of many of Bryan's objections to collective security has been demonstrated by experience.

[4]Taft and Bryan, *World Peace,* 63–8, 74–9. See also Bryan's speech of April 17, 1907, in American Peace Congress, *Proceedings, 1907,* 357.

[5]Taft and Bryan, *World Peace,* 124–5.

[6]*Commoner* 16 (Mar. 1916), 1–2. Bryan repeated the proposal in a speech to the Lake Mohonk Conference on International Arbitration on May 18, 1916. See ibid. (Aug. 1916), 10.

[7]Ibid. 18 (Jan. 1918), 2; Bryan to Wilson, Jan. 15, 1918, BP. Like Wilson, Bryan was a candidate for the Nobel Peace Prize in 1918—surely a measure of his international standing. See S.K. Huntsman to Bryan, July 17, 1918, BP. Bryan pursued his campaign to be appointed to the peace delegation with relentless vigor, bombarding friends in both the executive and legislative branches with his requests for support. They, often even without his urging, pressed the president. Large amounts of this correspondence can be found in

the Bryan, Wilson, and Josephus Daniels Papers in the Manuscripts Division, Library of Congress. It is pointless to cite all of these letters, but note especially Bryan to Wilson, Jan. 15, 1918, with marginal note from Wilson to his secretary, Joseph Tumulty, and Wilson to Bryan, Jan. 22, 1918, in Wilson Papers.

[8]Cronon, *Cabinet Diaries,* 356; Bryan to Dr. James Brown Scott, Jan. 23, 1919, Edwin E. Slosson to Bryan, Feb. 10, 1919, Louis J. Alber to Bryan, Feb. 15, 1919, BP; *Commoner* 18 (Jan. 1918), 1; ibid. 19 (Feb. 1919), 3, 5.

[9]*Commoner* 19 (Mar. 1919), 1; Coletta, *William Jennings Bryan,* III, 90. Bryan's plan to divide up the underdeveloped world strikes a later generation as rank imperialism, or at the very least, as a result of an appalling cultural arrogance. There was, of course, a strong sense of cultural superiority behind his missionary drive. Bryan thought that his idea of buying out property owners in the areas to be taken over removed the taint of imperialism; in fact, he described the idea as "one of my greatest contributions to world politics"— a practical application of idealism. See Bryan to Charles W. Bryan, Mar. 13, 1919, NBP.

[10]Bryan objected especially to the proposed treaty of alliance with France that Wilson submitted to the Senate at the same time as the Treaty of Versailles. He pointed out, quite correctly, that the treaty would not only pull the United States into European affairs, but more important, that it gave the United States no authority to *prevent* actions by its ally that might lead to war. *Commoner* 19 (May 1919), 1.

[11]Ibid. (Mar. 1919), 1; ibid. (Apr. 1919), 3; ibid. (May 1919), 2; ibid. (Aug. 1919), 1, 4; Bryan to Charles W. Bryan, Mar. 2, 13, 1919, Bryan to Dan Bride, Mar. 2, 1919, Dan Bride to Colonel [Callahan?], Feb. 4, 1930, NBP. In particular, Bryan regretted that specific arms reduction agreements had not been written into the treaty. Bryan to David Lloyd George, Mar. [?], 1919, BP.

[12]Rosser, *Crusading Commoner,* 260; *Commoner* 19 (Mar. 1919), 1. Bryan and Lodge took equally consistent but diametrically opposite positions, with Bryan believing that the league should eschew force and rest only on persuasion, and Lodge convinced that it would succeed only if backed by solid, credible force. Widenor, *Henry Cabot Lodge,* 258–9, and passim.

[13]*Commoner* 19 (Oct. 1919), 1; Bryan to Josephus Daniels, Sept. 25, 29, 1919, Daniels Papers; Senator Gilbert M. Hitchcock to Bryan, Oct. 4, 1919, Secretary of the Interior Franklin K. Lane to Bryan, Oct. 6, 1919, BP. Hitchcock and Bryan had long battled to control the Nebraska Democratic party. Most recently, Hitchcock had defeated Bryan's bid to become a delegate to the 1916 Democratic convention, and Bryan would retaliate in kind in 1920, but for the moment they were allies in a common cause.

[14]Bryan to "My Dear Senator," Nov. 24, 1919, Hitchcock to Bryan, Nov. 30, 1919, Senator Henry F. Ashurst to Bryan, Nov. 18, 1919, Senator Porter J. McCumber to Bryan, Nov. 30, 1919, David Starr Jordan to Bryan, Dec. 12, 1919, Manton Wyvell to Bryan, Dec. 26, 1919, Bryan to Arthur Dunn, Feb.

1, 1923, BP; *Commoner* 19 (Dec. 1919), 1–2; copy of speech by G.M. Hitchcock, Dec. 10, 1919, Gilbert M. Hitchcock Papers, Manuscripts Division, Library of Congress, Washington, D.C.

[15]Cronon, *Cabinet Diaries,* 481–2; *Commoner* 20 (Jan. 1920), 1; ibid. (Feb. 1920), 1; ibid. (Apr. 1920), 6, 8–9; Bryan to Robert J. Thompson, Mar. 1, 1920, BP; James W. Gerard, *My First Eighty-Three Years in America: The Memoirs of James W. Gerard* (Garden City, N.Y., 1951), 290–1; Levine, *Defender of the Faith,* 141–6; Coletta, *William Jennings Bryan,* III, 94–100.

[16]*Commoner* 20 (June 1920), 1; William Jennings Bryan, "Democratic Policies at San Francisco," *American Review of Reviews* 42 (July 1920), 42–5; Coletta, *William Jennings Bryan,* III, 100–2; Edwin Weinstein, *Woodrow Wilson: A Medical and Psychological Biography* (Princeton, N.J., 1981), 364–8.

[17]*Commoner* 20 (July 1920), 8–14; ibid. (Oct. 1920), 1; ibid. (Nov. 1920), 2; Bryan to Charles W. Bryan, Jan. 3, [Feb.?] 23, 1920, Bryan's July 2, 1920, speech to the 1920 Democratic convention, NBP; Cronon, *Cabinet Diaries,* 356; Senator Pat Harrison to Bryan, Aug. 5, 1920, Bryan to "My dear . . . ," Sept. 20, 1920, R.W. Woolley to Bryan, Sept. 24, 1920, BP; "League of Nations" plank, Democratic National Committee and Democratic Congressional Committee, *The Democratic Text Book, 1920* (New York, 1920), 6; Mark Sullivan, *Our Times: The United States, 1900–1925* (New York, 1926), 108–9; Rixey Smith and Norman Beasley, *Carter Glass: A Biography* (New York, 1939), 210–12; Cox, *Journey Through My Years,* 410–11.

[18]*Commoner* 20 (Nov. 1920), 1; ibid. 21 (Jan. 1921), 2; ibid. (Mar. 1921), 1; Warren Harding to Bryan, Nov. 13, 1920, George B. Christian, Jr. (Harding's private secretary) to Bryan, Dec. 9, 1920, BP; Levine, *Defender of the Faith,* 183–94. Bryan did not by any means leave the party. He campaigned hard and effectively for Democrats in 1922 and took an active role in 1924, although by then he was out of harmony with the rising leadership of the party. See Cordell Hull (chairman of the Democratic National Committee) to Bryan, Nov. 11, 1922, BP.

[19]Coletta, *William Jennings Bryan,* III, 140–1; *Commoner* 21 (Jan. 1921), 2.

[20]*Commoner* 21 (Feb. 1921), 1; ibid. 22 (Apr. 1922), 2; ibid. (July 1922), 4; ibid. 23 (Feb. 1923), 6; Bryan to William J. O'Brien, Apr. 25, 1923, Bryan to T.A. Watkins, Feb. 24, 1923, BP.

[21]Bryan to John Mez, Oct. 13, 1921, Hitchcock to Bryan, Dec. 1, 1922, Bryan to Frank D. Pavey, Feb. 2, 1923, BP; *Commoner* 23 (Jan. 1923), 1; ibid. (Feb. 1923), 1; William Jennings Bryan, "Our Responsibility for the Ruhr Invasion," *Current History* 17 (Mar. 1923), 898–9.

[22]Cronon, *Cabinet Diaries* (June 2, 1920), 537. This is the earliest reference to this particular idea I have found; Coletta dates it in August of 1920 *(William Jennings Bryan,* III, 135), and Levine in July at the Democratic convention *(Defender of the Faith,* 201–2). See also Bryan's speech to the 1920 convention in NBP; *Commoner* 20 (July 1920), 9; ibid. (Nov. 1920), 9, 11; ibid. 21 (Jan. 1921), 3; ibid. 23 (Aug. 1922), 1; Herrick and Herrick, *Life of William Jennings Bryan,* 310. In fact, Bryan suggested in March of 1920 that the United States offer to take over debts owed by Latin American nations to

the Allies in exchange for the Allied debts owed to the United States—the intention being to benefit both the Allies and the Latins. See *Commoner* 20 (Mar. 1920), 4.

²³Cronon, *Cabinet Diaries,* 537; Bryan to Frederick Lynch, Feb. 9, 1921, Bryan to Senator William E. Borah, Aug. 5, 1922, Borah to Bryan, Aug. 8, 1922, Bryan to President Coolidge, Jan. 1, 1925, Coolidge to Bryan, Jan. 5, 1925, BP.

²⁴*Commoner* 21 (May 1921), 1; Bryan to Frederick Lynch, Feb. 9, 1921, Bryan to George A. Speese, Mar. 6, 1923, "World Peace by William Jennings Bryan" (address to quadrennial meeting of Federal Council of Churches at Atlanta, Dec. 8, 1924), BP. Bryan's desire to commit the churches to an active political and social role was not shared by many fundamentalists, and his efforts met with little success.

²⁵*Commoner* 20 (Feb. 1920), 14; ibid. 23 (Jan. 1923), 2; George A. Finch to Bryan, Sept. 11, 1920; John Bassett Moore to Bryan, Sept. 29, 1922, James Brown Scott to Bryan, Mar. 3, 1923, Edward W. Bok to Bryan, July 26, 1923, Bryan to Secretary of State Frank Kellogg, May 1, 1925, Calvin Coolidge to Bryan, May 4, 1925, BP; *Houston Chronicle,* (Jan. 9, 1921); John Bassett Moore to R. Walton Moore, Dec. 7, 1934, in Borchard et al. *Collected Papers of John Bassett Moore,* VII, 8; James T. Shotwell, "Alternatives for War," *Foreign Affairs* 6 (Apr. 1928), 461–2; James T. Shotwell, *War as an Instrument of National Policy and Its Renunciation in the Pact of Paris* (New York, 1929), 259; Curti, *Bryan and World Peace,* 162–4, 251–2.

²⁶Bryan to Henry Goddard Leach, Apr. 7, 1925, BP; James Brown Scott, "Remarks on Bryan's Peace Treaties (Apr. 26, 1929)," *Proceedings of the American Society of International Law at Its Twenty-third Annual Meeting, 1929* (Washington, D.C., 1929), 174.

²⁷Borah to Bryan, Dec. 27, 1920, M. Doyle to Bryan, July 14, 1921, Florence Kling Harding (Mrs. Warren G.) to Mary Baird Bryan, July 28, 1921, Graham Patterson to Bryan, Aug. 2, 1921, Senator William S. Kenyon to Bryan, Aug. 4, 1921, Ross A. Collins to Warren G. Harding, Aug. 17, 1921, Grace Bryan Hargreaves, "The Last Decade, 1915–1925," manuscript biography of Bryan, II, 8, BP; Bryan to Josephus Daniels, Jan. 13, 1921, Daniels Papers; *Commoner* 21 (Jan. 1921), 3; ibid. (Nov. 1921), 1.

²⁸For Bryan's views on the conference, see *Commoner* 21 (Nov.–Dec. 1921); ibid. 22 (Jan.–Apr. 1922); Borah to Bryan, Dec. 13, 1921, Bryan to Dan Bride, Dec. 14, 1921, Bryan to Warren G. Harding, Jan. 26, 1922, Harding to Bryan, Jan. 31, 1922, Senator Oscar W. Underwood to Bryan, Mar. 14, 1922, Senator Key Pittman to Bryan, Mar. 16, 1922, BP; Coletta, *William Jennings Bryan,* III, 145–6. Bryan did not have much success in his efforts to influence Democratic senators; 23 of 35 opposed the Four-Power Treaty.

²⁹*Commoner* 18 (Sept. 1918), 4; Ellis O. Jones to Bryan, Dec. 6, 1920, BP; Coletta, *William Jennings Bryan,* III, 200.

³⁰In 1919, Bryan joined the Washington firm of Douglas, Obear and Douglas as a specialist in international law. In 1922 he agreed with Boaz

Long, former head of the Latin American Division of the State Department, to represent several Central American states in their efforts to secure loans in the United States. His agreement with Charles Douglas specified that Bryan would not take cases unless both he and Douglas agreed they were suitable. Bryan seems, however, to have been none too scrupulous about what clients he actually agreed to represent. For example, he represented an appeal for recognition by Federico Tinoco of Costa Rica, although Tinoco was widely thought a creature of American oil and banana interests who had come to power through revolution, and he agreed to represent American claimants, including Standard Oil, against the Mexican government. Aside from lending his name to the firm, however, it is not clear that he actually had much to do with these cases. For somewhat sketchy documentation of these and other similar activities, see BP, boxes 33, 34, 36, 37, 39, 40; Wilson to Bryan, July 18, 23, 1918, Wilson Papers; Coletta, *William Jennings Bryan*, III, 147–8. Coletta gives the firm's name as Obear, Douglas, and Obear.

[31]Metcalfe, *Real Bryan*,, 174–5.

[32]Koenig, *Bryan*, 655.

[33]Clipping (source unknown) dated July 27, 1915, in NBP, scrapbook, 12.

NOTES TO CHAPTER 9

[1]Fensterwald, "Anatomy of American 'Isolationism,' " 117–19.

[2]Quoted in ibid., 122n6.

[3]DeConde, "On Twentieth Century Isolationism," 8–9.

[4]A convenient summary of various theories about the causes of isolationism is Justus D. Doenecke, *The Literature of Isolationism: A Guide to Non-Interventionist Scholarship, 1930–1972* (Colorado Springs, Colo., 1972).

[5]John M. Cooper, Jr., "Progressivism and American Foreign Policy: A Reconsideration," *Mid-America* 51 (Oct. 1969), 265–6.

[6]Between 1914 and 1917 the prohibition issue overshadowed isolationism for Nebraska German-Americans, and they deserted Bryan. By 1918, when Charles Bryan ran for governor, the war issue had become paramount to German-Americans, and they supported Bryan despite his prohibitionist stand. See Burton W. Folsom, "Tinkerers, Tipplers, and Traitors: Ethnicity and Democratic Reform in Nebraska during the Progressive Era," *Pacific Historical Review* 50 (Feb. 1981), 66–7.

[7]Cooper, "Progressivism and American Foreign Policy," 264–5.

[8]Metcalfe, *Real Bryan*, 253.

[9]Herbert McCloskey, "Personality and Attitude Correlates of Foreign Policy Orientation," in James N. Rosenau, ed., *Domestic Sources of Foreign Policy* (New York, 1967), 63.

[10]Ibid., 57.

[11]On rural attitudes in the 1920s, see Don S. Kirchner, *City and Country: Rural Responses to Urbanization in the 1920s* (Westport, Conn., 1970).

[12]William E. Leuchtenburg, "Progressivism and Imperialism: The Progres-

sive Movement and American Foreign Policy, 1898–1916," *Mississippi Valley Historical Review* 39 (Dec. 1952), 483–504. For analyses that make it clear that this view was a minority one even among Republican progressives, see Barton J. Bernstein and Franklin A. Leib, "Progressive Republican Senators and American Imperialism, 1898–1916: A Reappraisal," *Mid-America* 50 (July 1968), 163–205; Cooper, "Progressivism and American Foreign Policy."

[13]Cooper, "Progressivism and American Foreign Policy," 261–4; Widenor, *Henry Cabot Lodge*, 121–70 and passim.

[14]See chapter 1, above, for a fuller comparison of Bryan and Wilson. Two excellent studies of the place of religious and political idealism in American foreign policy are Edward McNall Burns, *The American Idea of Mission: Concepts of National Purpose and Destiny* (New Brunswick, N.J., 1957), and Ernest L. Tuveson, *Redeemer Nation: The Idea of America's Millennial Role* (Chicago, 1968).

[15]Bernstein and Leib, "Progressive Republican Senators and Imperialism," 164.

[16]Bryan, *Memoirs,* 501.

[17]For an interpretation stressing the importance of strategic interests in the Wilson as well as Roosevelt-Taft eras, see Wilton B. Fowler, "American Diplomacy in the Progressive Era: The Dictates of Strategy and Defense," in Louis L. Gould, ed., *The Progressive Era* (Syracuse, N.Y., 1974), 153–80. In the Western Hemisphere, at least, strategic concerns diminished with the outbreak of World War I in 1914.

Bibliographical Essay

The study of William Jennings Bryan's role in the development of American foreign policy must be pursued through a very large body of materials. Notes to the chapters provide specific references to materials used in this study. This essay does not attempt to reiterate all sources cited in the notes; its aim is to discuss, briefly, the major primary and secondary sources relating to the topic. Additional bibliographical information can be found in Frank Freidel, ed., *Harvard Guide to American History* (2 vols., Boston, 1974), and Wilton B. Fowler, ed., *American Diplomatic History Since 1890* (Northbrook, Ill., 1975).

PRIMARY SOURCES

Study of Bryan begins with the William Jennings Bryan Papers, which unfortunately are somewhat scattered. The largest collection is in the Manuscripts Division of the Library of Congress, Washington, D.C. Additional collections, sometimes called the Bryan-Wilson Correspondence, are in the National Archives, Washington, D.C.; the Nebraska State Historical Society at Lincoln; and the library of Occidental College in Los Angeles. Other collections of special importance to the study of Bryan are also found in the Manuscripts Division of the Library of Congress; they include: the Ray Stannard Baker Papers, the Albert S. Burleson Papers, the Josephus Daniels Papers, the Charles Hamlin Diary and Papers, the Gilbert M. Hitchcock Papers, the Robert Lansing Diary and Papers, the William Gibbs McAdoo Papers, and the Woodrow Wilson Papers. Also of great value are the Edward M. House Diary and Papers in the Sterling Library of Yale University; the Department of State Decimal Files for the years Bryan was secretary of state, 1913–1915, in the Foreign Affairs Division of the National Archives; and the British Foreign Office Files, in the Public Records Office, London.

Printed documents of particular importance to this study include the *Congressional Record,* the U.S. Department of State's *Papers Relating to the Foreign Relations of the United States,* including the special *Supplements* published for the war years, and *The Lansing Papers, 1914–1920.* Among the published private papers for the period, the most valuable are Arthur S. Link et al., *The Papers of Woodrow Wilson* (34 vols. to date, Princeton, 1966–). *The Letters of Theodore Roosevelt* (8 vols., Cambridge, Mass., 1951–4), edited by Elting E. Morison, is also excellent, but Charles Seymour's often cited *The Intimate Papers of Colonel House* (4 vols., Boston, 1926–8) is unreliable, and the forthcoming new microfilm edition being prepared by Wilton Fowler will be most welcome.

BRYAN'S OWN WORKS

Bryan was a prolific writer and a prodigious speaker. As far as I know, no one has ever compiled a complete bibliography of his books, articles, and printed speeches. What follows represents only those items that I found particularly useful in studying his foreign policy. The place to start is with *The Memoirs of William Jennings Bryan* (Chicago, 1925). This volume, completed and published by Bryan's widow, contains some chapters written by him and some by her, but it is always clear which is which, and the inclusion of some of Bryan's letters and memoranda makes the book useful even if it is not very analytical. Two books, *The First Battle: A Story of the Campaign of 1896* (Chicago, 1896), and *The Second Battle* (Chicago, 1900), assess Bryan's first two presidential campaigns, and a third, *A Tale of Two Conventions* (New York, 1912), describes the Republican and Democratic conventions of 1912. *The Old World and Its Ways* (St. Louis, 1907) is a collection of articles Bryan wrote for the Hearst papers during his world tour. It reveals a boundless optimism about the prospects for peace and democracy in the world. Similar views can be found in Bryan's collections of Chautauqua lectures and sermons, such as *Heart to Heart Appeals* (New York, 1917) and *In His Image* (New York, 1922). *Letters to a Chinese Official, Being a Western View of Eastern Civilization* (New York, 1906) revealed Bryan's ignorance about Asia and his confidence that Asiatic nations would soon be westernized. Some of Bryan's public speeches on various subjects are found in *Speeches of William Jennings Bryan, Revised and Arranged by Himself* (2 vols., New York, 1911); *Republic or Empire? The Philippine Question* (Chicago, 1899); *The Forces That Make for Peace,* in World

Peace Foundation Pamphlet Series, no. 7, pt. 3 (Boston, 1912). Occasional transcripts of speeches can be found in the Bryan Papers, but these are rare, and for the most part the student must rely on newspaper accounts except for major speeches that Bryan thought worth recording and publishing.

Bryan also published an enormous number of articles. Some of the most important for the topic of the present volume include: "Citizenship in a Republic," *School and Society* 4 (July 15, 1916), 86–88; "Colonialism: How Could the United States, If Necessary, Give Up Its Colonies?" *World To-Day* 14 (Feb. 1908), 151–4; "The Democratic Party's Appeal," *Independent* 65 (Oct. 15, 1908), 872–5; "The Election of 1900," *North American Review* 171 (Dec. 1900), 788–801; "Foreign Influence in American Politics," *Arena* 19 (April 1898), 433–8; "The Issue in the Presidential Campaign," *North American Review* 170 (June 1900), 753–71; "The Next Awakening," *Public Opinion* 38 (May 27, 1905), 805–7; "Our Foreign Policy," *Independent* 76 (Oct. 9, 1913), 73–5; "The Path to Peace," *Independent* 61 (Aug. 30, 1906), 483–9; "The United States in Porto Rico," *Independent* 69 (July 7, 1910), 20–3; "The World Missionary Movement," *Outlook* 95 (Aug. 13, 1910), 823–6; "Why the Philippines Should Be Independent," *Everybody's Magazine* 19 (Nov. 1908), 640d–f.

Special mention should be made of Bryan's own newspaper, *The Commoner,* published by him from 1901 to 1923. Although he and his brother, Charles, and others shared editorial duties and there were periods when Bryan was too busy to pay very close attention to the paper, it nevertheless reflects throughout its publishing history the strong impress of Bryan's views. Practically every issue carried one or more editorials by Bryan, reports of his speeches, or articles describing his activities. He took an enormous interest in the paper and regarded it as one of the major channels through which he could keep in touch with his millions of followers across the country. It represents a unique source of Bryan's own ideas and of what his admirers and supporters were thinking as well.

BIOGRAPHIES OF BRYAN

Bryan has continually fascinated biographers, both scholarly and popular. The standard biography is now Paolo E. Coletta's *William Jennings Bryan* (3 vols., Lincoln, Neb., 1964–9), the first volume of which seems to me the best. Paul Glad's *The Trumpet Soundeth: William Jennings Bryan and His Democracy, 1896–1912* (Lincoln, Neb., 1960) is brilliant in placing Bryan in the context of middle western culture. In *Defender of the Faith: William Jennings Bryan, The Last Decade, 1915–1925* (New York, 1965), Lawrence W. Levine has made a difficult period of Bryan's life comprehensible to a modern audience and has treated his last crusades with sympathetic understanding that is by no means uncritical. The only studies that concentrate on aspects of Bryan's foreign policy views are "William Jennings Bryan," by Anonymous (J.V. Fuller), in S.F. Bemis, ed., *American Secretaries of State and Their Diplomacy*, (New York, 1929), vol. X, and *Bryan and World Peace*, by Merle E. Curti, Smith College Studies in History, (Northampton, Mass., 1931), vol. XVI. Neither is a full study, and both need to be supplemented in light of new materials now available; Louis W. Koenig's *Bryan: A Political Biography of William Jennings Bryan* (New York, 1971), is the best modern one-volume biography. Its emphasis on Bryan's support of reforms that were later adopted, however, seems to me to distort reality somewhat by making the Commoner sound more "modern" than was the case. Charles Morrow Wilson's *The Commoner: William Jennings Bryan* (Garden City, N.Y., 1970) is frequently unreliable.

For the most part, the modern biographies have supplanted those published soon after Bryan's death, but a few of the earlier ones retain some value for various reasons. Two of them, Genevieve Forbes Herrick and John Orgien Herrick's *The Life of William Jennings Bryan* (Chicago, 1925) and Charles M. Rosser's *The Crusading Commoner: A Close-up of William Jennings Bryan and His Times* (Dallas, 1937), were written by people who were friends of Bryan and thus had personal recollections of him. Wayne C. Williams wrote two biographies, *William Jennings Bryan: A Study in Political Vindication* (New York, 1923) and *William Jennings Bryan* (New York, 1936); a draft of the first was actually submitted to Bryan for correction. Finally, I should note the biography by Paxton Hibben and C. Hartley Grattan, *The Peerless Leader: William Jennings Bryan* (New York, 1929), a volume so savagely hostile yet engaging in style that it might have made H.L. Mencken himself envious.

Scholarly articles dealing with aspects of foreign policy in the Bryan years are cited in the notes to each chapter, but special mention should be made of a few. Selig Adler's "Bryan and Wilsonian Caribbean Penetration" (*Hispanic American Historical Review* 20 [1940], 198–226) presented an original and critical overview of a subject that up until that time had received very little attention from scholars. Richard

Challener's essay on Bryan as secretary of state ("William Jennings Bryan, 1913–1915," in Norman A. Graebner, ed., *An Uncertain Tradition: American Secretaries of State in the Twentieth Century* [New York, 1961], 79–100) is a brief and fair assessment of Bryan's role. A series of fine articles by Paolo E. Coletta often give more detail and documentation on various aspects of Bryan's career than is available in the compressed text of his biography. Of particular value to the student of Bryan's foreign policy are "Bryan, Anti-Imperialism and Missionary Diplomacy," *Nebraska History* 44 (1963), 167–87; "Bryan, McKinley, and the Treaty of Paris," *Pacific Historical Review* 26 (1957), 131–46; "McKinley, the Peace Negotiations, and the Acquisition of the Philippines," *Pacific Historical Review* 30 (1961), 341–50; " 'The Most Thankless Task': Bryan and the California Alien Land Legislation," *Pacific Historical Review* 36 (1967), 163–87; "William Jennings Bryan and the United States–Colombia Impasse, 1903–1921," *Hispanic American Historical Review* 47 (1967), 486–501; "William Jennings Bryan's Plans for World Peace," *Nebraska History* 58 (1977), 193–217; "The Youth of William Jennings Bryan—Beginnings of a Christian Statesman," *Nebraska History* 31 (1950), 1–24.

MISSIONARY ISOLATIONISM

Particularly central to this study is *The Vanity of Power: American Isolationism and the First World War, 1914–1917* (Westport, Conn., 1969) by John M. Cooper, Jr., not only because Cooper is one of the first historians to attempt a detailed study of isolationism in the pre–World War I period, but because his delineation of various categories of isolationism—most notably, "idealistic isolationism"— is very helpful to understanding Bryan and his role in the development of American foreign policy. The classic study of isolationism in the United States is, of course, Selig Adler's *The Isolationist Impulse: Its Twentieth Century Reaction* (New York, 1957). Despite its title, Adler's work touches very little on the pre–World War I period, although its central thesis that isolationism was an "impulse" is valid for the whole period from 1900 to after World War II.

For the missionary aspect of missionary isolationism, see Edward McNall Burns, *The American Idea of Mission: Concepts of National Purpose and Destiny* (New Brunswick, N.J., 1957); Ernest L. Tuveson, *Redeemer Nation: The Idea of America's Millennial Role* (Chicago,

1968); and Frederick Merk, *Manifest Destiny and Mission in American History: A Reinterpretation* (New York, 1963).

THE ELECTION OF 1896 AND THE SPANISH-AMERICAN WAR

Central to any understanding of the election of 1896 are Stanley L. Jones's *The Presidential Election of 1896* (Madison, Wis., 1964) and J. Rogers Hollingsworth's *The Whirligig of Politics: The Democracy of Cleveland and Bryan* (Chicago, 1963). Two important articles bearing on the little-studied foreign policy implications of the silver issue are Roger V. Clements's "The Farmers' Attitude toward British Investment in American Industry" *(Journal of Economic History* 15 [1955], 151–9) and Jeannette P. Nichols's "Silver Diplomacy" *(Political Science Quarterly* 48 [1933], 565–88). On the general subject of Anglo-American relations in this period, see Bradford Perkins, *The Great Rapprochement: England and the United States, 1895–1914* (New York, 1968), and R.G. Neale, *Great Britain and United States Expansion: 1898–1900* (East Lansing, Mich., 1966).

The topics of the war with Spain and imperialism are still extremely controversial. A generation after Julius Pratt apparently laid to rest the notion that business promoted the war with Spain in *Expansionists of 1898: The Acquisition of Hawaii and the Spanish Islands* (Baltimore, 1936), Walter LaFeber seemingly revived it again in *The New Empire: An Interpretation of American Expansion, 1860–1898* (Ithaca, N.Y., 1964), and William Appleman Williams discerned an even more militant farmers' imperialism in the same period in *The Roots of the Modern American Empire: A Study of the Growth and Shaping of Social Consciousness in a Marketplace Society* (New York, 1969). I have found no evidence that Bryan or his followers accepted the economic expansionism that Williams attributed to farmers; Bryan favored economic expansion only if it were strictly regulated and guided by moral principles. More general studies of the phenomenon of imperialism include Ernest May's *Imperial Democracy: The Emergence of American as a Great Power* (New York, 1961) and his excellent study of the role of public opinion in foreign policy formulation, *American Imperialism: A Speculative Essay* (New York, 1968) and David Healy's *U.S. Expansionism: The Imperialist Urge in the 1890s* (Madison, Wis., 1970). In a famous article, "Progressivism and Imperialism: The Progressive Movement and American Foreign Policy, 1898–1916"

(Mississippi Valley Historical Review 39 [1952], 483–504), William E. Leuchtenburg argued a correlation between domestic progressivism and imperialism. One obvious problem with his argument is that all of his examples are Republicans; Bryan and other progressive Democrats did not share Roosevelt's views. For a useful critique of the Leuchtenburg article, see Barton J. Bernstein and Franklin A. Leib, "Progressive Senators and American Imperialism, 1898–1916: A Reappraisal," *Mid-America,* 50 [1968], 163–205.

Göran Rystad, in *Ambiguous Imperialism: American Foreign Policy and Domestic Politics at the Turn of the Century* (Stockholm, 1975), uses a sophisticated combination of historical and political science techniques to explicate the tangled motives of the imperialists and their opponents. For an overview of the anti-imperialist movement, see E. Berkeley Tompkins, *Anti-Imperialism in the United States: The Great Debate, 1890–1920* (Philadelphia, 1970). Also useful, though more limited, is Robert L. Beisner's *Twelve Against Empire: The Anti-Imperialists 1898–1900* (New York, 1968). Surprisingly, Beisner does not discuss Bryan. Useful articles include Harold Bryan's "Anti-Imperialism and the Democrats" *(Science and Society* 21 [1957], 222–39) and Christopher Lasch's "The Anti-Imperialists, the Philippines, and the Inequality of Man" *(Journal of Southern History* 24 [1958], 319–31).

THE REPUBLICAN ERA, 1900–1912

Standard studies of aspects of Theodore Roosevelt's diplomacy include: Howard K. Beale, *Theodore Roosevelt and the Rise of America to World Power* (Baltimore, 1956); Dana G. Munro, *Intervention and Dollar Diplomacy in the Caribbean, 1900–1921* (Princeton, N.J., 1964); Raymond A. Esthus, *Theodore Roosevelt and Japan* (Seattle, 1966); and Charles E. Neu, *An Uncertain Friendship: Theodore Roosevelt and Japan, 1906–1909* (Cambridge, Mass., 1967). The diplomatic history of the Taft administration is described by Walter V. Scholes and Marie V. Scholes in *The Foreign Policies of the Taft Administration* (Columbia, Mo., 1970) and by Paolo E. Coletta in *The Presidency of William Howard Taft* (Lawrence, Kans., 1973).

More work needs to be done on the role of the opposition party in American foreign policy in general, and on the role of the Democrats between 1900 and 1912 in particular. A good starting point for the general topic is *The American Party Systems: Stages of Political Development* (New York, 1967), edited by William Nisbet Chambers and

Walter Dean Burnham. On the Democrats, see Hollingsworth, *The Whirligig of Politics,* and Glad, *The Trumpet Soundeth,* both cited above. One source of common Democratic attitudes is suggested by John B. Wiseman in "Racism in Democratic Politics, 1904–1912" (*Mid America* 51 [1969], 38–58).

SECRETARY OF STATE, 1913–1915

Arthur Link's multivolume biography of Woodrow Wilson, *Wilson* (Princeton, N.J., 1947–), has supplanted all other biographies and many of the more specialized studies as well. The second volume of Paolo Coletta's biography of Bryan, titled *Progressive Politician and Moral Statesman, 1909–1915* (1969), covers this period and is the best available study of Bryan's role as secretary of state. Curti's *Bryan and World Peace* is also useful, although much new documentary material has come to light since its publication.

Because the United States first contemplated a major internationalist role during the Wilson years, the overall interpretation of Wilson's foreign policy has been a topic of lively and continuing interest among historians. Perhaps the best modern version of the traditional interpretation that Wilson was an idealist seeking to improve the world is contained in the two highly readable volumes by Arthur Walworth, *Woodrow Wilson* (Boston, 1958). At the opposite pole, interpreting Wilson as an ardent imperialist seeking to "Americanize" the world is Sidney Bell's *Righteous Conquest: Woodrow Wilson and the Evolution of the New Diplomacy* (Port Washington, N.Y., 1972). Other views include Edward Buehrig's argument that Wilson sought to achieve a traditional balance of power (an argument not widely accepted by other scholars), in *Woodrow Wilson and the Balance of Power* (Bloomington, Ind., 1955), and Arthur Link's assertion that Wilson's idealism was actually defensible as a "higher realism," argued to some extent in his biography, but more explicitly in a collection of essays, *The Higher Realism of Woodrow Wilson and Other Essays* (Nashville, Tenn., 1971). See also the rewritten version of Link's *Wilson the Diplomatist* (Baltimore, 1957), which strongly defends Wilson as the first world leader to attack imperialism and to understand such modern revolutions as those in Mexico and Russia. The new edition is called *Woodrow Wilson: Revolution, War, and Peace* (Arlington Heights, Ill., 1979). A persuasive, moderately revisionist interpretation of Wilson as an exponent of "liberal capitalism" is argued by N. Gordon Levin, Jr., in *Woodrow Wilson and World Politics: America's*

Response to War and Revolution (New York, 1968). A careful, judicious study of the roots of Wilson's policy views is provided by Harley Notter in *The Origins of the Foreign Policy of Woodrow Wilson* (Baltimore, 1937), but Notter should be supplemented now by careful study of the published *Wilson Papers*. Psychological dimensions of Wilson's personality have been explored with some success by Alexander L. George and Juliette L. George in *Woodrow Wilson and Colonel House: A Personality Study* (New York, 1956), and with more venom but less insight by Sigmund Freud and William C. Bullitt in *Thomas Woodrow Wilson: A Psychological Study* (Boston, 1967). Building on a seminal article published some years ago, Edwin Weinstein has recently published a full medical biography of Wilson that illuminates many otherwise inexplicable aspects of the president's behavior, particularly in 1919–20. It is *Woodrow Wilson: A Medical and Psychological Biography* (Princeton, N.J., 1981). A provocative and thoughtful review essay about the interpretation of Wilsonian diplomacy is by Samuel F. Wells, Jr., "New Perspectives on Wilsonian Diplomacy: The Secular Evangelism of American Political Economy; A Review Essay," *Perspectives in American History* 6 (1972), 389–419.

Bryan's spoilsmanship has aroused a good deal of interest. A sympathetic and intelligent contemporary view was expressed by George Harvey in "The Diplomats of Democracy" (*North American Review* 199 [1914], 161–74). Modern studies of the issue include Paolo E. Coletta's "Secretary of State William Jennings Bryan and 'Deserving Democrats' " (*Mid America*, 48 [1966], 75–98) and Seward W. Livermore's " 'Deserving Democrats': The Foreign Service under Woodrow Wilson" (*South Atlantic Quarterly* 69 [1970], 144–60). Rachel West, in *The Department of State on the Eve of the First World War* (Athens, Ga., 1978), holds Bryan and his diplomatic appointees up against modern professional standards and finds both wanting. Richard Hume Werking, in *The Master Architects: Building the United States Foreign Service, 1890–1913* (Lexington, Ky., 1977), offers useful background on the department as Bryan inherited it and presents a much more sympathetic sketch of how he managed it than does West.

For the decision to move toward independence for the Philippines, see Roy Watson Curry, "Woodrow Wilson and Philippine Policy," *Mississippi Valley Historical Review* 41 (1954), 435–52; Francis Burton Harrison, *The Corner-Stone of Philippine Independence: A Narrative of Seven Years* (New York, 1922); and Peter Stanley, *A Nation in the Making: The Philippines and the United States, 1899–1921* (Cambridge, Mass., 1974).

Thomas A. Bailey's "California, Japan, and the Alien Land Legisla-

tion of 1913" *(Pacific Historical Review* 1 [1932], 36–59) was for
many years the standard work on the subject, but more recently it has
been supplemented if not supplanted by Roy Watson Curry's *Woodrow Wilson and Far Eastern Policy, 1913–1921* (New York, 1957);
Paolo E. Coletta's " 'The Most Thankless Task,' " cited above; and
Eldon Penrose's " 'Grape Juice Diplomacy and a Bit of Political
Buncombe' " *(Pacific Historical Review* 37 [1968], 159–62).

Latin American policy during the Wilson era has been, and remains,
the subject of much historical controversy, especially in regard to
Mexico. Standard studies of the Dominican Republic's troubles in
this period are Sumner Welles's *Naboth's Vineyard: The Dominican
Republic, 1844–1924* (New York, 1928) and Melvin M. Knight's *The
Americans in Santo Domingo* (New York, 1928). For Haiti, see David
Healy, *Gunboat Diplomacy in the Wilson Era: The U.S. Navy in Haiti,
1915–1916* (Madison, Wis., 1976); Hans Schmidt, *The United States
Occupation of Haiti, 1915–1934* (New Brunswick, N.J., 1971). Especially revealing in regard to Mexico are Peter Calvert's *The Mexican
Revolution, 1910–1914: The Diplomacy of Anglo-American Conflict*
(Cambridge, 1970), Charles Cumberland's *Mexican Revolution: The
Constitutionalist Years* (Austin, Tex., 1972), Mark T. Gilderhus's
*Diplomacy and Revolution: U.S.–Mexican Relations under Wilson and
Carranza* (Tucson, Ariz., 1977), Kenneth J. Grieb's *The United States
and Huerta* (Lincoln, Neb., 1969), P. Edward Haley's *Revolution and
Intervention: The Diplomacy of Taft and Wilson with Mexico, 1910–1917*
(Cambridge, Mass., 1970), and Larry D. Hill's *Emissaries to a Revolution: Woodrow Wilson's Executive Agents in Mexico* (Baton Rouge, La.,
1973).

For the student of Bryan, an essential study of American neutrality
during the first three years of World War I is Ernest R. May's *The
World War and American Isolation, 1914–1917* (Cambridge, Mass.,
1959). Not only is this volume a model of classical, multiarchival
diplomatic history, but it treats Bryan with perception and understanding. Less sympathetic to Bryan, though unmatched for charm of
style, sweep of narrative, and reasoned judgment of all parties, is
Patrick Devlin's *Too Proud to Fight: Woodrow Wilson's Neutrality* (New
York, 1975). Other useful studies include Arthur Link's biography of
Wilson and Coletta's biography of Bryan. Two short volumes of
considerable value are Daniel M. Smith's *The Great Departure: The
United States and World War I, 1914–1920* (New York, 1965) and
Ross Gregory's *The Origins of American Intervention in the First World
War* (New York, 1971). On Bryan and other "idealistic isolationists,"
see John M. Cooper, *The Vanity of Power,* cited above. Colin Simp-

son's sensational volume, *The Lusitania* (Boston, 1973), has been sunk by the broadsides of Thomas A. Bailey and Paul B. Ryan in *The Lusitania Disaster* (New York, 1975).

Many articles have cast light on some of the technical and complex issues of American neutrality in this period. Some of the best are Paul Birdsall's "Neutrality and Economic Pressure, 1914–1917" *(Science and Society* 3 [1939], 217–28), Joseph V. Fuller's "The Genesis of the Munitions Traffic" *(Journal of Modern History* 6 [1934], 280–93), Richard W. Van Alstyne's "The Policy of the United States Regarding the Declaration of London, at the Outbreak of the Great War" *(Journal of Modern History* 7 [1935], 434–47); Clifton J. Child's "German-American Attempts to Prevent the Exportation of Munitions of War, 1914–1915" *(Mississippi Valley Historical Review* 25 [1938], 351–68); and Daniel M. Smith's "Robert Lansing and the Formulation of American Neutrality Policies, 1914–1915" *(Mississippi Valley Historical Review* 43 [1956], 59–81).

The Wilson administration's difficulties in dealing with China and Japan are described in Curry's *Woodrow Wilson and Far Eastern Policy,* cited above; Tien-yi Li's *Woodrow Wilson's China Policy, 1913–1917* (New York, 1952); Meribeth E. Cameron's "American Reognition Policy toward the Republic of China, 1912–1913" *(Pacific Historical Review* 2 [1933], 214–30); and Ernest R. May's "American Policy and Japan's Entrance into World War I" *(Mississippi Valley Historical Review* 40 [1953], 279–90).

For Bryan's postresignation career, see Paolo Coletta's third volume, subtitled *Political Puritan, 1915–1925* (1969), and Lawrence Levine's *Defender of the Faith,* both cited above. Standard studies of Wilsonian peacemaking include Thomas A. Bailey's *Woodrow Wilson and the Lost Peace* (New York, 1944) and *Woodrow Wilson and the Great Betrayal* (New York, 1945). Background of the League of Nations and its forerunners can be traced through Ruhl H. Bartlett's *The League to Enforce Peace* (Chapel Hill, N.C., 1944); Lawrence E. Gelfand's *The Inquiry: American Preparations for Peace, 1917–1919* (New Haven, Conn., 1963); and Warren F. Kuehl's *Seeking World Order: The United States and International Organization to 1920* (Nashville, Tenn., 1969). Students of Wilsonian peacemaking should also consult *Henry Cabot Lodge and the Search for an American Foreign Policy* (Berkeley, Calif., 1980), by William C. Widenor. Widenor depicts Lodge as a thoughtful, consistent critic of Wilsonian policy whose background and ideas were, at every point, polar opposites of Bryan's. The contrast between the two is instructive to students of both.

Index

Adams, Henry, 34
Adee, Alvey A., 62
Aguinaldo, Emilio, 68
Allen, William V., 28
Allies, 98, 137; reject German peace terms, 120
American Anti-Imperialist League, 32, 34, 36
Anglophobia, 18, 35, 67; and silver in 1890s, 23–5
anti-imperialism, 145; and isolationism, 18–19; after Spanish-American War, 28–39; unites Democrats in 1898, 30
anti-imperialists, cool to Bryan in 1900, 34–5
applied Christianity, 6, 36, 40; *see also* religion, service
Arabic, 114, 117
arbitration, Taft's proposed treaties, 54, 56
Argentina, 41
Arlington National Cemetery, 142
Armed Ship Bill, 121
arms sales to belligerents, 98, 107
Army Appropriation Bill (1901), 41–2
Article 10 (of League of Nations Covenant), 133
Asia, 24, 36, 49

Bacon Resolution, 34, 35
Baéz, Ramon, 85
Banco Nacional (Santo Domingo), 63
Banker's Club (Tokyo), 54
Banque Nationale d'Haiti, 87–9
Bernstorff, Johann von (Count), 114
Beveridge, Albert, 150
bimetallism. *See* silver
Boer War, 38; *see also* South Africa
Bok Peace Prize, 139
Borah, William E., 5, 82, 120, 135, 137, 139

Bordas, José (Bordas) Valdés, 83–5
Borden, Robert Laird, 140
Boxer Rebellion, 41
Brazil, 41
British imperialism, 41
Bryan, Mariah Jennings, 3–4; influence on WJB, 5–6
Bryan, Mary Baird (Mrs. WJB), 20, 64, 142
Bryan, Silas, 3; influence on WJB, 5–6, 10
Bryan, William Jennings, youth and education, 3–6; influence of youth on mature opinions, 3, 5; childhood, 4–5; early ambitions, 4–5; and farming, 5; education, 20
———accepts silverite conspiracy theory, 24; Anglophobia, 24–5; warns against foreign influence in U.S., 24–5; attitude toward Cuban revolution, 26–8; endorses intervention in Cuba, 27–8; urges recognition of Cuban government, 28; supports Turpie Amendment, 29; and Teller Amendment, 29; military service, 29–30; first anti-imperialist speech, 29–30; foreign policy ideas shaped by events of 1898, 30; resigns from army, 30
———and Treaty of Paris (with Spain, 1898), 32–4; influence on Senate vote, 34; anti-imperialist arguments, 32–3, 35–6, 38; inevitable candidate in 1900, 34; sees election as test of principle of imperialism, 35; position in 1900 similar to McKinley's, 38; recommends protectorate for Philippines, 33, 41; favors American naval bases in Philippines, 32, 41; visits Philippines, 41; opposes Spooner Amendment, 41–2; and Philippine independence, 68–70

Bryan, William Jennings (*cont.*)
————favors annexing Puerto Rico, 32, 41; urges self-government for Puerto Rico, 41; favors coaling stations in Puerto Rico and Cuba, 32; and U.S. Caribbean policy, 44–6, 48; opposes Platt Amendment, 41–2; opposes Panama Canal treaty, 43; rejects Roosevelt Corollary and dollar diplomacy, 45–6; traditional attitude toward Monroe Doctrine, 45; evolving Asian policy, 49
————foreign travel, 20, 41, 46, 52, 54; peace plan, 12, 51–4, 65–7, 109; and Nobel Peace Prize, 67; believes peace plan could have averted war, 127; influence of peace plan in 1920s, 138–9; believes peace treaties most important achievement, 172n27
————favors low tolls for Panama Canal, 48; favors exemption of American ships from Panama tolls, 67; reluctantly supports repeal of toll exemption, 67–8
————supports Taft's Canadian reciprocity treaty, 166n38; supports Taft's arbitration treaties, 54–6; learns from failure of Taft's treaties, 56–7; policy proposals contrasted to those of Roosevelt and Taft, 49, 51; contrasted with Theodore Roosevelt, 152
————secretary of state, 59–65; value to Wilson, 59; grape juice diplomacy, 59–60; Chautauqua lectures, 60; patronage, 60–4; State Department morale, 64; poor administrator, 64; wants to be secretary of agriculture, 168n3; compared with Woodrow Wilson, 20–1, 151, 152, 154–5
————favors exclusion of Oriental immigrants, 49, 70; and California land law, 70–5; California trip, 71–2; supports new treaty with Japan, 74; effect of racial prejudices on policy, 36, 75; influence on Japanese-American crisis, 75; suggests dispersing California Japanese throughout U.S., 175n48; proposes neutralizing China area in WW I, 102; and Twenty-one Demands, 102–5; disagrees with Wilson about China policy, 103–4
————aims in Latin America, 77; use of force, 77; opposes revolutions,

Bryan, William Jennings (*cont.*)
77–8; given free hand in policy, 77; definition of dollar diplomacy, 77; attitude toward American businessmen abroad, 77–9; proposes new loan program, 78–9; Pan-American non-aggression treaty, 79; treaty of apology with Colombia, 79; Nicaraguan policy, 81–3; loans to Nicaragua, 81; Dominican policy, 83–7; Haitian policy, 87–90; limited influence on Wilson's Mexican policy, 90–5; supports intervention in Mexico, 94–5; failure of Latin American policy, 94–5; urges withdrawal of Pershing expedition, 188n16; suggests U.S. take over Latin American debts to Europe, 192n22
————neutrality policy in WW I, 96–101, 105–11; war evokes isolationism, 96; neutrality policy contrasted with Wilson's, 96, 110–11; sets initial neutrality policy, 98; loan ban, 98; opposes ban on sale of arms, 98–9; urges postponing issues with Germany, 107, 116; suggests suspending some neutral rights during war, 107; theory of "contributory negligence," 107, 117; proposes ban on American travel in war zone, 109, 117; differs with Wilson about submarines, 108; shocked by Wilson's first *Lusitania* note, 108; seeks way out of crisis with Germany, 109; resignation, 110–11; neutrality program evaluated, 124–5
————urges mediation in WW I, 105, 118–19; compared to Wilson in regard to mediation, 105–6; avoids Ford peace ship, 119; considers peace trip to Europe, 119; urges support for Wilson's peace efforts, 120; praises Wilson's "peace without victory" speech, 121; opposes preparedness, 114–16; proposes referendum on declaration of war, 12, 117, 139; and German-Americans, 113–14; supports Gore-McLemore Resolutions, 117–18; endorses Wilson for reelection, 118; opposes Armed Ship Bill, 121; opposes severing diplomatic relations with Germany, 121; last efforts to avert war, 121; supports government during war, 122; and wartime dissent, 122–4

Bryan, William Jennings (*cont.*)
———and international organization, 12; concerned about post-war settlement, 113; sees opportunity for progress in war, 113; moves away from isolationism, 116, 120, 127, 132–3; endorses Fourteen Points, 123, 131; debates program of League to Enforce Peace with Taft, 128; alternatives to League to Enforce Peace, 129–30; hopes to be appointed to peace delegation, 130–1; urges elimination of secret treaties, 131; advocates disarmament, 131, 137–8; warns against reparations, 131, 136–7; suggests amendments to Treaty of Versailles, 131–2; supports U.S. membership in League of Nations, 132; praises League of Nations as better than League to Enforce Peace, 133; describes Article 10 of league covenant as "excess baggage," 133; urges unconditional ratification of Treaty of Versailles, 133–4; proposes compromise on Treaty of Versailles, 134–5
———praises establishment of Russian republic, 121; distressed by Bolshevik takeover, 122, 140
———pessimistic about world situation, 134; turns from politics to moral issues, 135; favors joining World Court, 136; urges U.S. to join any international effort to preserve peace, 136; warns against French takeover of Ruhr, 137; proposes forgiving Allied war debts in return for disarmament, 137–8; at Washington Naval Conference, 139–40
———influence of religion on policy, 9–10; religious principles, 6–7, 8–9, 157n7; belief in heart as guide, 8–11, 12; on universality of morality, 9–10; faith in moral progress, 51–2, 140–141; on man's nature, 8–9; supports foreign missions, 6–8; favors export of American culture, 48; urges education of foreign students in U.S., 48; missionary isolationism, 48, 156; isolationism, 12, idealism, xiv–xv; conflict of idealism and political concerns, 75–6; intuitive methods, 155; political principles, 10–12; faith in political progress, 11–12, 49; belief in democracy influences foreign poli-

Bryan, William Jennings (*cont.*)
cy, 153; suggests U.S. give up use of force to collect foreign debts, 46, 48; and pacifism, 114; and use of force, 152–5; limits on use of force, 153–4; evolving opinions, xiii, 143; relations with followers, xi, xiii–xv, 15–19 (tables, 16–17, 19), 21–2, 149–50; influence on American foreign policy, xv; criticisms of, 10, 40, 49, 57; prohibition and fundamentalism, 141, 150; "Great Commoner," xi; "Monkey Trial," xi, 141–2, *see also* Scopes; and woman suffrage, 3; death and burial, 142
Burke, Edmund, 152
Burleson, Albert, 68

Cabrera, Luis, 92
California land law (Webb Act), 70–5
Caribbean policy (1900–1912), 44–8
Carnegie, Andrew, 32, 34, 36
Carr, Wilbur J., 62
Carranza, Venustiano, 94
Central America, 82, 139
Central American Court of International Justice, 82
Central Powers, 98; *see also* Germany
Chautauqua lectures, 21, 60
China, 41; U.S. withdraws from loan to, 101; recognition of, 101–2; and Twenty-one Demands, 102–5; Bryan's and Wilson's policies compared, 105
Chinda, Sutemi (Viscount), 72, 74
Christian. *See* religion
Clayton-Bulwer Treaty (1850), 42
Cleveland, Grover, 13, 34, 36
Colombia, 43, 79
Commoner (Bryan's nickname), xiv
Commoner, The, 21
Constitutionalists, 91
consular service, 62
Coolidge, Calvin, 137
Cooper, John Milton, Jr., xii, 18, 19–20
Cox, James M., 135
"Cross of Gold," xi, 24
Cuba, 38, 41; revolution, 25, 41; Grover Cleveland's policy toward revolution in, 25, 26; revolution in election of 1896, 25–6; William McKinley's policy toward revolution in, 26; recognition of belligerency, 25, 27, 160n13; "bond conspiracy," 28
Cushing, 108

Daniels, Josephus, 72, 122, 130, 137
Darrow, Clarence, 141
Dayton, Tennessee, 141–2, 155
Declaration of London, 99–100; provisions of, 181n8
de Lôme letter, 27
"deserving Democrats," 62, 63, 64
Dewey, George, 29
Dewey, John, 152
Díaz, Porfirio, 91
disarmament, 137–8
dollar diplomacy, 45, 77, 148
Dominican Republic, 153; Sullivan scandal, 63–4; Wilson-era policy, 83–7
Douglas, Charles, 193n30
Douglas, Obear and Douglas, 193n30
Dumba, Constantin, 109

Edinburgh peace conference (1910), 54
election, of 1896, 23–5; of 1900, 34–9, 42; of 1904, 40–1; of 1912, 167n2; of 1916, 118; of 1920, 134–5
El Salvador, 65
example, as foreign policy method, xii–xiii, xiv, 6, 36, 38, 46, 49, 130, 136, 153, 156

Fairview, 5
Falaba, 107, 108
Farnham, Roger, 87–90
Filipinos. See Philippines
First Battle, The, 26
Five-Power Treaty, 140
Foraker, Joseph B., 29
Ford, Henry, 119
Ford, Henry Jones, 68–9
"foreign policy elite," xii
Foreign Relations Committee (Senate), and Bryan peace treaties, 65; and Nicaragua, 81–2
Four-Power Treaty, 140
Fourteen Points, 123; see also League of Nations
France, 54, 88–90, 136–7
Fukien, 103
Fuller, Paul, Jr., 90
fundamentalist. See religion

Garrison, Lindley M., 69
Gerard, James W., 119
German-Americans, 98, 147, 194n6
Germany, 14, 136–7; and Bryan peace treaty, 67; reported planning in-

Germany (cont.)
tervention in Haiti, 88–9; declares war zone, 106; orders submarines not to attack liners, 109; asks for U.S. help in arranging peace conference, 119; calls for peace conference of belligerents only, 120; announces unrestricted submarine warfare, 121
Glad, Paul, 21
Gompers, Samuel, 71
Gore, Thomas P., 117
Gore-McLemore Resolutions, 117, 147, 148
Gorman, Arthur Pue, 43–4
Grace, W.R. and Company, 87
Great Britain, 14, 42, 54, 99, 136–7; and Bryan peace treaty, 67, 68; and Panama Canal tolls, 67–8; and Mexico, 91–2; and Declaration of London, 99–100; U.S. protest to regarding neutral rights, 100–1; makes cotton contraband, 114
Grey, Sir Edward, 68
Guam, 32
Guantanamo Naval Base, 78, 87
Gulflight, 108

Haiti, 78, 153; Wilson-era policy, 87–90
Hale, William Bayard, 92
Hamill, James, 63
Hamilton, Alexander, 143–4
Harding, Warren, 149; friendly to Bryan, 135; "association of nations," 135–6; and Washington Naval Conference, 140
Harrison, Francis Burton, 69
Hawaii, annexation, 26
Hay, John, 42
Hay-Bunau-Varilla Treaty. See Panama Canal treaty
Hay-Pauncefote Treaty (1901), 67, 148
Hitchcock, Gilbert, 134, 191n13
Hoar, George F., 34
Hobart, Garret, 34
Hofstadter, Richard, 26
Holt, Hamilton, 128
House, Edward M., 100, 131; influence on diplomatic appointments, 62; and Panama tolls repeal, 68; and Pan-American non-aggression treaty, 79; European trip (1915), 106; preferred by Wilson to Bryan as agent, 106

Huerta, Victoriano, 91–3
Hughes, Charles Evans, 140

idealism, 39, 70; and WW I, xiii; sources in Bryan's followers, xiv; in American foreign policy, 151–2; makes extremes of policy likely, 154
idealistic isolationism, xii, 18, 19–20, 138, 151; *see also* isolationism, ultra-nationalist isolationism, missionary isolationism
imperialism, xi, xii, xiii, 69, 145; and isolationism, 14; after Spanish-American War, 28–39
India, 41
"Insular Cases," 40
international court, at The Hague, 45–6
internationalism, xi, xii, xv, 18, 19–20, 136, 146, 151
Interparliamentary Union, 54
isolationism, xi, xi–xii, xv, 12–15, 136, 143–51; and WW I, xiii; in late nineteenth century U.S., 12–13; origins and development, 13–14; and technological change, 14; and trade, 14; economically undermined in 1920s, 146–7; and missionary movement, 14; and missionary instinct, 144–5; and navy, 14; sectional variations, 14–15, 147, 148; and rural protests in late nineteenth century U.S., 14–15; in West and South, 14–15, 42, 158n31; and silver, 18; challenged in early twentieth century, 18; and anti-imperialism, 18–19; ideological influences on, 147–8; limits idealism, 154–5; *see also* idealistic isolationism, ultranationalist isolationism, missionary isolationism
Italy, 109; and Bryan peace treaty, 67

Jackson, Andrew, 11
James, William, 152
Japan, 14, 49, 139–40; and Bryan peace treaty, 67; and California land law, 70–5; suggests new treaty with U.S., 72, 74; declares war on Germany, 102; Twenty-one Demands, 102–5
Japanese-American Treaty of Commerce and Navigation (1911), 70
Jefferson, Thomas, 5, 32, 99, 143–4, 147–8, 152

Jiménez, Juan Isidro, 85
Johnson, Hiram, 70–1, 135
Jones, James K., 28

Kellogg-Briand Pact, 139
Kent, William, 71
Kenyon, William S., 135
Kiaochow, 102
Kitchin, Claude, 117
Knox, Philander Chase, 54, 56, 81

LaFollette, Robert M., 121, 135
Lansing, Robert, 131; counselor of state department, 62; and Haiti, 89; and Mexico, 94; and Bryan's loan ban, 98; and Declaration of London, 99–100; proposes "practical" agreements with Great Britain, 100; suggests application of non-recognition to China, 104; drafts protest about German war zone, 106; and *Falaba* case, 107; opposes debate with Germany over *Lusitania*, 109
Latin America, xiii, 12, 41, 44–8, 153, 154; and silver, 24; Bryan's policy, 77–95; proposed non-aggression treaty, 79
Latin American Division, of state department, 88
League of Nations, xiii, 67, 131, 132, 134, 143, 144; controversy over U.S. membership, 131–6; *see also* Treaty of Versailles
League to Enforce Peace, 120, 128–30, 132, 133
Lind, John, 92
Lloyd George, David, 119
loan ban, 98; abandoned, 114
Locarno treaties, 139
Lodge, Henry Cabot, 13, 18, 25, 133, 134, 144, 151, 185n45
Long, Boaz, 62, 193n30
Lusitania, 104, 108, 114, 117

Madero, Francisco, 91
Mahan, Alfred Thayer, 18
Maine, 27
Malone, Dudley Field, 62, 169n13
Manifest Destiny, 18, 30
Manila Bay, battle of, 29
Marburg, Theodore, 128
Marshall, Thomas, 62
McAdoo, William G., 68
McCloskey, Herbert, 149

McEnery Resolution, 162n37
McGuffey readers, 4, 6
McKinley, William, 27, 29, 30, 34, 38
McLemore, Jefferson, 117
Mencken, H.L., 5
Mexico, 152, 153; Wilson-era policy, 90–5; and American business, 91; arbitration offered by Argentina, Brazil, Chile, 93
missionary isolationism, 57–8, 142, 156; see also idealistic isolationism, isolationism, ultranationalist isolationism
Môle Saint Nicolas, 78, 87, 88, 89, 90
Monroe Doctrine, 13, 36, 45
Moore, John Bassett, 62, 169n14

National City Bank of New York, 87
Navy League, 115
"New South," 15
New York World, 63
Nicaragua, 154; proposed canal, 26, 78; Wilson-era policy, 81–3
Nine-Power Treaty, 140

O'Gorman, James A., 63
oil, and Colombia, 79; and Mexico, 92
Olney, Richard, 13, 34
Open Door policy, 41, 74, 101, 103
Osborne, John E., 62, 87

Page, Walter Hines, 99, 100
Panama, 42–4
Panama Canal, 70, 154; favored by Democrats, 42–4; Wilson administration concerned with protection of, 78
Panama Canal tolls, 48, 67–8
Panama Canal Treaty (1903), 42–4, 46, 148
partisanship, and foreign policy, 148–9
peace movement, 52
Permanent Court of International Justice (World Court), 136, 139
Persia, 117
Philippines, xiii, 32, 36, 38, 40–1, 72, 75, 146; independence promised, 69–70; see also imperialism
Phillips, William, 62, 169n13
Platt Amendment, 41–2, 148; provisions, 164n8; and Nicaragua, 81–2
Populism, 15, 34, 150
preparedness, 114–16, 147
Prohibitionists, 34
Protestant. See religion

public opinion, xii, xiii
Puerto Rico, xiii, 32, 38, 41, 48; see also imperialism
Putney, Albert H., 62

Quezon, Manuel, 69

Reed, Thomas, 29
Reinsch, Paul, 103–4
religion, Bryan's, 6–10, 141–2, 157n6, 7; and Bryan's support of foreign missions, 6–8; and Bryan's hopes for world peace, 129
reparations, 131, 136–7
Republicans, conservative, and foreign policy, 150–1; progressive, and foreign policy, 150–1
rivers and harbors bill (1901), 42
Roosevelt Corollary, 45, 46
Roosevelt, Theodore, xi, xv, 42, 49, 146, 150–1, 154; and U.S. Caribbean policy, 44–6; opposes Taft's arbitration treaties, 56; "Gentlemen's Agreement," 70; and California land law, 71; and Colombian treaty, 79; supports preparedness, 114–15; contrasted with Bryan, 49, 51, 152
Root, Elihu, 82
Round Robin, 131
Russia, 121, 122, 140
Russo-Japanese War, 49

St. Louis World's Fair, 42
Sam, Vilbrun Guillaume, 90
Scopes, John Thomas, 141
Scott, James Brown, 139
service, xi, 6, 136
Shantung, 102
silver, and foreign policy in the 1890s, 23–5; conspiracy theory, 24; and isolationism, 24; foreign trade benefits, 24; and ultranationalist isolationism, 25; and Spanish-American War, 28
sisal, 93
Slayden, James L., 79
Social Darwinism, 14
Social Gospel, 14; see also applied Christianity
Socialists, 34
South Africa, 41; see also Boer War
Spanish-American War, 13, 15, 25–39, 42, 153
Speyer and Company, 87
Spooner Amendment, 41–2, 148

State Department, press leaks, 64; appointments, 60–4; morale, 64
states' rights, and California land law, 70–1
Stephens, Dan V., 117
Stewart, William M., 82
Stone, William J., 28
Straus, Oscar, mediation proposal, 183n27
"strict accountability," 106–7
submarines, 106–10
Sullivan, James Mark, 63–4, 83–4
Sussex, 118
"*Sussex* pledge," 118, 119

Taft, William Howard, 131, 154; and U.S. Caribbean policy, 44–5; and Bryan peace plan, 54, 56; arbitration treaties with Great Britain and France, 54, 56; and California land law, 71; treaty with Colombia, 79; intervention in Nicaragua, 81; Dominican policy, 83; Haitian policy, 87; Mexican policy, 91; China policy, 101; and League to Enforce Peace, 128; contrasted with Bryan, 49, 51
Tampico Incident, 93
Teller Amendment, 29, 41, 161n25
Théodore, Davilmar, 88–9
Thrasher, Leon C., 107
Tolstoi, Lev Nikolayevich (Count), 52
trade with belligerents, differences between Bryan and Wilson, 99
Trans-Mississippi Commercial Congress (1897), 26–7
Treaty of Paris, with Spain (1898), 32–4
Treaty of Versailles, xiii, 130, 134, 137, 148; *see also* League of Nations
Tumulty, Joseph, 63
Turpie Amendment, 28–9, 34
Turpie, David, 28–9
Tyrrell, Sir William, 68

ultranationalist isolationism, 18, 19, 38, 136; and silver, 25; *see also* isolationism, idealistic isolationism, missionary isolationism
United Nations, 67

Valdés, José Bordas. *See* Bordas
Venezuela, 41, 46
Veracruz, 93
Villa, Pancho, 94

war debts, 137–8
War of 1812, 99
Washington, George, 13, 24
Washington Naval Conference, 139–40
Watson, Tom, 28
Webb Act, 72, 74
Wells, H.G., 140
Western Hemisphere, 36; *see also* Latin America
Williams, Edward Thomas, 62
Wilson, Henry Lane, 63
Wilson, Woodrow, xi, xv, 100, 143, 146, 148, 154, 155; compared with Bryan, 20–1, 151–2, 154–5; appoints Bryan secretary of state, 59; keeps consular service under civil service, 62; appoints campaign contributors to diplomatic posts, 62, 63; special agents bypass state department, 64; supports repeal of Panama tolls exemption, 67–8; and Philippine independence, 68–9; Latin American policy, 78; rejects Bryan's loan plan for Latin America, 79; changes mind about Mexico, 92; and California land law, 70–5; delays sending Japanese treaty to Senate, 74; and Twenty-one Demands, 102–5; disagrees with Bryan about China policy, 103–4; applies non-recognition to China, 104–5
———and WW I, xiii; contrasted with Bryan on neutrality policy, 96, 110–11; and Bryan's loan ban, 98; opposes ban on sale of arms, 98–9; overrules Bryan about protest to Great Britain, 101; differs with Bryan over policy on submarines, 107–8; drafts sharp protest note to Germany, 108; authorizes "tip" to press, 108; withdraws permission for "tip," 108–9; opposes debate with Germany over *Lusitania,* 109; rejects Bryan's plans for ban on war zone travel or protest to England, 109; drafts second *Lusitania* note, 109–10; opinion of Bryan after Bryan's resignation, 185n44
———converted to preparedness, 114; fights Gore-McLemore Resolutions, 117; calls on belligerents to state aims, 120; "peace without victory" speech, 120; asks declaration of war, 121; refuses to appoint Bryan to

Wilson, Woodrow *(cont.)*
  peace delegation, 130–1; illness, 133–4; contemplates third term, 134–5
Winthrop, John, 13, 156
World Court. *See* Permanent Court of International Justice
World War I, 153, 154; and Bryan peace treaties, 65; American neutrality policy, 96–101, 105–11; impact on European balance of power, 146;

World War I *(cont.)*
  impact on American opinions of foreign policy, 148–9, *see also* names of major figures and specific issues

Yamashita, Yachachiro, 165n24
Yucatan, 93

Zamor, Oreste, 88
Zimmermann telegram, 121

William Jennings Bryan, Missionary Isolationist was composed into type on a Mergenthaler Linotron 202N phototypesetter in ten-point Galliard with one and one-half points of spacing between the lines. The book was designed by Jim Billingsley, composed by Williams of Chattanooga, printed offset by Thomson-Shore, Inc., and bound by John H. Dekker & Sons. The paper on which the book is printed bears the watermark of S.D. Warren and is designed for an effective life of at least three hundred years.

The University of Tennessee Press : Knoxville